Postmodern Social
Analysis and
Criticism

Postmodern Social Analysis and Criticism

John W. Murphy

CONTRIBUTIONS IN SOCIOLOGY, NUMBER 79

GREENWOOD PRESS
New York • Westport, Connecticut • London

Library of Congress Cataloging-in-Publication Data

Murphy, John W.
    Postmodern social analysis and criticism.

    (Contributions in sociology, ISSN 0084-9278 ; no. 79)
    Bibliography: p.
    Includes index.
    1. Sociology—Philosophy. 2. Postmodernism.
3. Philosophy and social sciences. 4. Civilization,
Modern—Philosophy. I. Title. II. Series.
HM26.M87   1989   301'.01   88-35774
ISBN 0-313-26683-2 (lib. bdg. : alk. paper)

British Library Cataloguing in Publication Data is available.

Library of Congress Catalog Card Number: 88-35774
ISBN: 0-313-26683-2
ISSN: 0084-9278

First published in 1989

Greenwood Press, Inc.
88 Post Road West, Westport, Connecticut 06881

Printed in the United States of America

The paper used in this book complies with the
Permanent Paper Standard issued by the National
Information Standards Organization (Z39.48-1984).

10 9 8 7 6 5 4 3 2 1

Contents

Preface

At this time, a controversy surrounds deconstruction in particular and postmodernism in general. Critics claim that these viewpoints culminate in the destruction of reason, culture, and thus morality. And the recent revelations about Paul de Man's wartime activities have made this situation worse. Writers such as Geoffrey Hartman, Jonathan Culler, and Jacques Derrida have attempted to rescue deconstruction from an ignoble fate. After all, if de Man was a fascist, many commentators will conclude that deconstruction (and postmodernism) leads automatically to this intolerable political position. In this book, no attempt is made to examine de Man's character, or to speculate about traces of fascism in his work. The time for public handwringing is over. Therefore, this text explores the social implications of postmodernism. It treats postmodernism as a philosophy that is worthy of serious study.

Postmodernism contains an epistemology, a methodology, and a social ontology, along with cultural and political dimensions. Subsequent to the advent of postmodernism society must be conceptualized anew. Yet stifling and repressive social imagery is not the product of this change. If anything, the number of possible realities is increased as a result of postmodernism. Whereas fascists constrict reality, postmodernists revel in the options exposed by imagination. However, postmodernists do not destroy order. In general, those who profit from ideology will not gain solace from postmodernism.

Postmodernism offers an alternative to the traditional macro- and micro-approaches to conceptualizing and studying social life. Neither the individual nor the collective is the focus of attention. Social reality, instead, is said to exist between these two extremes. Rules of order emerge from and are institutionalized through discursive practices, claim postmodernists. This means that the polity can assume a variety of forms, for language is constantly expanding. Each style of order, moreover, can be thoroughly assessed. Nonetheless, neither science nor reality is reified.

Social philosophers must abandon their traditional prejudices if postmodernism is to be properly understood. The standard renditions of knowledge and order must be jettisoned. If this is accomplished, a new way of viewing social existence can be entertained. At the heart of postmodernism is risk; it is hoped that postmodernism will become more accessible to readers after they consult this book.

Postmodern Social
Analysis and
Criticism

1

The Historical Development of Modernism

DUALISM AND THE WESTERN TRADITION

The aim of modern philosophy and science is the discovery of truth. In fact, as noted by Paul de Man, "the One, the Good, and the True" are central to the Western intellectual tradition.[1] Identifying the basis of truth, however, has been problematic. Subsequent to the work of Aristotle, truth has been defined perennially as *adaequatio rei et intellectus*. Stated simply, this phrase suggests that a statement is truthful if it correctly reflects the events occuring in the world. Using the imagery popularized by Richard Rorty, valid knowledge can be obtained only when the mind is trained to "mirror" reality.[2] The key implication of this position is that the mind is differentiated from whatever is known. For otherwise, reality could not be reflected in the mind, because these two elements would be identical. An object has a "referential liability," states Gerald Graff, when the world is conceived dualistically.[3]

Separating the mind from reality is not simply an offbeat requirement resulting from the use of particular imagery. Throughout Western philosophy the belief has been maintained that truth and opinion must originate from different sources. If these two types of knowledge were not sequestered from each other, the discovery of truth would be seriously impaired. Indeed, allowing truth to be defiled by opinion might culminate in the evisceration of culture. How can opinion, which by definition is situation-bound, provide a sound base for order? Durkheim writes, for example, that unless truth is "impersonal" the survival of society will be placed in jeopardy.[4] In other words, without a universal basis for reality, an abstract universal, truth will remain esoteric. Talcott Parsons agrees that truth must embody an "ultimate reality,"[5] while Durkheim contends that only a "reality *sui generis*" can sustain this sort of knowledge.[6]

How has this exalted reality been justified? Can knowledge that is context-free be adequately conceptualized, without a passel of accompanying problems? In order to establish a foundation for truth that is unencumbered by situational exigencies, objectivity was removed from the influence of subjectivity. Subjectivity, also referred to as interpretation or opinion, was assumed to be located within the individual. Objectivity, on the other hand, was imagined to have an autonomous existence, unaffected by the process whereby events are perceived. This distinction between subjectivity and objectivity is the centerpiece of dualism. Jean-François Lyotard charged recently that this schism has culminated in the "realist pretensions" exhibited currently by many social scientists.[7] His point is that many critics assert blithely that facts exist, regardless of how these phenomena are interpreted. Furthermore, a variety of methodological techniques have been invented to enable researchers to capture data, without any interference from human values. Yet value-free science has proven to be quite problematic, for knowledge deprived of a context is difficult to envision. As Robert Scholes has put it, "there is no recording, only constructing [reality]."[8]

Nonetheless, dualism, or what postmodernists call the internal/external distinction, has been central to mainstream philosophy. To use the language made famous by Descartes, the world has been divided into two mutually exclusive realms, referred to as *res extensa* and *res cogitans*. In this way, truth is protected from the deleterious consequences of cognition. Through a leap of faith, in other words, knowledge that cannot be encountered is posited to exist. Because this stock of information is immaculately conceived, a pristine base for truth and order is available. Yet this source of truth is predicated on a risky maneuver: the presence of the self must be negated. Passion must be desiccated. This is why postmodernists suggest that traditional social science is nihilistic. Specifically, order and truth are possible only if human vitality is undermined. As will be noted, dualism and the negative consequences that follow from this standpoint are ubiquitous to every facet of traditional social analysis.

This dualism has assumed a myriad of forms. For example, first principles, gods, scientific knowledge, and structural metaphors have all been used at one time or another. Coincident with these ideas, however, is the belief that reality is not contaminated by interpretation. Because these principles are not impaired by cognition, they are assumed to be unlimited. What this means is that an absolute framework is available for enacting truth and order. Consequently, truth is not restricted by human capriciousness and order is not easily subverted by the promise of personal gain. Achieving this ahistorical insight, accordingly, has been a highly valued prize. Philosophers have engaged in many acts of mortification, in order to prepare themselves to receive this knowledge. The reason for this, stated simply, is that truth supposedly has the power to prevent society from devolving into chaos.

Truth is thus the product of pure vision, or *theoria*.[9] Consistent with the tradition inaugurated by the Greeks, valid knowledge is acquired as a result of persons overcoming their contingent nature. Specifically, the limits imposed by subjectivity must be transcended before an accurate assessment of nature or social life can be made. One author has argued recently that "methodologically indiced immortality" serves currently to ground knowledge.[10] Only in this way can the foundation, sometimes known as an *archē*, of truth be reached. As John Ruskin recalls in his *Modern Painters*, *theoria* is associated with the generation of "grateful perception."[11] *Theoria*, in other words, is the pure vision that is essential to the acquisition of knowledge unsullied by corporeal concerns. Morality emerges from *theoria*, in that norms of behavior accompany the institution of reality. Western writers have tended to assume that morality and certainty arrive simultaneously. Yet, the question remains, how has this reality *sui generis* been conceived throughout the history of Western philosophy? What has justified placing *doxa*, or opinion, at the periphery of philosophy?

Although a more elaborate discussion of postmodernism is forthcoming, at this juncture the thrust of this philosophy must be mentioned. Dualism, in short, is destroyed by postmodernism. To use Derrida's term, a postmodern world is characterized by "radical alterity," whereby opposites are conflated.[12] Separating inside from outside is thought to be illegitimate. The world is not an object, but a "text" that is simultaneously read and interpreted. Camus describes adequately this position when he writes in the *Myth of Sisyphus*: "I have no concern with ideas or with the eternal. The truths that come within my scope can be touched with the hand. I cannot separate from them."[13] Accordingly, sounding like a postmodernist, Scholes states that "we do not imitate the world, we construct versions of it."[14]

Postmodernism does not refer to a historical period, presumably the one that follows modernity, but an approach to understanding reality. Antidualism is the centerpiece of this position. While many contemporary writers question the legitimacy of dualism, the separation of objectivity from subjectivity (along with the distinctions made between fact and value, appearance and reality, and truth and opinion) has been viewed as dubious for quite some time. Various artists, scientists, philosophers, and social critics have recognized the fatuity of dualism. Nonetheless, the Western tradition has been overwhelmingly dualistic. Faith in an undefiled reality is still very prevalent. The mediational effects of the human present are revealed by postmodernism—that is, the background that other philosophies presuppose but ignore.

THE EARLY GREEKS

To some readers this point of departure may seem inappropriate, for the early Greeks are usually assumed to have directed their attention to nature and not necessarily to social life.[15] In fact, only later on in their history are the Greeks thought to deal adequately with ethical issues. Nonetheless, valuable insight can be gained into social existence by understanding how these "lovers of wisdom" viewed the natural world. Particularly important is how the parts and the whole of nature were related, and how this relationship was legitimized and regulated.

As revealed by Aristotle and others, Western philosophy is thought to have begun with Thales.[16] Thales was a monist, for he argued that all phenomena emanated from "primary stuff," usually referred to as water. Whether this factor was actually water is irrelevant. Most important is the manner in which Thales explained the existence of reality. To him, water was the "substratum" that sustained every other "element"; it was the basis or "first principle" of existence. Rather than Thales' imagery, the way he conceptualized nature should be the focus of attention. Specifically, he suggested that the elements or parts of nature are regulated by a source that they do not control.

Anaximander also developed a cosmology. The principle that underpins the world was referred to by him as the "boundless" (*apeiron*). Yet he made clear a point that was merely suggested by Thales: namely, that this ultimate principle controls all the elements, without being affected by them. *Apeiron* was the "all-steering" provider of order and thus was accorded a quasi-divine status. Anaximander, furthermore, hinted that his rendition of nature has social implications. He is known for having recognized the existence of "innumerable worlds" (*apeiroi kosmoi*), organized by *Apeiron*. In more contemporary parlance, he implied that society is pluralistic and thus is comprised of numerous "world-views."

As should be noted, a few key themes pervaded the ideas of these inaugural Greek philosophers. First, that a single factor serves to sustain everyday life. Second, that this base is removed from daily existence and is conceived to be infinite. And third, that this primordial source is presumed to be the origin of everything that can be known. Not only were these themes expressed by other figures of this era, similar concepts used by later writers became progressively complex and more sociologically suggestive.

Pythagoras, for instance, is known to have maintained that the four elements (fire, water, earth, and air) are regulated by a fifth. This extra factor, or the "Whole," he claimed, is responsible for engendering the harmony that is witnessed in the universe. Furthermore, elements one through four possess a property that causes them to coalesce. Number, in other words, transforms the parts of existence into a coherent body. In addition to making a distinction between the parts and the whole, Pythagoras noted that an essential tension is present between the various components of nature. Each part is thus ascribed a specific role to play in the cosmic plan.

Heraclitus identified *logos* as the "steering mechanism" that organizes the world.[17] In more sociological terms, justice is posited by *logos*, so that a universal standard is available to verify the accuracy of an individual's judgments. In fact, as a result of the action of *logos* persons are introduced to norms that are universal, for these rules are divinely inspired. Whereas his predecessors were vague on this point, Heraclitus emphasized that laws are legitimate because they originate from a single, implacable authority.

After Heraclitus, Greek philosophers concentrated on describing how laws function. Empedocles was concerned with understanding how the various elements of the universe combine to form new ones, while Anaxagoras attempted to unlock the secrets of *nous*, the omnipotent source of both natural and social laws. In general, the Atomists were devoted to discovering how the primal elements of life, or atoms, operate. By the time this period of philosophy came to a close, the world was no longer portrayed as an amorphous mass, regulated by mythical forces. Instead, fixed laws, although in a manner similar to the earlier *archai*, were believed to underpin every sort of order. In later periods, the identity of these laws became much more elaborate.

GREEK CLASSICS: PLATO AND ARISTOTLE

Plato sought to erect an indubitable ground of knowledge, commonly referred to as the Forms, which was divorced from the contingencies of everyday life.[18] The implication of this démarche is that common sense is inferior to the knowledge associated with these ahistorical archetypes. Moreover, the Forms are indirectly related to everything that is visible. Those who endure the arduous philosophical preparation specified by Plato have a chance to catch a glimpse of eternity. Most important for this discussion is that the Forms provide an inviolable framework for justice and order.[19]

Plato described the social world as a system or, as Martin Buber states, a "pure construct."[20] The term system in this instance refers to an absolute structure that regulates interpersonal relationships, but is unaffected by human desire. Hence Buber's claim that Plato's rendition of order is ideal, or abstract, is easy to understand. Order does not result from convention, in that persons are constrained by an apparatus that is responsible for all knowledge. This process of control is illustrated when Plato reveals how persons are assigned their respective social roles. Persons are given positions according to their natural talents. For example, Plato believed that some persons are destined to be leaders and others followers.[21] Every individual is simply a part of the grand design, or "Grand Narrative," as postmodernists call it, that is provided by the Forms. Although he did not formulate a theory of natural law, Plato based valid knowledge, and thus order, on universal principles that pervade nature.

Aristotle is recognized traditionally as having tried to make social or political philosophy concrete, due to his rejection of Plato's Forms. According to Aristotle, the origin of order is not ethereal, but found within nature. Knowledge and society, specifically, are the product of physical laws. In line with this type of thinking, Aristotle imagined society to be a living organism. Consequently, every city "must be allowed to be the work of nature."[22]

While Aristotle did not rely on esoteric Forms to sustain society, like Plato he placed truth beyond the reach of normal individuals. Every aspect of life has a telos, or purpose, that is disassociated from interpretation. Thus the state is accorded a raison d'être that dictates the organization of the polity. Similar to a living body, every part of society is assumed to have a function that contributes to the survival of the whole. In fact, Aristotle claims in his *Metaphysics* that the components of nature are unquestioningly subordinate to the grand design of the cosmos. As he writes, the "whole must necessarily be prior to the parts."[23] By this statement he means that society exists prior to the individual, and, additionally, that when divorced from the whole no individual segment of the polity has any significance. Modern functionalists advance a similar argument. Nonetheless, the upshot of Aristotle's theory is that human action is ancillary to the discovery of truth and the formation of order.

THE NATURAL ORDER OF THE MEDIEVAL PERIOD

Medieval philosophy can be characterized as a search for the indubitable truth found in God. Faith instead of reason, accordingly, was the primary concern. Medieval philosophers held that truth cannot be discovered through ratiocination, or human effort, but only as a result of a leap of faith that carries an investigator beyond the categories of logic and experience.

Several themes are ubiquitous in medieval philosophy. First, the entire universe, including humans, is created by God. Second, the world is organized in accordance with a Divine plan. Third, God is the ontological justification of everything that exists. And fourth, knowledge about this base of reality can be obtained only indirectly. The most obvious corollary of this outlook is that the individual is a microcosm of the universe, or whole. Clearly, social actors were envisioned to be passive and ineffectual in generating sound information, unless they were assisted in this endeavor by God. As might be expected, this image of human behavior did not necessarily foster self-governance; it was assumed that only by adhering to the divinely inspired laws of the cosmos would order prevail.

The idea that God created the universe is very important for understanding the government of the medieval period. Because authority was considered to be derived from a divine act, those who governed were given inscrutable legitimacy. Augustine, for instance, stated that Christians owe unswerving allegiance to those in authority, while Gregory the Great argued that the majority of persons are incompetent to lead and must obey their rulers.[24] Peter Lombard was more direct; he stated that government is always justified, because leaders are inherently superior to other persons. Although Thomas Aquinas equivocated at times on this point, he adhered to the Pauline interdiction that persons should submit to the Lord's will, in order to settle equitably any dispute.[25] Most important, the asymmetrical relationship between leaders and plebians was considered a natural condition ordained by God.

Due to God's intervention, social order is reinforced by immutable laws. Because of the direct link between Divine authority and law, legal categories are believed to reflect the mind of God. Social order is thus not invented, because society is predicated on Divine intervention. In fact, each one of God's creations is presumed to have a specific function to perform within what medieval writers called the *unum corpus Christi*. Persons have a unique calling, in other words, that can be fulfilled only when they are well integrated into the social whole. Accordingly, the *bonum universale* results from citizens following the rules that are prescribed. As Ullman describes, the *utilitas publica* is given primacy over the *utilitas privata* by most medieval philosophers.[26] In this respect, to use St. Paul's phrase, a ruler is a *"minister Dei."* Hence the so-called microcosm is dominated by the macrocosm.

CONTEMPORARY "CLASSICAL" RENDITIONS
OF SOCIETY

Although the theories that emerged after the medieval period represented a wide range of viewpoints, a common theme was present. Consistent with Descartes' declaration that only "clear and distinct" knowledge is valuable, truth and order were no longer understood to be related to rarefied principles. Rather than faith in God, knowledge was said to be derived from empirical events. According to Wolin, the social world was constructed "by intellect alone, without appeal to super-sensory authority and without relying on non-rational and non-sensory faculties."[27] One would assume this type of empiricism results in the generation of human knowledge that is connected with human action. During this period, however, such an assumption would be unwarranted.

Similar to most of his predecessors, Hobbes recognized that only a reliable base of knowledge can prevent anarchy. Yet contrary to Plato or Thomas Aquinas, for example, he contended that valid information originates from sense impressions. And in order to avoid obtaining a false image of reality, he said, persons must purge themselves of emotion and all other subjective influences; veridical knowledge can be acquired only when the mind "copies" accurately events as they occur. This "copy theory" is still adhered to by a gaggle of philosophers, including some Marxists. Hobbes also stated, however, that facts and values must be kept separate, or truth will remain forever hidden. Those who expect to acquire truth, that is, must become value-free. In this case, sense impressions represent causal factors that convey objective knowledge.

Yet Hobbes recognized that knowledge sustained by sense impressions could also be problematic. Because these impressions expose only one perspective at a time, are recorded in a linear manner, and do not provide a framework for comparing input, he was eventually convinced that through them people would receive a disjointed picture of the world. Indeed, this epistemology bothered Hume so much that he began to doubt whether he even existed. When presented in an atomistic manner, knowledge cannot be readily generalized and thus remains idiosyncratic. Hobbes' major concern was that the "war of all against all" he anticipated would be hastened through the inability of persons to have an all-encompassing view of reality. Without a "common present," as Chaim Perelman describes, how are persons supposed to predict successfully each other's actions?[28]

In order to avoid what he called "inconsistent signification," Hobbes proceeded to argue that the state must enforce a particular rendition of reality, which is accepted eventually by all rational persons.[29] By merging a variety of interpretations of reality into a commonly accepted point of reference, the state became in Hobbes' thought the "Great Definer."[30] He categorically separated private and public knowledge, because personal opinions cannot supply a sufficient base for social reality. Accordingly, Hobbes deified the state, for he claimed that the commonwealth is a "mortal god" that is directly related to the "immortal God."[31] Thus Hobbes portrayed political authority as divinely sanctioned. He touted obedience to laws, furthermore, as the highest possible form of worship. In the true mythological sense, the state in Hobbes' work becomes a Leviathan.

Like Hobbes, Locke stated that knowledge has an empirical foundation. He thought that sense perceptions impinge on the mind, which he referred to as a tabula rasa. Central to Locke's epistemology is the rejection of deductive logic. Deduction relies on the acceptance of specific categories of thought that are accepted a priori as legitimate. Locke argued that such an abstract conceptual scheme will surely distort knowledge. Instead, he maintained that because sense data exist a posteriori, knowledge is perceived always in situ. Contextualized in this way, information is concrete and easily adapted to meet situational requirements. However, eventually Locke began to recognize that universal principles of morality cannot be inductively generated.

Therefore, as is commonly known, Locke championed a contractual theory of law, so as to avoid the authoritarianism he believed to be pivotal to Hobbes' portrayal of order. Locke justified his view that law is established spontaneously by accepting a simple idea. That is, because no one has complete knowledge, situational exigencies cannot be ignored by the state. Publicly verifiable knowledge, nonetheless, is not necessarily an outgrowth of individual preferences. In other words, concern for the common weal is not automatically related to personal gain. Consequently, Locke declared that all citizens must surrender their natural rights to the community, thereby implying that the government represents significantly more than the sum of individual desires. Actually, he believed that social institutions are best suited to supply order because they are unsullied by internecine rivalries and thus are global in scope. This contention becomes apparent in his distinction between "private judgments" and those expressed by legislators.[32] Moreover, Locke charged that the survival of society depends on God and Nature, as opposed to political discourse. The vox populi is thus obliquely related to preserving the polity. Like Hobbes, Locke gave primacy to a source of knowledge that can control opinion.

A similar type of dualism is also found in the work of Rousseau. Although he is sometimes called a radical contract theorist, he subordinated the "private will" to the "general will." Rousseau hoped to liberate people from the strictures imposed by the modern world, yet he was unsuccessful in this endeavor. For if the private will is ancillary to a collective good that is abstractly defined, order cannot be said to result from intersubjectively recognized commitments. Rousseau's understanding of the social contract does not give individuals the responsibility to create and protect social relationships. In point of fact, he wrote that a social contract requires the "total alienation of each associate, all his rights, to the community."[33] In other words, the final product is superior ontologically to those who negotiate a contract.

Rousseau went on to admit that a contract does not embody a voluntary association among persons, but an "obligation to a collective body of which oneself constitutes a part."[34] As opposed to the vox populi, or particular will, the survival of a community depends on the General Will. Unlike the particular will, Rousseau said, the General Will cannot err because it is impartial. While the particular will is merely the "sum of all private wills," the mélange of claims that compete to dominate the political landscape is transcended by the General Will. Because private wills are undisciplined and capricious, the General Will must impose order or otherwise none would exist. Persons are not emancipated from the constraints stipulated by the modern world, but are tethered to norms that are beyond their control. In a manner of speaking, for Rousseau the General Will is the savior of humanity.

A PRELUDE TO MODERN SOCIOLOGY

Auguste Comte and Emile Durkheim are usually considered the key forerunners of modern sociology. They both argued that only non-speculative, empirical knowledge can provide society with a permanent justification. While they claimed that metaphysical knowledge is unreliable, they eventually abandoned this position. In other words, they introduced an abstract base to substantiate order.

To appreciate the position advanced by Comte and Durkheim, their historical context must be recalled. France was in turmoil in the mid-nineteenth century as a result of the many dramatic social and political changes that were taking place. In fact, both writers believed that the collapse of French society was imminent, unless "moral order" could be restored.[35] Societal fragmentation was resulting from rapid industrialization, thus transforming communities into *Gesellschaften*. Individualism was encouraged to the extent that society was beginning to be plagued by anomie, which Durkheim identified as a proliferation of norms. Therefore, as Durkheim wrote, "reality seems valueless. . . . Reality is abandoned."[36] According to both Comte and Durkheim, however, erecting an imperial state would not correct this condition. This remedy would be simply ephemeral, because of the political character of government. They claimed that order must be given a seigneurial status, before anomie can be prevented.

Comte believed that disorder stems from persons acting with reference to contradictory knowledge bases. According to his Law of Three Stages, during theological and philosophical periods knowledge is unreliable, because gods and other unconfirmed factors are invoked to explain social and natural occurrences.[37] In the third stage, positive science reigns, and thus knowledge is revealed that is assumed to be universal. Because science is allegedly value-free or unbiased, truth is finally within the grasp of those who are scientific. Comte wrote that science provides the means for generating "Public Opinion," a body of information that appeals to every segment of society. Because this knowledge is not subject to interpretation, social cohesion can be maintained or, possibly, increased.

Although Durkheim disagreed with Comte's metaphysics and many of his solutions to curb social discord, both writers contended that truth must be impersonal. Durkheim opposed Kant, utilitarians, and pragmatists, arguing that reality is unrelated to cognition or any other form of human calculation. In other words, the survival of truth does not depend on the accuracy of a person's judgments. Truth, stated simply, "must correspond to something real."[38] Likewise, Durkheim contended that society should not be assumed to satisfy human needs, while "moral order" should not be viewed as related to personal salvation. Society, he said, is possible only when order is understood to exist *sui generis*, removed from psychological proclivities. Through "collective effervescence," which Durkheim believed erupts during public ceremonies, persons become aware of a normative referent that is absolute. They overcome their idiosyncracies and begin to appreciate that society is a comprehensive system. Unaffected by existential concerns, Durkheim maintained that society operates as a coercive force ("collective force") and secures order.

Durkheim wrote that "reality is none other than society."[39] This reality, moreover, is a collective body that is greater than the sum of individuals: "Society transcends the individual's consciousness."[40] Social symbolism elevates persons to a sphere uncontaminated by opinion, and thus knowledge is available that can condition perception. Accordingly, this exalted framework is given the latitude necessary to control behavior. Intellectual anarchy is averted, Durkheim said, because truth is distinguished from illusion by a "collective consciousness." Persons are controlled by a collective mind that both recollects a society's past and contains its future. Thus, the moral constraint that Durkheim says is the key to maintaining social decorum can be guaranteed. As he is famous for emphasizing, society is a "thing" that has objective validity, unrelated to personal expressions of discontent and satisfaction. Simply put, society is a "reality *sui generis*." According to Durkheim, the "social always possesses a higher dignity than what is individual."[41]

MODERN SOCIOLOGY AND MODERNITY

Modern sociology is usually identified with the work of Talcott Parsons. As is well documented, he was almost obsessed with the issue of how order is maintained, which he referred to as the "Hobbesian problem." Specifically, how is it possible to secure order without utilizing the metaphysical props adopted in the past? For as long as society is regulated by unsubstantiated principles, Parsons feared that chaos could occur at any time.

To impede the outbreak of the "war of all against all" predicted by Hobbes, Parsons invented new social imagery. He described society as a system having various parts that are structurally linked together. Most important are the roles that specify in any situation the behavior expected from persons. Roles are the basic structures of society. These fundamental units are united according to "reciprocal expectations," whereby the demands of any one role are understood to have implications for others.[42] For example, the roles of doctor and nurse are thought to be complementary and thus essentially related. Anyone who operates within the parameters prescribed by his or her roles will be automatically attuned to the expectations of other persons. As should be noticed, Parsons is concerned with the maintenance of roles and their relationships, and not necessarily with the way persons actually conduct their daily affairs.

An institution consists of the appropriate roles and their interrelationships. For this reason, Parsons has been criticized for transforming social existence into an assembly of role networks. De Man, for example, suggests that in a system such as Parsons', persons become marionettes and obey blindly those who are in authority.[43] After all, outside of the boundaries outlined by roles nothing but a wilderness exists. Conceived as a system of interlocking roles, society no longer has to be associated with abstract doctrines to insure that persons are adequately controlled. Since these social structures are the locus of institutional and personal meaning, behavior inconsistent with role expectations is by definition irresponsible. As a result of the asymmetry present between roles and their inhabitants, persons are confronted by a plethora of structural imperatives.

Parsons' work on the role system was undertaken mostly during the 1940s and 1950s. During the 1960s he became a proponent of cybernetics. Like Norbert Wiener, Parsons argued that social and natural systems consist of information and energy. Systems high in information, accordingly, control those high in energy. As might be suspected, he said that social structure is the source of information, while the human being supplies the energy required to keep the system operating. This scenario specifies, however, that persons have no direction until they are given an orientation by their roles. In this sense, persons are incapable of subverting social structures. How could anyone undermine the origin of their identity? Guiding the entire cybernetic system, moreover, is what Parsons called "ultimate reality," an unimpeachable source of information. Hence society is completely reified.

What Parsons did, consistent with his reliance on Freud, was to differentiate cultural from individual rationality. Specifically, he envisioned roles as objective embodiments of formal reason, while he cited human action as irrational and a threat to order. This message was unmistakably conveyed through his use of structural metaphors. As is commonly assumed, structures are not subject to interpretation and are neutral. Therefore, they prescribe an indubitable framework for order. Parsons, for example, established the rationale necessary to bureaucratize society. Bureaucracies are deemed to be valuable because they proffer an extremely formalized scheme for making decisions. Judgments are based on standardized criteria, thus allowing large amounts of data to be routinely processed. According to

Peter Berger and his colleagues, the success of a bureaucracy depends on "emotional control."[44] That is, persons must be thoroughly convinced that their concerns will only obscure reality. As a result, citizens are expected to refrain from public debate and transfer all decision making to technical experts, who are familiar with institutionalized modes of assessment. Most important, these technocrats are assumed to be scientific and unimpressed by personal appeals. The central theme of bureaucratization, stated simply, is that persons are less rational than institutions.

With decision making organized by role requirements, efficiency is thought to improve. Nonetheless, persons begin to complain regularly about the impersonal treatment they receive from bureaucrats. The reason for their dissatisfaction is quite simple: the human element is reduced in importance. In a workplace, for example, bureaucratization may be disastrous, because the formalization of a job may result in apathy and reduced productivity. Moreover, patrons of a business expect to be treated with courtesy, or they will shop elsewhere. Therefore, on a practical level, bureaucracy may not be as efficient as at first thought. The human costs may begin to outweigh any gain in technical expertise. In general, the impersonalization attendant to organizational formalization may begin to infect every aspect of society and cause widespread dissatisfaction. This sort of alienation, moreover, may not be cured simply by a political revolution. Perhaps the history of social order will have to be rethought to correct the problems attendant to bureaucratization.

CONCLUSION: THE DECLINE OF MODERNITY

The externalization of the human will, indigenous to bureaucratization, is often identified as the hallmark of modernity. Because of the ubiquity of bureaucracies and the unfortunate belief that persons are basically capricious, Lucien Goldmann has called modernity a tragedy.[45] He believes that when citizens cannot be trusted to formulate laws through discourse, the resulting society will inevitably be stifling. Although modernity can be said to epitomize this tendency, this trend can be found throughout Western philosophy. Particularly noteworthy, for example, is the ideal of self-denial, which is not the most auspicious theme for use in developing an open society. With human action relegated to an obscure position, reality can emerge undefiled. Accordingly, an unfailing belief in the efficacy of science, the view that formal logic is the paragon of reason, and the complete rationalization of institutions are usually associated with modernity. Max Weber, for instance, referred to this as the "routinization of charisma."[46] Modernism suggests that reducing the impact of the human element will increase the efficiency of any undertaking. Hence the sacrifice of human freedom is portrayed as noble and necessary for society to function properly.

Subsequent to the onset of modernity, persons are levelled to a common denominator, for a mass society is spawned. As is clearly visible today, conformity to well established roles is the measure of an individual's integrity. Rebellion is viewed with suspicion. Behavior is further standardized due to the infiltration of science into practically every sphere of life. Because society operates in a mechanistic manner, initiative is vanquished. Also, as large bureaucracies begin to dominate the social scene, the classification and regulation of activities are of paramount importance. Replaceable persons are required by what Peter Drucker has called the "Corporate Society." Persons, in other words, who are mass produced are essential for the survival of modernity. In sum, modernity consists of a search for scientific rationales to justify social arrangements, thereby fostering the image that order represents what Jean-Francois Lyotard calls a "unicity," or a self-perpetuating machine.[47] Yet modernity is considered decadent by postmodernists, because it seeks order at the expense of creativity. In a Kafkaesque sense, persons are trapped within a labyrinth of edicts issued by authorities who remain anonymous, while organizations that cannot be penetrated regulate existence.

In general, according to postmodernists, the major shortcoming of the Western tradition is that knowledge and order are conceived dualistically and underpinned by "metanarratives." This problem culminates in the alienation that pervades modernity. A metanarrative is a style of knowledge that is used to buttress norms, for example, but is unaffected by quotidian problems. As stated by Lyotard, "there is a universal 'history' of spirit, spirit is 'life,' and 'life' is its own self-presentation and formulation in the ordered knowledge of all its forms contained in the empirical sciences."[48] Although society may be legitimized in this manner, the cost is quite high. Specifically important to postmodernists is that persons are enslaved to their own creations, in that all social phenomena are autonomous. The dimensions of the human spirit are defined by cultural objects. As Marx and Engels wrote in the *German Ideology*, the life-process appears to be upside down, as in a *camera obscura*.[49] Yet as postmodernists demonstrate, the dualism that perpetuates this travesty is outmoded. Metanarratives, they show, cannot be justified any longer. Moreover, they claim that this rejection of dualism is liberating. Whereas dualism and metanarratives are characteristic of mainstream Western philosophy, postmodernism provides a grounded epistemology and social ontology. Accordingly, Gilles Deleuze states that "there is no *Logos*, there are only hieroglyphs."[50] There is only the text, which Julia Kristeva defines as a "*practice* calling into question [symbolic and social] *finitudes* by proposing *new signifying devices*."[51] The text disrespects authority, for anything that is written invites interpretation.

Postmodernism is thus "pagan," according to Lyotard.[52] Postmodernists do not aspire to bask in the pure light of truth, but rather to wallow in the mire of opinion. They work with slimy concepts, rather than rigorous axioms of logic. In this sense, truth, knowledge, and morality are not founded on themes that are immune to evolution. For example, the primitive mind is considered by Lévy-Bruhl to be illogical, simply because the cognitive style of so-called primitive persons does not fit neatly into the scheme outlined by modern psychologists. The mind of Lévy-Bruhl's natives is corporeal and informed by existential considerations, and thus is not formalized. His primitives live a poetic existence, because in it dreams and reality are intermixed.[53] The postmodern mind is also "wild," and not restricted by scientific protocol. Barthes aptly describes postmodern society as "a body of bliss consisting solely of erotic relations."[54] Obsessed by normativeness, even Aristotle treated persons who were not Greek as barbaric. Nowadays that designation is retarded or deviant. Nonetheless, because of the association between postmodernism and savagery, this recently developed philosophy has been severely criticized. Culture, in short, is presumed to be decimated. Without pristine truth, many critics feel, culture is impossible; insanity reigns supreme.

The aim of this book is not only to introduce the main tenets of postmodernism, but to answer the critics of this philosophy. The question is: Why does reality have to be sanitized, instead of poetic? Also, is a poetic reality synonymous with chaos? As will be shown, the usual renditions of knowledge and order are defiled by postmodernism, yet culture is not destroyed. Instead, postmodernists talk about developing a society "without criteria," or, more specifically, without a priori guidelines. Deconstruction, a variant of postmodernism, according to Jonathan Culler "seeks to undo (to deconstruct) oppositions that in the name of unity, purity, order, and hierarchy try to eliminate difference."[55] While this prospect may frighten many readers, the opponents of postmodernism are simply incorrect when they state that a non-dualistic conception of society is impossible: a culture intimately connected to human action is not sheer fantasy. This inability to overcome dualism may testify to the current impoverishment of the human spirit, rather than the bankruptcy of postmodernism. Maybe Heidegger was expressing profound insight, instead of despair, when he lamented that possibly only a God can save humanity, due to the present level of alienation.

No one ever said that living a non-alienated existence would be easy, but only possible. Many traditional ideas must be rethought before this can occur. Truth and order, particularly, must be conceptualized anew. Postmodernism facilitates this process. Yet rethinking these basic notions may frighten some readers. Doubtless, the key to understanding postmodernism is perseverance. This book seeks to promote a correct reading of postmodern philosophy. Actually, postmodernism may prove to be quite liberating, as opposed to condemning humankind to chaos and slavery to the so-called dark forces of life. Expressing a postmodern theme popularized by Nietzsche, postmodern critics place themselves constantly at risk. Critique and interpretation, in other words, are allowed to intermingle, and they produce a very potent concoction. Expectations are questioned and norms dissolve, as society expands through creative acts.

NOTES

1. Paul de Man, *Allegories of Reading* (New Haven: Yale University Press, 1979), p. 119.
2. Richard Rorty, *Philosophy and the Mirror of Nature* (Princeton: Princeton University Press, 1979).
3. Gerald Graff, *Poetic Statement and Critical Dogma* (Chicago: University of Chicago Press, 1980), p. 25.
4. Emile Durkheim, *Pragmatism and Sociology* (Cambridge: Cambridge University Press, 1983), p. 74.
5. Talcott Parsons, *Societies: Evolutionary and Comparative Perspectives* (Englewood Cliffs, N.J.: Prentice-Hall, 1966), p. 8.
6. Durkheim, *Pragmatism and Sociology*, p. 87; Emile Durkheim, *Sociology and Philosophy* (New York: Macmillan, 1974), pp. 80–97.
7. Jean-François Lyotard, *The Postmodern Condition: A Report on Knowledge* (Minneapolis: University of Minnesota Press, 1984), pp. 12, 37.
8. Robert Scholes, "The Fictional Criticism of the Future," *TriQuarterly* 34 (Fall 1975), pp. 233–247.
9. Paul de Man, *The Resistance to Theory* (Minneapolis: University of Minnesota Press, 1986), pp. 3–20.
10. John W. Murphy, "The Importance of Schutz's Phenomenology for Computerization," *Worldly Phenomenology: The Continuing Influence of Alfred Schutz on North American Human Science*, ed. Lester Embree (Washington, D.C.: University Press of America, 1988), pp. 137–149.
11. Herbert Read, *The Philosophy of Modern Art* (Greenwich, Conn.: Fawcett Publications, 1967), pp. 77–81.
12. Michael Ryan, *Marxism and Deconstruction* (Baltimore: Johns Hopkins University Press, 1982), p. 14.
13. Albert Camus, *The Myth of Sisyphus and Other Essays* (New York: Alfred A. Knopf, 1961), p. 89.
14. Scholes, "The Fictional Criticism of the Future," p. 236.
15. Samuel Enoch Stumpf, *Socrates to Sartre: A History of Philosophy* (New York: McGraw-Hill, 1975), pp. 3–30; W.K.C. Guthrie, *A History of Greek Philosophy*, vol. 1 (Cambridge: Cambridge University Press, 1962), pp. 1–25.
16. Milton C. Nahm, *Selections from Early Greek Philosophy* (New York: Appleton-Century-Crofts, 1964), pp. 37–39.

17. Philip Wheelwright, *Heraclitus* (Princeton: Princeton University Press, 1959), pp. 44, 107 (Fragments 120, 35).

18. Ludwig Landgrebe, *Major Problems in Contemporary European Philosophy* (New York: Frederick Ungar, 1966), pp. 126ff., 157ff.

19. G. C. Field, *The Philosophy of Plato* (London: Oxford University Press, 1961), pp. 66–84.

20. Martin Buber, *On Judaism* (New York: Schocken, 1967), pp. 115, 145–148.

21. Plato, *Laws* 964e, in *The Collected Dialogues of Plato*, ed. Edith Hamilton and Huntington Cairns (Princeton: Princeton University Press, 1961), p. 1509; Frederick Copleston, *A History of Philosophy*, Vol. 1 (Westminster, Md.: The Newman Press, 1963), pp. 225ff.

22. Aristotle, *Politics*, 1252b, in *Everyman's Library,* 605, ed. Ernest Rhys, trans. William Ellis (New York: E. P. Dutton, 1939), p. 3.

23. Ibid., 1253a.

24. Walter Ullman, *The Individual and Society in the Middle Ages* (London: Methuen, 1967), pp. 12–13.

25. Thomas Gilby, *The Political Thought of Thomas Aquinas* (Chicago: University of Chicago Press, 1958), pp. 150ff.

26. Ullmann, *The Individual and Society*, p. 43; see also D. J. O'Connor, *Aquinas and Natural Law* (London: Macmillan, 1967), pp. 42ff.

27. Sheldon S. Wolin, *Politics and Vision* (Boston: Little, Brown, 1960), p. 245.

28. Chaim Perelman, *The New Rhetoric and the Humanities* (Dordrecht, Netherlands: D. Reidel, 1979), pp. 17–18.

29. Thomas Hobbes, *Leviathan*, ed. Michael Oakeshott (Oxford: Basil Blackwell, 1946), pp. 7–8.

30. Wolin, *Politics and Vision*, p. 260.

31. Hobbes, *Leviathan*, pp. 112, 140.

32. John Locke, *The Second Treatise on Government* (New York: Macmillan, 1956), p. 98.

33. Jean Jacques Rousseau, *The Social Contract* (New York: Hefner Publishing Co., 1965), p. 15.

34. Ibid., p. 17.

35. Emile Durkheim, *Selected Writings*, ed. Anthony Giddens (Cambridge: Cambridge University Press, 1972), pp. 97–100.

36. Emile Durkheim, *Suicide* (New York: The Free Press, 1951), p. 256.

37. Christopher G. A. Bryant, *Positivism in Social Theory and Research* (New York: St. Martin's Press, 1985), pp. 27–33; see also Leszek Kolakowski, *The Alienation Of Reason* (Garden City, N.Y.: Doubleday, 1968), pp. 47–72.

38. Durkheim, *Selected Writings*, p. 252.

39. Durkheim, *Pragmatism and Sociology*, p. 87.

40. Durkheim, *Sociology and Philosophy*, p. 54.

41. Durkheim, *Selected Writings*, p. 253.

42. Talcott Parsons, *The Social System* (New York: The Free Press, 1951), pp. 36–45.

43. Paul de Man, *The Rhetoric of Romanticism* (New York: Columbia University Press, 1984), pp. 262–290.

44. Peter L. Berger, Brigette Berger, and Hansfried Kellner, *The Homeless Mind* (New York: Random House, 1973), pp. 34ff.

45. Lucien Goldmann, *The Hidden God* (London: Routledge and Kegan Paul, 1970).

46. Max Weber, *Economy and Society*, Vol. 1 (Berkeley: University of California Press, 1978), pp. 246–254.

47. Lyotard, *The Postmodern Condition*, p. 12.

48. Ibid., p. 34.

49. Karl Marx and Frederick Engels, *The German Ideology* (Moscow: Progress Publishers, 1976), p. 42.

50. Gilles Deleuze, *Proust and Signs* (New York: George Braziller, 1972), p. 167.

51. Julia Kristeva, *Revolution in Poetic Language* (New York: Columbia University Press, 1984), p. 210.

52. Jean-François Lyotard and Jean-Loup Thébaud, *Just Gaming* (Minneapolis: University of Minnesota Press, 1985), pp. 16ff.

53. Lucien Lévy-Bruhl, *How Natives Think* (Princeton, N.J.: Princeton University Press, 1985).

54. Roland Barthes, *The Pleasure of the Text* (New York: Hill and Wang, 1975), p. 16.

55. Jonathan Culler, "It's Time to Set the Record Straight About Paul de Man and His Wartime Articles for a Pro-Fascist Newspaper," *The Chronicle of Higher Education*, 13 July 1988.

2

The Making of the Postmodern World

INTRODUCTION: THE BREAKDOWN OF DUALISM

Gradually the dualism endemic to mainstream philosophy became problematic around the turn of the twentieth century. The chasm existing between a knower and that which is known could no longer be tolerated. Although the result of this distinction was supposed to be the revelation of pristine facts, theoretically and practically this could not be the case. For if experience is unrelated to the acquisition of knowledge, how can anything be known? A phenomenon unmediated by the human presence is thoroughly abstract; facts, for example, are contextless and thus without meaning. Dualistically conceived knowledge may be uncontaminated by opinion, yet this unadulterated truth can never be grasped. According to Waldenfels, because *doxa* is despised, the aim of philosophy is paradoxical.[1] The discovery of truth consists of finding knowledge that is unquestionably valid but likely to be irrelevant.

Perhaps most problematic are the social implications of a dualistic epistemology. Specifically, this rendition of knowledge is thought by postmodernists to lead to social repression. Viewing knowledge as abstract, they conclude, will surely result in moral, ethical, or political principles becoming differentiated from human needs. After all, if the focus of attention is something loosely referred to as society, what happens to the individual? Persons may be treated as functional elements of a system that is insensitive to human needs. As was the case in Germany during World War II, the state may acquire the power, with meager opposition, to murder innocent citizens. Nonetheless, the point is that when order is substantiated by dualism, persons may easily become viewed as ancillary to the perpetuation of culture.

As noted in Chapter 1, dualism encourages the adoption of grand narratives to explain the origin and purpose of society. As a result, the advent of a particular philosophy, for example capitalism, may be associated with evolutionary development. Lyotard makes this point by stating that events may be perceived as located on the "itinerary of the Spirit." This allusion to Hegel suggests that the destiny of society owes nothing to the commitment exhibited by its citizens. In this sense, Lyotard's criticism of Hegel is identical to that voiced by Marx. In any case, leaders may claim to have received a divine mandate, while plebians are consigned permanently to their lowly status. History serves to justify politics, even pogroms, rather than the decisions of policymakers, who are fallible. Hence the human spirit may be crushed under the weight of history and society. For Natural History— historical descriptions based on divine or natural laws—disrespects the inclinations that motivate persons. Such disregard can only result in disaster, according to postmodernists.

In essence, the dehumanization spawned by dualism prompted the move toward what Lyotard calls "postmodernism."[2] Of course, others have used this term, yet he popularized its adoption. The 1984 translation of his book, *La condition postmoderne: rapport sur le savoir*, originally published in 1979, brought instant recognition to this topic. Nonetheless, the rejection of dualism was not necessarily inaugurated by Lyotard and his fellow travellers. Themes associated with postmodernism can be found in the works of a variety of earlier writers. Along with Lyotard, these authors believe that dualism renders the human condition untenable, because truth is speculative and thus unverifiable. Truth, accordingly, can be espoused by any fanatic. Additionally, the rationalization of the world that is required for the discovery of knowledge unmarred by interpretation undermines the postmodernist belief that society should cultivate spontaneity. In today's world, emphasis is placed overwhelmingly on social control; advocates of positive science and bureaucracy, the key elements of modernity, do not stress divergent thinking.

Broadly speaking, as defined by Jean Wahl, postmodernism is a "philosophy of existence."[3] Hence the aim of philosophy should not be to reveal immutable truths or ideals, but to appreciate the intimate association between human action (praxis) and the meaning of life. In order to comprehend how fact and illusion are differentiated, Wahl suggests, the human presence must be penetrated. Both inductively and deductively derived schemes are irrelevant to this process, in that neither of these approaches is sensitive to the role praxis plays in the generation of knowledge. Postmodernists loathe the use of explanatory models (or heuristic devices), because all phenomena are described in such a way that their social significance is distorted. In opposition to Plato, Aristotle, Aquinas, and

Durkheim, for example, postmodernists assume that nothing exists divorced from human expression. Therefore, postmodern philosophers search within the realm deployed by experience to explain adequately the human condition. Existence and "system" are thus treated as contradictory notions. Reminiscent of Nietzsche's views, postmodernists believe that those who strive to establish philosophical systems lack integrity.

Postmodernists contend that social life can best be understood as a "world without opposite," to use Jean Gebser's phrase.[4] In other words, meaning and purpose are not found in rarefied formulae, but emerge from discourse, which is integral to the search for truth. As Martin Buber says, truth is found in the "between" that spans the distance which separates subjectivity from objectivity. This is the arena where Nietzsche's tightrope walker works. To surrender the "opposite" means simply that human action and the world are inextricably united; they cannot be separated in order to insure the integrity of facts or authority. "In this togetherness the thou," Gebser writes, "be it a partner, world, or divine, is no longer thought, understood, or grasped as an opposite."[5] In this way, nothing is inherently antagonistic to the human condition. A postmodern world, therefore, might best be imagined as embodied, as a corporeal framework. As both Nietzsche and Marx might state, nothing is really alien to the human condition.

At this juncture, the use of the term "embodied" must be further explained. In opposition to dualism, knowledge is understood in postmodernism to be submerged in the affairs that comprise everyday experience. In point of fact, Deleuze notes that " 'interpreting' dissolves the one [subjectivity] no less than the other [objectivity]."[6] Desire, hate, and love, for example, are part of any laws that might be formulated. As should be noted, the idea of corporeality suggests that knowledge has a purpose, even if it is labelled as scientific. Rather than contemplative, truth is practical and seduced into existence. Knowledge, according to Merleau-Ponty, is a "interiorly worked-over mass."[7] In this regard, Schutz remarks that facts always exist "for someone."[8] Yet contrary to the view held by Descartes, who feared the advances of the evil genius and thus distrusted intuition, this consequence is not necessarily bad. For knowledge that is implicated in human action cannot be hostile, treating sadistically those who pursue truth. Truth is not a martinet, but a friend who cajoles and entices persons to acquire insight. In this regard, truth is a bodily experience. Further, as a bodily function, truth has social importance, and is not simply a metaphysical conundrum.

PHILOSOPHY

In philosophy this movement toward understanding reality in an integrated or "integral" manner is thought to have begun in earnest with

Kant. His so-called Copernican Revolution changed dramatically the nature of philosophy. Most important, he proposed that the presuppositions built into human cognition, rather than empirical reality, determine the parameters of facts. Space and time, simply put, are considered to be experiential constructs. For this reason, temporality is referred to by Minkowski as "lived time," while the term associated with Bergson is *durée*. In either case, the dimensions of daily life are presumed to be affected by changes in cognitive intensity. Rather than constrained by time, human behavior emerges as temporal movement. Accordingly, Gebser writes that "temporal freedom" is central to postmodernism.[9] Time, in a manner of speaking, originates from the most mundane activities. The time whereby events are revealed subtends any chronology of facts.[10]

Postmodernists were influenced particularly by Kant's conflation of imagination and reality. Sartre captures adequately what postmodernists value about imagination: "To be able to imagine, it is enough that consciousness be able to surpass the real in constructing a world, since the negation of the real is always implied by its construction of the world."[11] Uniting imagination and the world both creates and suppresses reality. Derrida calls this endeavor writing "under erasure." For example, if Derrida writes that "God exists," he conveys the idea that by "putting the existence of God under erasure," he has "both affirmed it and called it into question."[12] Reality is thus "determinable indeterminancy": reality is created and then held in abeyance.[13]

Kant's rejection of dualism was not complete, for his belief in the "*Ding an sich*" remained firm. Of course, Hegel tried to reunite history and the human spirit, although he was unsuccessful in this endeavor. His reliance on *Geist* to reconcile disparate events undermined the possibility of viewing seriously human destiny as an outgrowth of praxis. With regard to interjecting life into empirical events, Husserl advanced beyond both Kant and Hegel. When Husserl argued that all knowledge is "intentional," he subverted dualism. His simple phrase "consciousness is always consciousness of something" altered forever how persons must understand their relationship to the world.[14] According to Alfred Schutz, who was influenced by Husserl, the world is sustained by a "pragmatic motive." Intentionality, writes Schutz, transforms "natural things into cultural objects, human bodies into fellow-men, and the movements of fellow-men into acts, gestures, and communications."[15] Therefore, facts are no longer moribund empirical referents, but phenomena that have a humanly inspired texture. Indeed, Husserl contrasted the empirical world to what he called the *Lebenswelt*, or "life-world." The *Lebenswelt* is the "construct of a universal, ultimately functioning subjectivity."[16] His point was that the world is not the eviscerated object described by empiricists and positivists. Rather than being lifeless, reality shimmers as a result of consciousness burrowing into every facet of existence.

Due to Husserl's use of the term "intentionality," Heidegger argued that Husserl's thesis was simply too psychological and, possibly, medieval. Heidegger, therefore, reformulated Husserl's position into his now famous "question of Being." Persons, stated differently, should not be concerned with the meaning of events, which can be settled easily by a logician or scientist, but instead with the fundamental nature of whatever is known. In fact, Heidegger contended that neither medieval theologians nor modern positive scientists think, and that they may actually prevent serious questioning. Both are concerned primarily with categorizing events, Heidegger claimed, and do not raise fundamental questions about their identity. Because of his interest in Being, Heidegger labelled his work fundamental ontology. His ontology is foundational because it is not speculative, or based on factors that are naively accepted. For Heidegger, Being is an "event" and not something hidden from view.[17] In other words, Being can be found only *"proximally and for the most part*—in its average *everydayness."*[18] Being, as Otto Pöggeler notes, is "appropriation."[19] "Being is *what requires creation of us* for us to experience it," claims Merleau-Ponty.[20] In sum, Being is not ahistorical and absolute.

Being is not pure, Heidegger said, but is embroiled in the activities of *Dasein*. Literally translated as "being there," the use of this term suggests that Being does not exist in the abstract. Being is always connected to a situation, wherein human action unfolds. Actually, humans are involved closely in the disclosure of Being. Whereas the human side of facticity is diminished in importance by positive science, Heidegger claimed that Being resides in a "clearing" established by language use. Consequently, he declared language to be the "house of Being." Within language Being stands, always shifting according to the various nuances of speech. Therefore, borrowing from Hölderlin, Heidegger wrote that "poetically man dwells" on this earth.[21] Through the use of language, the opportunities that constitute a person's life are exposed as both radiant and fragile. The world is not represented, but is brought to presence through language.

The general thrust of Heidegger's ontology is that things do not have an essence outside of their linguistically inscribed identity. Sartre made this point with his now famous statement, "existence precedes essence." Nonetheless, according to Roland Barthes, Jacques Derrida, Paul de Man, and Michel Foucault, Heidegger's study of Being is not sufficiently radical. These writers believe that language is not a conduit for Being, but the source of reality. Language and reality, they argue, can be distinguished in Heidegger's work. Derrida, for example, is attempting to subvert this bifurcation when he states that "nothing exists outside of the text."[22] Rather than a surrogate for some higher reality, language is the source of all meaning. Jacques Lacan, too, applauds this change in thinking and suggests that truth is derived from language, not reality.[23]

Writers such as Derrida bring to fruition the trend begun by Kant. Leaping beyond experience to encounter eternal truths is no longer deemed appropriate for a philosopher or anyone else. Consistent with what Nietzsche had to say on this issue, the search for truth consists of nothing more than a return to history, specifically the parade of meaning enacted through the use of language. This is not the traditional view of history, which assumes that all differences will be reconciled and complete knowledge will be available. History in the postmodern sense speaks in a multitude of ways. Whereas Nietzsche could only believe in a God who could dance, postmodernists refuse to recognize knowledge that does not have a voice.

According to postmodernists, a text, or the world, is never simply read. Much more fundamental, reading consists of textual or world construction. Every time an event is read, its identity must be reinforced through language use. This is the same as saying that Being is supported by language. For this reason, postmodernists do not search for the essence of Being. De Man, for instance, states that postmodernism is "free from the fantasy of unmediated expression."[24] Accordingly, the ways in which language contaminates Being are considered to be important. As suggested by Barthes, the way Being is spoken should be of paramount importance.

SCIENCE

Following the lead of Frederick Ferré, Stephen Toulmin declares that the age of postmodern science has arrived.[25] Werner Heisenberg contends that this radical change in science began in the late nineteenth century. Pivotal to this transformation is that facts are no longer thought to reside in a substance called ether, equally dispersed throughout the cosmos. With this theoretical maneuver, the absolute reference point used traditionally to verify measurements in classical physics was abandoned. Specifically, the conceptions of space and time invented by Newton were no longer justified. According to Heisenberg, the scheme proposed by Newton idealized nature, and thus was not really concerned with reality. Similarly, Einstein noted that physicists should be concerned with everyday temporality and not necessarily time.

Whereas scientists have tried traditionally to describe the origin of the universe, postmodernists do not.[26] In other words, the ability of scientists to procure so-called objective knowledge has been curtailed, because researchers cannot assume their usual role of "detached observers." Therefore, knowledge cannot be viewed as readily accessible to any rational observer who has mastered research techniques. Postmodernists adhere to Heraclitus' dictum that nature likes to hide, yet they do not opt for his solution to this dilemma. Facts are not obtrusive "things," but are concealed by presuppositions, measurements, and other conceptual considerations. Matter is not pure, but context-bound.

For example, Michael Faraday indicated that electromagnetic phenomena should be understood to exist within a "field of force," rather than within abstract space and time. His point is that the concepts of mechanics are inappropriate. This finding was confirmed by Einstein's suggestion that space and time are not separate entities. His work indicated that there is not a "unique present," from which measurements can be made.[27] Temporal duration is inextricably united to an object's movement. In this regard, Einstein urged scientists not to distinguish time from daily events. The implication is that a multitude of temporal frameworks are possible.

Quantum theory further threatened the Newtonian position. In classical physics, knowing an object's antecedent conditions was thought to be sufficient to predict its future position. Yet particles of matter proved to be more difficult to circumscribe than originally imagined by the Greek Atomists. Planck discovered uncertainty in matter, and thus argued that only statistical statements can be made pertaining to an object's identity. In quantum theory, an object consists of a "collection of possible states."[28] This point is reinforced by Heisenberg's "indeterminacy principle," whereby he shows that the measurement process influences whatever is measured.[29] If the initial conditions of an object cannot be unquestionably ascertained, how can the Cartesian rendition of objectivity be retained?

Postmodernists charge that "undecidables" associated with the interpretive nature of research contribute to the meaning of a phenomenon. Interpretation enters research in many ways, yet mostly through assumptions that go unexamined. Tacitly held beliefs about knowledge, reality, and methodology, for example, begin to shape whatever is perceived. In effect, because knowledge resides in domains that are defined as real, only "best estimates" of truth can be produced. Furthermore, according to René Thom, only "islands of determinism" exist, which are circumscribed by a particular modality of experience.[30] Gone is Newton's absolute ground of certainty.[31] Hence determinism pertains to the connections that are assumed to exist between events. Given certain values that are accepted as valid, a limited range of propositions can be advanced about reality.

Heisenberg claims that Descartes' differentiation between cognition and matter has little importance nowadays.[32] The reason for this is that value-freedom does not guarantee access to truth. In fact, value-freedom is impossible. Does this conclusion imply that science is destroyed? Karl Popper, for instance, illustrates that the answer to this query is No.[33] Knowing the

assumptions or values that sustain a context enables a researcher to comprehend a specific modality of reality. The acquisition of truth is thus not
precluded, but can occur only within a limited domain. Hence truth is embodied. In view of his belief in indeterminacy, Heisenberg writes that the
"subject matter of research is no longer nature itself, but nature subjected
to human questioning, and to this extent man, once again, meets only with
himself."[34] Certainly truth mediated by interpretation in this manner is
valuable, although this knowledge is not automatically generalizable to any
situation. As with Heisenberg, postmodern scientists are not concerned with
metaphysical speculation but with facts that are socially constituted. Unfor-
tunately, the discovery of facts no longer rests simply on technical skills, as
was once thought.

THE ARTS

Impressionism was an outgrowth of the obsession with science and
technology prevalent during the late nineteenth century. In concert with the
requirements of empiricism, impressionists were concerned with reducing
reality to its elementary particles. Painting, for example, reproduces objects
"through *parts* of the material of which they are made up."[35] The aim of art
is to remove conceptualization from perception, so that pure matter may
come into relief. As a result of relying on retinal stimulation, impressionists
assumed that reality uncontaminated by passion could be captured.
Neutralizing art in this way was supposed to make aesthetics scientific. The
subtleties of nature, accordingly, could be mastered and this knowledge
disseminated throughout society.

Anti-impressionistic art, on the other hand, does not preserve but violates
nature. Instead of mimesis, expression is central to art. The attempt is made,
therefore, to unshackle the spontaneity sublimated through impressionism.
This theme is reiterated by Kristeva when she states that postmodern art is
situated "outside art, through art."[36] Similar to anti-impressionists,
postmodernists reject the fantasy that reality can be seized once certain
techniques are perfected. The point of postmodern art is to affirm life, and
not to describe a fate that is waiting to be fulfilled. In the view of postmodernism, writes Deleuze, "the work of art is nourished by the truths it
engenders."[37] Describing postmodernists, John Cage insists that "we are intimate with whatever will happen."[38] Hence artists should not simply strive to
chart Minerva's flight because artistic inspiration does not depend on reality.
Accordingly, impressionism and other styles of realism are anathema to
postmodernism. Postmodern art does not depend on reality.

Anti-impressionism is usually thought to have begun with the work of
Cézanne.[39] In his work, space is no longer three-dimensional, but multidimensional. The parameters of an object are defined by shifts in color. As a

result of this technique, even simple objects appear to have contours, which would be invisible if space were flat. Merleau-Ponty is correct when he remarks that Cézanne's paintings are corporeal, for the planes of color require an onlooker to quell their movement.[40] In this sense, according to Gaston Bachelard, "Being is round." Space is historical and thus imperfect. Actually, Cézanne recognized what would later be stressed by cubists—space is not homogeneous, but constructed with respect to the painter's field of vision. Although Matisse was not employing the cubist method, in both *Dance* and *The Red Studio* he demonstrated clearly that persons are not merely inserted into space. Rather, space is a "living medium."[41] Of course, the compositions of Kandinsky de-objectified space completely. Like Jackson Pollock, Kandinsky deployed space through fulminations of emotion. Kandinsky dissolved objects and allowed viewers to stroll within his paintings. In general, the purpose of these anti-impressionistic tendencies is to delegitimize the mechanistic world image proposed by Newton and to illustrate that space is a human creation.

While the views promulgated by Cézanne and the other nineteenth- and twentieth-century artists just mentioned were certainly radical, space may still treated as something to be traversed, albeit from a variety of directions. Max Ernst, however, had a premonition that sooner or later the so-called inner and outer world would begin to overlap. In postmodern language, the internal/external distinction would be obliterated. With the onset of surrealism, Ernst's dreams were realized. Art, in other words, came to "represent the flow of *jouissance* into language," claims Kristeva.[42]

Surrealists scoffed at naturalists and argued that reality is imaginary. André Breton suggested in his *Manifesto of Surrealism* (1924) that dreaming should not be limited to the nighttime.[43] For dreams and reality, he noted, can not be easily distinguished. Because no form of knowledge emerges unscathed by imagination, surrealists contended, reality must be invented. For example, music is inherently noise, according to Cage, until sound is transubstantiated into something meaningful by creativity. Consider Magritte's painting *Pipe*, which is a picture of a pipe with the words "this is not a pipe" scrolled across the bottom.[44] This statement is not absurd if the visual and linguistic messages conveyed by Magritte are understood to be mediated by interpretation. After all, an interpretation is never final. Is the identity of a pipe certain? Due to the pervasiveness of interpretation, reality is displaced by surrealists and revealed to be something that is possible rather than actual. A pipe is not empirical, but cultural. Nowhere among its empirical elements will a pipe be found.

Displaced in this case means that justification for an ultimate *archē* is undermined. This finding, as might be expected, is thought to be personally and socially liberating. The Marxists associated with the Frankfurt School, for example, find the music of Sch¨oenberg to be revolutionary for this reason.[45] His atonal construction does not rely on a center, around which a musical score can be organized. The resulting music does not appear to have a single telos, but unfolds simultaneously in numerous directions. Walter Benjamin writes, accordingly, that history is portrayed to consist of simply debris piled skyward.[46] Deprived of a destiny, persons have no other option but to make their existence out of uncertainty.

As suggested by Paul Klee, postmodern artists devote their effort to reviving the "prehistory of the visible."[47] Merleau-Ponty calls this the "invisible."[48] Described another way, attention is paid to the human side of art, the element that turns interpretation into reality. For example, space is no longer envisaged to be obtrusive, but, in Mir´o's words, is illuminated by the "light of freedom." Rather than a spectacle, the human condition is an ongoing creation. A postmodern artist, accordingly, captures reality by penetrating the domain ignored by empiricists.

When this gambit is understood, a circuitous route to reality is all that is possible. Only in terms of the question of reality can the real be known. As in the Theater of the Absurd, what is most absurd about life is that there is no justification for accepting a particular interpretation of reality, other than personal gratification. Ionesco states: "Realism does not exist. Everything is invention. Even realism is invented. Reality is not realistic."[49] Yet postmodern artists recognize that the will to create is at the basis of existence, and should never be forgotten. With all due respect to Barthes, the birth of art requires the assassination of both the artist and the consumer, or any other abstraction that limits expression. If art is not to be redundant, as is suggested by Ionesco, reality must allow for creation—reality must be porous.

Postmodern art is not a matter of painting, writing, or composing, but of inventing realities. Harold Rosenberg, in his *The De-definition of Art*, quotes an artist as saying, in a postmodern fashion, "I choose not to make objects. Instead, I have set out to create a quality of experience that locates itself in the world."[50] The artist, in a manner of speaking, is no longer confined by art. The first stroke across a canvas, for example, does not represent the horizon or the backdrop for a city. This inaugural action defines a milieu, the framework wherein reality is to be constructed. Rather than being an onlooker, the artist is in the midst of the creative process. As the artist moves, so does reality. The human presence, rather than reality, is the focus of a work of art. Yet when conceived in this way, an art object is not at all an object. At this juncture Mir´o's suggestion is certainly germane: a product of artistic effort is the manifestation of freedom. Postmodern artists work without rules and objects, or, simply put, restrictions. The sublime and experience intermingle, thus producing the real. In this way, both consumers and artists create works of art.

CULTURAL SCIENCES

Until the late nineteenth century, a naturalistic model was used almost exclusively to describe social life.[51] Humans were thought to be a part of nature, and thus should be conceptualized in a manner similar to other natural phenomena. Natural laws were assumed to underpin society, while persons were believed to be equipped sufficiently to adjust to their environment. In short, persons and institutions, like the organs of the body, existed to insure the survival of the social whole. Implied by this scenario, however, was that the meaning of an individual's life is prescribed by society or, as believed by the Greeks, the cosmos. Indeed, persons were given the latitude to act merely within the strictures imposed by nature. Hence human action was thought to be just one of the many forces present in nature; humans had a well-defined place in the universe.

In line with the work of Max Scheler, and later Gabriel Marcel and Merleau-Ponty, anthropologists began in the early twentieth century to question the physicalistic imagery used to depict humans and their relationship to culture. Humans, simply put, were classified as "problematic." Von Üxküll and von Bertalanffy, for example, rejected the idea that persons are aligned in a causal manner with their environment.[52] Accordingly, the term "world-openness" was introduced to characterize the basic quality of human existence. This theme became increasingly important to writers such as Arnold Gehlen and Helmuth Plessner.[53] Plessner claimed that persons are "ek-static," while Gehlen's research convinced him that humans are unfinished products. In each case, the point was that human nature is invented, rather than something that is specified before birth. For example, Simone de Beauvoir suggests that women are made, not born.[54] The human essence, in other words, is thoroughly social. Theorists as diverse as Marxists and phenomenologists have adopted this view, in order to account for social change.

Writers in other disciplines such as psychology and economics also recognized the untenability of understanding behavior as regulated by an abstract social system. Subsequent to the development of gestalt psychology, only with great difficulty can persons be portrayed as motivated by stimuli or unconscious drives. These psychologists demonstrated that the meaning of a phenomenon is derived from cognitive activity. Additionally, Ludwig Binswanger, Viktor Frankl, Carl Rogers, and a host of so-called humanistic psychologists diminished the importance of reality, particularly with respect to conducting therapy.[55] They were more concerned with understanding the social significance of behavior, than with determining whether or not a client is "normal." Rather than normalcy, these humanists were interested in how health and illness are interpreted.

This shift was prompted by their discovery that reality is elusive, because conceptual categories are the source of its meaning. Reality, therefore, has no relevance outside of the interpretive milieu where a person resides. Binswanger, for instance, referred to reality as a mode of a person's "being-in-the-world."[56] Accordingly, he favored *Daseinsanalyse*, because the focus of therapy is the way a client relates to the world. Hence simply classifying behavior is not believed to be an especially productive method to facilitate treatment, for insanity has no inherent traits. Insanity does not violate reason.

This notion that reality is localized altered the character of economics. According to some economists, the rationale for macroeconomics has been destroyed. All that is possible is an economics that begins with the categories persons use to organize everyday life, rather than abstract schemes that depict the behavior of buyers and sellers. Popularized initially by the members of the Austrian School, this opinion is currently extolled by critics of Keynes, such as monetarists and rational expectationists.[57] They charge that any attempt to manipulate "aggregate demand" is fruitless, because this sort of abstraction does not represent actual economic exchange. Trading, instead, proceeds according to how persons interpret market signals, rather than grand laws about economic life. Since no one has complete or absolute knowledge, the Austrians contended, the framework for trading can only be negotiated at the marketplace. Market order, states Hayek, is "spontaneous." Therefore, the belief is that less government intervention into the economy will allow trading signals to be correctly deciphered. These conservative economists, in short, question the wisdom of a policy that presupposes the existence of an exchange system unfettered by values, commitments, and judgments. While the Austrian School's political views may be naive, their rejection of abstract economic systems is consistent with postmodernism.

Perhaps the most dramatic move toward an anti-dualistic conception of culture has been made by a group of theologians. In the wake of the Death of God movement, religion has been radicalized in many respects.[58] Borrowing from Nietzsche, some theologians contend that the traditional or medieval rendition of God is not viable, because anything that is separated categorically from experience is ineffable. Postmodern theologians do not attempt to acquire eternal knowledge, but understand that God is revealed in experience.[59] All questions about God must be raised with reference to solving human problems. Social justice is believed to be essential for redemption. "Human involvement," contends Wolfhart Pannenberg, is essential for the development of a religious ethics. In a postmodern sense, he believes that ethical action does not spring from eternal formulae. "*Respons-abilité*" must be central to ethics, charges Derrida. Accordingly,

Buber, Tillich, and, most notably, Dietrich Bonhoeffer maintain that without social justice God is not worthwhile.[60] In this sense, escape from the world is not essential to discover God, but rather, according to Jürgen Moltmann, the desire to interject hope into history.[61]

Deprived of God as an absolute point of reference, salvation must come through a transformation of society that enhances the human condition. This is what Nietzsche had in mind when he stated that the question of ethics goes "beyond good and evil." Instead of arcane principles, ethical action is based on responsbile behavior toward others. Postmodern religion represents a call for justice in the midst of barbarism. Ethical issues can be addressed only between humans, and not in abstract terms. Religion binds persons together, instead of manacling them to rarefied notions.

In sum, in a postmodern culture the idea is abandoned that society constitutes a totality or complete system. Due to the absence of absolute knowledge, both a person's existence and social order are plagued with uncertainty. Out of this mélange of competing claims, moreover, society must emerge. And as postmodern theologians argue, preventing culture from devolving into a series of misinterpretations has religious significance. Society is not something natural, comprised of various laws. Persons do not simply respond to stimuli, while the economy does not respond automatically to particular events. Key to a postmodern society is that persons do not react to occurrences. In fact, as Lacan states, every response is shaped by a question. What he means is that no social phenomena, including human nature or God, have inherent meaning. According to postmodernists, every aspect of society is imaginary, or connected inextricably to a plan of human action. These plans, moreover, are society. And merging these plans is essential to preserving culture.

POSTMODERNISM: THEORETICAL JUSTIFICATION

The foregoing historical exposition was not exhaustive, but was planned to illustrate how the traditional dualistic worldview has begun to collapse in various fields of study. In fact, as already noted, postmodernism is identified with this rupture with dualism. As early as the late nineteenth century, researchers began to realize that persons do not simply possess an environment, and thus do not confront the world. A clear distinction cannot be made between human action, knowledge, and order, for these factors are fundamentally interrelated. Lyotard, for example, refuses to accept the long-standing belief that imagination merely supplements reality.[62] Roland Barthes and de Man are similarly anti-dualistic when they suggest that reading is never innocent. What they mean is that perceptual acts defile or shape whatever is seen. "There is always and only bias, inclination, prejudgment, swerve," writes Harold Bloom.[63] As an adventure in interpretation, acquiring knowledge is often referred to by postmodernists as an erotic activity. According to André Green, truth can be attained only in terms of its deformations. Clearly, therefore, the "metanarratives" used regularly to protect truth have no justification. For knowledge that is interpreted can never be accorded the status associated with this method for securing truth and order.

Lyotard attempts to summarize the various trends away from dualism by stating that knowledge is a product of "language games."[64] In other words, the rationale behind the failure of dualism is that the influence of language cannot be overcome, no matter what type of strategy might be concocted for this purpose. Neither Newton nor the impressionists, for example, could escape from the foibles of language. While relying on Wittgenstein, Lyotard's point is that reality is conceptualized through language use. Julia Kristeva's notion of *"intertextualité"* is relevant at this juncture.[65] Her point is that language can only be shuffled from one text to another, with no escape from this cycle of textuality. Once an interpretation is reached, this process begins anew. In fact, intertextuality reminds one of the myth of Sisyphus. Reality, accordingly, originates from linguistically instituted assumptions about truth and error. Escape from these assumptions is impossible. The rules that constitute language are neither naturally disposed nor divinely inspired, but are legitimized through speech acts.

Rather than technical, postmodernists argue, the thrust of language is "pragmatic."[66] As Barthes says, the alphabet is not impersonal, because language use is an event that penetrates to the core of reality. No matter what attempts were made in the past to separate language from the world, these ploys could never succeed, according to postmodernists. Simply put, the influence of language can never be avoided. The reason for this is quite simple: symbols do not point to, indicate, or stand for facts, as if the world is autonomous.[67] Speech is not a surrogate for a more profound reality, but, as noted by Derrida, "is *the* representation of itself."[68]

What Derrida and other postmodernists mean is that truth can be approached only indirectly, or in terms of changes in patterns of speech. Hence, Derrida writes, "there are only contexts without any center or absolute anchoring [*ancrage*]."[69] While expanding on Barthes' comparison, there is nothing other than the "this-side" of language. The so-called "other" or objective side of speech is simply an extension of linguistic acts—reality is the result of speech building on speech. A primordial *archē* is thus out of reach. Actually, reality proliferates when it comes into contact with language, because speech acts are dense and always subject to further interpretation. Due to the excess of the signifier, Merleau-Ponty laments that people always say both more and less than they intend. Even the axioms of logic cannot deny their linguistic heritage, and thus are never finally stable.

Human beings do not simply speak, but live within language. Heidegger has this idea in mind when he remarks that language speaks, rather than persons. Or, as described by Derrida, speech annihilates the distance that is thought typically to be inserted between persons and the world.[70] Their point is that no one can be catapulted outside of language, in order to revel in knowledge uncontaminated by interpretation. Very poignant at this juncture is Jackson Pollock's statement, "I am nature." He is not advocating hylozoism, but merely admitting that imagination is not a substitute for reality. According to postmodernists, there is nothing outside of language. This realization has prompted Barthes' charge that objectivity is nothing but another level of signification.[71] As a result of unifying truth and pathos, postmodernists have introduced a new model of social science. With realism shattered, obtrusive forms cannot be sought to describe knowledge and order. A non-referential science must be developed, one that does not search outside of human action to substantiate its claims.[72]

Subsequent to postmodernism, the simple representation of reality is impossible. Neither knowledge nor order is denotative. The reason for this is that language blocks access to indubitable standards. Existence is a game played with language, from which no one escapes. Therefore, Barthes writes, a linguistic message is present in every image.[73] Even the ancient *archai* were linguistically inspired. Social analysis, consequently, must be undertaken from within language. The praxis that empiricists and other realists render impotent must be resurrected as the focus of research. For, as postmodernists remind social analysts, nothing objective is ever expressed; "evident truths are . . . only choices," writes Barthes.[74] Again consistent with what Nietzsche has to say, postmodernists contend that only research ers who get their hands dirty in the world will be successful.

NOTES

1. Bernhard Waldenfels, "The Despised Doxa: Husserl and the Continuing Crisis of Western Reason," in *Husserl and Contemporary Thought*, ed. John Sallis (Atlantic Highlands, N.J.: Humanities Press, 1983), pp. 21–38.

2. Lyotard, *The Postmodern Condition*, p. xxiv. For a brief history of the term postmodern, please consult Richard Kearney, "The Crisis of the Post-modern Image," in *Contemporary French Philosophers,* ed. A. Phillips Griffiths (Cambridge: Cambridge University Press, 1987), pp. 113–122.

3. Jean Wahl, *Philosophies of Existence* (New York: Schocken, 1969).

4. Jean Gebser, *The Ever-Present Origin* (Athens: Ohio University Press, 1985), p. 481.

5. Ibid., p. 481.

6. Deleuze, *Proust and Signs*, p. 143.

7. Maurice Merleau-Ponty, *The Visible and the Invisible* (Evanstons, Ill.: Northwestern University Press, 1968), p. 147.

8. Alfred Schutz and Thomas Luckmann, *The Structures of the Life-World* (Evanston, Ill.: Northwestern University Press, 1973), pp. 3–8.

9. Gebser, *Ever-Present Origin*, p. 289.

10. Paul Tillich, *The Religious Situation* (New York: Henry Holt, 1932), pp. 136–143.

11. Jean-Paul Sartre, "Consciousness and Imagination," in *European Literary Theory and Practice*, ed. Vernon W. Gras (New York: Delta, 1973), pp. 61–68.

12. Gerald Graff, *Literature Against Itself* (Chicago: University of Chicago Press, 1979), p. 193.

13. Schutz and Luckmann, *Structures of the Life-World*, p. 9.

14. Edmund Husserl, *The Paris Lectures* (The Hague: Nijhoff, 1975), p. 13.

15. Schutz and Luckmann, *Structures of the Life-World*, p. 5.

16. Edmund Husserl, *The Crisis of European Sciences and Transcendental Phenomenology* (Evanston, Ill.: Northwestern University Press, 1970), p. 113.

17. Martin Heidegger, "The Turning," in *The Question Concerning Technology and Other Essays* (New York: Harper and Row, 1977), pp. 36–49.

18. Martin Heidegger, *Being and Time* (New York: Harper and Row, 1962), pp. 37–38.

19. Otto Pöggeler, "Being as Appropriation," in *Heidegger and Modern Philosophy*, ed. Michael Murray (New Haven: Yale University Press, 1978), pp. 84–115.

20. Merleau-Ponty, *The Visible and the Invisible*, p. 197.

21. Martin Heidegger, ". . . Poetically Man Dwells. . . ," in *Poetry, Language, and Thought* (New York: Harper and Row, 1971), pp. 213–229.

22. Jacques Derrida, *Of Grammatology* (Baltimore: Johns Hopkins University Press, 1976), p. 158.

23. Jacques Lacan, *Ecrits* (New York: Norton, 1977), p. 306.

24. De Man, *Allegories of Reading*, p. 18.

25. Stephen Toulmin, *The Return to Cosmology: Postmodern Science and the Theology of Nature* (Berkeley: University of California Press, 1982).

26. Werner Heisenberg, *Across the Frontiers* (New York: Harper and Row, 1974), pp. 104–121, 154–165.

27. Werner Heisenberg, *Physics and Philosophy* (New York: Harper and Row, 1962), pp. 110–127; see also Alfred North Whitehead, *Science and the Modern World* (New York: Macmillan, 1967), pp. 113–127.

28. Jonathan Powers, *Philosophy and the New Physics* (New York: Methuen, 1982), pp. 124–135.

29. Heisenberg, *Across the Frontiers*, pp. 8–29.

30. Lyotard, *The Postmodern Condition*, pp. 58–59; see also René Thom, *Structural Stability and Morphogenesis: An Outline of a General Theory of Models* (Reading, Mass.: Benjamin, 1975).

31. Murad D. Akhundov, *Conceptions of Space and Time* (Cambridge, Mass.: MIT Press, 1986), p. 98.

32. Heisenberg, *Physics and Philosophy*, p. 79.

33. Karl Popper, *The Open Universe* (Totowa, N.J.: Rowman and Littlefield, 1982).

34. Aldous Huxley, *Literature and Science* (New York: Harper and Row, 1963), p. 76.

35. Arnold Hauser, *The Social History of Art*, vol. 4 (New York: Vintage Books, 1951), p. 171.

36. Kristeva, *Revolution in Poetic Language*, p. 211.

37. Deleuze, *Proust and Signs*, p. 136.

38. John Cage, "Diary: How to Improve the World (You Will Only Make It Worse) Continued," *TriQuarterly* 18 (Spring 1970), pp. 94–111.

39. Dora Vallier, *Abstract Art* (New York: Orion Press, 1970), pp. 1–42; see also Ellen H. Johnson, *Modern Art and the Object* (New York: Harper and Row, 1976), pp. 65–71.

40. Maurice Merleau-Ponty, "Eye and Mind," in *The Primacy of Perception* (Evanston, Ill.: Northwestern University Press, 1964), pp. 159–190.

41. Dore Ashton, *A Reading of Modern Art* (Cleveland, Ohio: Case Western Reserve University Press, 1969), p. 16.

42. Kristeva, *Revolution in Poetic Language*, p. 79.

43. André Breton, *Manifestos of Surrealism* (Ann Arbor: University of Michigan Press, 1969).

44. Michel Foucault, *This is not a Pipe* (Berkeley: University of California Press, 1982).

45. David Held, *Introduction to Critical Theory* (Berkeley: University of California Press, 1980), pp. 88–89.

46. Walter Benjamin, "Theses on the Philosophy of History," in *Illuminations* (New York: Schocken, 1969), pp. 253–264.

47. Ashton, *A Reading of Modern Art*, p. 51.

48. Merleau-Ponty, *The Visible and the Invisible*, pp. 246–248.

49. Eugène Ionesco, "Eugene Ionesco in Defense of the Absurd," *New York Times*, 15 June 1988.

50. Harold Rosenberg, *The De-Definition of Art* (Chicago: University of Chicago Press, 1972), p. 11.

51. Gebser, *The Ever-Present Origin*, pp. 73–97.

52. Ludwig von Bertalanffy, *Perspectives on General Systems Theory* (New York: George Braziller, 1975), pp. 74–102.

53. Arnold Gehlen, *Man in the Age of Technology* (New York: Columbia University Press, 1980), pp. 1–23; Helmuth Plessner, *Laughing and Crying: A Study of the Limits of Human Behavior* (Evanston, Ill.: Northwestern University Press, 1970), pp. 32–40.

54. Simone de Beauvoir, *The Second Sex* (New York: Bantam, 1970), p. 806.

55. I. David Welch, George A. Tate, and Fred Richards, *Humanistic Psychology: A Source Book* (Buffalo, N.Y.: Prometheus Books, 1978).

56. Ludwig Binswanger, *Being-in-the-World* (New York: Basic Books, 1963).

57. John W. Murphy, "Conservative Economics and the Issue of Social Order at the Marketplace," in *Current Perspectives in Social Theory*, vol. 7, ed. John Wilson and Scott G. McNall (Greenwich, Conn.: JAI Press, 1986), pp. 69–86.

58. Harvey Cox, *Religion in the Secular City* (New York: Simon and Schuster, 1983).

59. John W. Murphy, "Cultural Manifestations of Postmodernism," *Philosophy Today* 30.4 (1986), pp. 346–353; see also Rudolf J. Siebert, *The Critical Theory of Religion* (Berlin: de Gruyter, 1985).

60. John A.T. Robinson, *Honest to God* (Philadelphia: Westminster Press, 1963).

61. Jürgen Moltmann, *The Crucified God* (New York: Harper and Row, 1974), pp. 317–340.

62. Lyotard, *The Postmodern Condition*, p. 52.

63. Harold Bloom, "Breaking the Form," in Harold Bloom et al., *Deconstruction and Criticism* (New York: Seabury Press, 1979), pp. 1–37.

64. Lyotard, *The Postmodern Condition*, p. 10.

65. Julia Kristeva, *Desire in Language* ((New York: Columbia University Press, 1980), pp. 36–38.

66. Lyotard, *The Postmodern Condition*, pp. 9–10.

67. W.J.T. Mitchell, *Iconology* (Chicago: University of Chicago Press, 1986), pp. 5–46.

68. Jacques Derrida, *Speech and Phenomena* (Evanston, Ill.: Northwestern University Press, 1973), p. 57.

69. Jacques Derrida, "Signiture Event Context," *GLYPH* 1 (1977), pp. 172–197.

70. Jacques Derrida, *Writing and Difference* (Chicago: University of Chicago Press, 1979), p. 69.

71. Roland Barthes, *The Rustle of Language* (New York: Hill and Wang, 1986), p. 160.

72. De Man, *The Resistance to Theory*, p. 39.

73. Roland Barthes, *Image-Music-Text* (New York: Hill and Wang, 1977), p. 38.

74. Roland Barthes, *Criticism and Truth* (Minneapolis: University of Minnesota Press, 1987), p. 39.

3

Postmodern Social Science

POSITIVISM

Positivists want to avoid making metaphysical claims when trying to explain behavior.[1] This desire is illustrated clearly in Auguste Comte's Law of Three Stages. In true Enlightenment fashion, only knowledge that is verifiable can be introduced as evidence. Speculation about gods or any other absolute factor that may influence the course of events is to be eschewed. Direct experience, accordingly, should be of paramount importance to anyone who is interested in acquiring valid knowledge. As argued by Bacon, those who are able to purge themselves of their "idols" have a chance of finding truth.

Although positivists claim that experience is the root of knowledge, they retain dualism. The focus of research is nature, rather than the human psyche, cognition, or any other source of interpretation.[2] The basis of information is assumed to be invariable, or, as they are sometimes called, natural laws. Facts are distinguished from values, and thus knowledge is imagined to be synonymous with physical events. Facts, as Durkheim writes, are "outside [of] the mind."[3] Factual knowledge, in other words, has an "independent existence outside of the individual consciousness."[4]

Knowledge is available to those who are able to perceive nature accurately. Because knowledge is believed to be related to physical properties, sense impressions are identified as the cause of perception. For this reason, positivists are frequently cited as advocating a "copy theory" of knowledge.[5] If the world is to be correctly apprehended, the mind must mimic nature. To use Locke's imagery, the mind must become a "blank slate" on which information can be easily imprinted. With the mind given a passive role in their epistemology, positivists conclude that knowledge is both objective and obtainable without contamination. "Far from being a product of the will, they [facts] determine it from without."[6] Facts are autonomous.

The problem, however, is that the human element must be extricated as much as possible from the research process. Even though the mind can only reflect nature, perceptual errors are always possible. While relying on observation as a key methodological principle, positivists contend that after rigorous training, perception can be entrusted to discover truth.[7] In other words, because everyday or naive perception may be unreliable, persons must be taught a particular way of analyzing events. Trained perception must be engendered. A type of surrogate vision must be systematically cultivated, for otherwise data may be adulterated by values and other non-empirical considerations. Researchers must be shown how to counter the effects of situational exigencies, in order to enhance their prospects for uncovering universal knowledge. The end product of this conditioning might be called a methodologically induced state of immorality.

In order to avoid being guided by unsubstantiated ideas, research must begin with an empirical referent. This point of departure, moreover, must represent the so-called real world, as opposed to a particular standpoint.[8] To begin a study in this auspicious manner, interpretive judgments must be excluded from a research project. Due to this requirement, data collection becomes overly instrumental. In short, logistical refinements are thought to lead naturally to the generation of valid data. Various techniques are mastered to foster standardization, which, in turn, serve to insure that a study is not replete with bias. The key assumption at this juncture is that the manipulation of techniques does not involve interpretation. Therefore, the more technological research becomes, the less likely it is that human error will influence a project's findings.

Positivism implies that methodological techniques are value-free. These "prosthetic aids," as postmodernists refer to them, enable researchers to have access to a reality that would otherwise be out of reach.[9] By following certain techniques, interpretation can be overcome and facts revealed. The illusion of objectivity is perpetuated by transforming judgments into methodological rubrics. Strict observation is reinforced, because research proceeds in terms of explicit, step-by-step guidelines. As a result of constricting the value base of research, the laws that underpin nature cannot be obscured by opinion. Minimizing the influence of interpretation, moreover, encourages the formulation of axioms unencumbered by contingencies. The generation of law-like regularities is thus expedited.[10]

Because of their unabashed belief in the efficacy of positive science, early writers such as Comte and Durkheim were able to claim that the impersonal truth vital to the survival of society can be discovered.[11] Accordingly,

Talcott Parsons, particularly during his cybernetic phase, argued that sociologists had the means necessary to explore the "ultimate reality" required to arrest the onset of anarchy.[12] Writers such as George Lundberg and George Homans believed that significant advances could finally be made by sociologists, once rigorous experimental studies were underway.[13] The optimism of these and other positivists reflect the dualism at the heart of positivism, which suggests that technical operations have nothing to do with cognition. No wonder technical devices are so highly touted as research instruments: the only obstacle preventing the unqualified generalization of research findings is the inability of a researcher to master a few technical procedures. More encompassing questions related to the social relevance of data, for instance, are dismissed as disruptive.

Nowadays this desire for an instrumental sociology is manifested in the attempt to formalize completely theory construction and research. Similar to the members of the Vienna Circle, writers such as Hans Zetterberg, and in some ways James Coleman and Hubert Blalock, have tried to transform reason into a system of abstract symbols.[14] Consistent with the Vienna philosophers, these and other like-minded sociologists assume that substituting mathematical signs for language will increase the validity of all propositions. Here again, the idea is that if perception, or in this case language use, can be significantly constrained, factual evidence can be readily procured.

Yet the success of this gambit depends on whether experience can be defined in terms of science, without any serious repercussions. Can humans be studied effectively if their behavior is reduced to its smallest, measurable components? Stated differently, without appreciating the way persons conceptualize reality, can their actions be understood? Postmodernists contend that the denial of the human element is not only unjustified, but that ignoring interpretation jeopardizes the discovery of facts. In *Proust and Signs*, Deleuze writes: "We are wrong to believe in facts; there are only signs. We are wrong to believe in truth; there are only interpretations."[15]

Moreover, is the framework adopted by positive science appropriate for delineating the range of experience that is available as evidence? If not, the social importance of information can be easily overlooked. In fact, the claim that certain forms of knowledge are automatically relevant may become ideological, particularly when others are rejected without question. Similar to their general critique of Western philosophy, postmodernists argue that the dualistic foundation of positivism should not be given credence. Accordingly, they raise the question of whether or not positivism can generate socially significant knowledge.

The self-denial that is central to Western philosophy is epitomized in positivism. That is, according to positivists, valid knowledge can be gained only at the expense of human action. Positivism imposes a set of methodological guidelines—not very different from those that sustained the asceticism practiced by medieval philosophers—that suppress the influence of opinion. Substituting technical procedures for cognitive operations is supposed to facilitate the collection of high quality data, because mental activity is made to conform to the strictures prescribed by research methodology. Merely by complying, in a step-by-step manner, with methodological rubrics, a pathway is supposed to be cleared to truth. Accordingly, the success of positivism depends solely upon whether or not researchers become technically proficient.

As already suggested, however, postmodernists disagree with positivism. Specifically, they contend that facts are not obtrusive, or "things," as Durkheim says, and that more than technical competence is required if accurate insight about social life is to be obtained. Due to the importance they attribute to language use, postmodernists insist that there is no substitute for communicative competence when conducting social research. In other words, the linguistic relevance of behavior must not be concealed by technical requirements. Any methodology that ignores the polyvalence of words should be avoided.

THE POSTMODERN REBELLION

For postmodernists, language is not simply a tool; it provides the only access persons have to the world. Instead of embellishing reality, language pervades everything that is known. To a significant extent, reality is a linguistic habit. Consistent with the Greek verb *sumballein,* symbols or language, is understood to "throw together" the meaning of an event.[16] According to Derrida writing is an "originary act," a gesture that establishes the dimensions of sensibility.[17] It is the "play of speech," rather than necessity (*ananke̅*), that legitimizes reality.

According to Barthes, language that is objectified and treated as a neatly structured classification system has only limited "exchange value."[18] But because speech mediates everything that is known, language is a domain that extends indefinitely. Barthes' point, therefore, is that language does not refer to anything; the implied dichotomy between speech and reality is undermined. "Everything is a message," declares Sartre.[19] The value of language is thus derived from the way persons speak to one another. Postmodern researchers are mostly interested in how language spans the gulf between birth and death, usually referred to as a person's existence. This symbolic plane is where reality arises and declines, and where postmodern research is conducted. Postmodernists operate within the language game of a society. For it must be remembered, in the postmodern world nothing exceeds language. And "the absence of the transcendental signified," writes Derrida, "extends the domain and the interplay of signification *ad infinitum*."[20]

A. Truth

Clearly, this rendition of language requires that the typical definition of truth be rethought. The correspondence theory of truth that has been prominent since the time of Aristotle is not viewed by postmodernists to be credible. Proponents of this view, however, contend that a truthful statement reflects adequately objective conditions. In this sense, the index of truth is an external referent over which persons do not exert any substantial influence. Accuracy, accordingly, becomes the measure of truth, for reality must be reflected precisely in the mind. Any means that improves precision is also thought to increase the likelihood that truth will be discovered. The query "Is it true?" is thus rhetorical, because the fundamental nature of truth is not questioned. All that is asked is whether a claim is properly attuned to reality. When truth is conceived in this manner, however, Lyotard suggests that knowledge loses its "use value."[21]

Although they adopt Marxist terminology, the point made by both Barthes and Lyotard is clear: divorced from the purpose it has in daily life, truth has no meaning. In fact, subsequent to adopting their view on language, postmodernists undermine the discovery of pristine knowledge. For "truth doesn't speak, *stricto sensu*; it works," writes Lyotard.[22] His point is that truth must struggle to emerge from interpretation. With knowledge and interpretation intertwined, truth has a precarious existence. Considering this relationship between language and knowledge, Heidegger refers to truth as *aletheia*, or "unconcealment."[23] Truth is not obtrusive, but resides within a clearing provided momentarily by language. Because language is volatile and always shifting with respect to its meaning, the "rustle" of speech must be quelled long enough for a particular interpretive modality of truth to be known.[24] For this reason, Derrida describes truth as a "trace," a "non-origin."[25]

Truth, stated differently, is originative, but not an origin. J. Hillis Miller, for example, uses the phrase *mise en abîme* to characterize this elusive notion of truth.[26] To paraphrase Miller, although meaning springs from truth, this exalted knowledge is deprived of the status for it to be an *archē*, or foundation. Symbols do not simply exist, but are "always becoming."[27] Derrida intends by this oblique reference to Nietzsche to convey the idea that knowledge is never settled, due to the presence of human action, or praxis. In practical terms, therefore, checking how closely a story corresponds to reality is insufficient to ascertain whether or not a statement is true. Instead, the particular language game that is operative must be consulted, so that the linguistic meaning of reality is grasped. A statement is true when it illuminates the rules of speech that sustain a particular linguistic community. The implication, of course, is that truth is local and not universal. As Lyotard remarks, "knowledge has no final legitimacy outside of serving the goals envisioned by the practical subject, the autonomous collectivity."[28] Truth is thus meaningful, yet something appreciably different from dogma.

This version of truth is different from that advanced, for example, by Stanley Fish and Karl Popper. These very different writers contend that informed members of a community can distinguish between correct and incorrect language use. Fish is concerned with literary critics and Popper with scientists. In each case, however, the rules adopted by these respective communities are assumed to exist a priori. While the language used by the literati and by scientists is certainly different from that present in everyday discourse, anyone who is educated in a manner similar to these experts is expected to have been introduced to a particular set of axioms related to logic and speech. The rules of language, therefore, are localized but not invented. Postmodernists advance the views of these authors a step further by stating that language games are locally constructed, rather than merely discovered. Communicative competence is not presupposed by language use, as assumed by Fish and Popper, but emerges through discourse.

B. Facts

Because postmodernists have up to now devoted a great deal of their time to literary criticism, this area of study will be used as a starting point to explore the nature of facts. Based on the postmodern rendition of truth, the views championed by Comte, Durkheim, and other positivists are outdated. Simply put, facts are not "things" that exist external to the individual.[29] Likewise, using structural metaphors to describe the operation of society is not legitimate. The use of structural props promotes the erroneous belief that social phenomena are autonomous, or unrelated to shifts in conscious experience. In general, a mechanistic image of social life is an anachronism, because facts cannot be separated neatly from judgments. Consequently, behavioral laws cannot be articulated in simple form $A \rightarrow B$.

Barthes warns that literature exists within language.[30] With this statement he is attempting to refute those who contend that texts are objects, structured in accordance with rational principles any trained person can eventually recognize. Texts, in other words, cannot be separated from how they are read or written. Contrary to Northrop Frye and supporters of the New Criticism, literature is significantly more than a "piled aggregate of works."[31] Although this point may sound quite banal, at issue is whether language merely conveys reality, or organizes it. In this respect, Félix Guattari notes that readers do not simply decipher but "over-encode" a text.[32]

A similar point is made by Barthes when he claims that language is infected by Eros, and compares writing to having an ejaculation.[33] What they are saying is that reading is always re-reading, thereby precluding ever reaching a starting point that antedates the intervention of interpretation. According to postmodernists, a text embodies a social space that is shaped by imagination. Therefore, the meaning of a text is revealed in the exchange that occurs between a reader and author.[34] Postmodernists agree with Blanchot that the subject (author) and the researcher (reader) may disregard each other, yet this insensitivity must be overcome or the social world (text) will be misunderstood.[35]

As postmodernists like to state, symbols float in a sea of signification. This is what Jorge Borges means when he states that authentic creations occur "in flight." In other words, no anchor is available to a sign other than that provided by language. Only after a reader has entered the world created by an author can a text be assumed to be understood. Accordingly, writes William Gass, "the novelist, if he is any good, will keep us kindly imprisoned in his language—there is literally nothing beyond."[36] Language is stabilized by nothing other than something as fleeting as another interpretation. Of utmost importance is that facts are not simply empirical. Similar to a text, the world is not a wasteland of objective indicators, which can best be described as lifeless. Barthes, in this regard, criticizes empiricists for "embalming" life, due to their penchant for reducing social existence to a few, easily measurable indices.[37] Following the suggestion of phenomenologists, society should be conceptualized as a living world, a *Lebenswelt*.

At this juncture the distinction made by Husserl between facts and meaning is instructive.[38] Meaning is certainly factual, yet facts do not necessarily have meaning. That is, events are factual because they have linguistically inscribed significance, whereas facts that are purely empirical may have no social relevance. The thrust of Husserl's argument is that facts are simply empirical, while meaning relates to the linguistic or interpretive importance of phenomena. Postmodernists contend that truth lurks within meaning and has little to do with facts. Researchers who are concerned with revealing truth, moreover, ought to pay attention to the social meaning of events, rather than categorizing facts. The voice with which facts speak should be the focus of interest. In fact, due to the ubiquitousness of language, values are understood by Barthes to antedate the discovery of facts.[39]

Is technical competence, therefore, sufficient to guarantee the successful procurement of knowledge? Obviously, postmodernists say no. In order to overcome the limitations imposed by subjectivity, however, positivists regard technical rigor as a defense against the introduction of bias into research. If judgments can be adequately sublimated into technical decisions, then the likelihood of human error is presumed to be reduced. For, as noted earlier, techniques do not think. Instead, technical methods operate like a fishing net, immobilizing whatever is caught. Positivism assumes that methodological procedures are value-free. Clearly, this reliance on technical precision is a ploy by positivists to convince readers that objective facts, untainted by language, can be generated by technically proficient researchers. Yet can socially relevant knowledge be obtained through detached contemplation?

Counterproductive to the discovery of truth, according to postmodernists, is the concealment of values.[40] Rather than obscuring values with a technological facade, postmodernists contend, researchers should attempt to comprehend the living milieu of persons who are studied. The existential interests that motivate actions hold the key to truth. For, it must be recalled, the assumptions conveyed through language subtend reality. While referring to Foucault, Derrida contends the *episteme* that brings reality into existence must be consulted.[41] Overlooking this framework can only result in a sterile portrayal of society. Actually, researchers who emphasize procedural refinement in the name of science may systematically distort data, and thus do a lot of damage through the creation of socially insensitive policies based on faulty information. Stated succinctly, because the assumptions that accompany the use of a particular technique are introduced in the guise of science, they may go unchallenged and begin to alter subtly the identity of data. Positive scientists pursue facts, rather than meanings.

The distinction Barthes makes between deciphering and disentangling texts is relevant at this juncture. Positivists decipher material, for they attempt to reduce an event to its material essence. All secondary traits, in other words, are explained by fundamental causes or other empirical factors. Postmodernists, contrary to this modus operandi, unravel a text with respect to the linguistic framework presupposed by an author. Passages, for example, are understood to be related because they have a similar destiny within the operative linguistic world. Spatial proximity, accordingly, is unrelated to causality. In terms of the social world, events should be classified similarly only when they have an identical linguistic identity. While referring to Kafka, Barthes, in a poignant manner, states: "[do] not make me believe what you are saying, but even more important, make me believe in your decision to say it."[42] Hence a postmodernist searches for existential rather than empirical justification for behavior.

POSTMODERN METHODOLOGY

The methodology advocated by postmodernists is known as "schizo-analysis."[43] Using this esoteric terminology has not helped to clarify their position. To critics of postmodernism, this is evidence that a postmodern science is impossible. Nonetheless, the thrust of this methodology is actually quite straightforward. Allegedly like a schizophrenic, postmodern researchers fail to recognize reality. Normally, such a faux pas may lead to a person being labelled as mentally ill. To a postmodern scientist, however, this lack of conceptual acuity can enhance the research process. According to Guattari, the reason why data collection is improved relates to the principle of "semiotic polycentrism" that postmodernism fosters.[44] Postmodern researchers are not limited by what they believe is rational. Reason does not make them blind to experience.

By using the phrase "semiotic polycentrism," postmodernists are claiming that phenomena may possess a variety of meanings simultaneously. The idea that there must be a "final reading" of a text is rejected as uninformed. Postmodernism also undermines the belief that a society's "dominant significations" are synonymous with reality and lead to truth.[45] Reality is thus recognized to be multivalent. As opposed to the position maintained by structuralists, facts do not constitute bricolage—something that is fully constituted and borrowed from one's predecessors or contemporaries. Liberated from the shackles imposed by logic and reason accepted a priori, reality can be experienced by postmodern researchers, instead of merely analyzed according to criteria that are clear but irrelevant.

A schizo-analyst, therefore, does not seek "to make subjectification fit in with the dominant significations and social laws."[46] The duty of a researcher, according to Derrida, is to subdue the "aggression of reason" indigenous to technological rationality, so that the fragile linguistic basis of facts is not destroyed.[47] In other words, even if an interpretation of reality appears to be irrational, the reason that is present must be given serious attention. As Barthes recommends, the "hysteria" of language should be given credence, for reality is not destroyed but inflated by speech.[48] Postmodern researchers recognize that statements which are "really real" must be distinguished from those which are "just stories," without ever having a complete picture of reality. In this sense, Deleuze writes, "the odor of a flower, when it constitutes a sign, transcends the laws of matter and the categories of the [abstract] mind."[49] The flower, in short, is an interpretive phenomenon. Accordingly, postmodernists are interested in the significance of an event. Kristeva describes significance as follows: "What we call significance . . . is precisely this unlimited and unbounded generating process, this unceasing operation of the drives toward, in, and through language; toward, in, and through the exchange system and its protagonists—the subject and his institutions."[50] Significance is the product of creativity.

Suggested by its Greek root *methodos*, methodology is a "way" to acquire knowledge. Hence methodological rigor should not be treated as an end in itself; standardization should not be extolled as an adequate maxim to guide research. Simply because a data collection strategy is precise and internally consistent, this is no guarantee that the meaning of a phenomenon will be apprehended. In order for meaning to be obtained, the researcher's sensitivity should be paramount. Sensitivity, in this case, does not refer to empathy, but "epistemological participation."[51] In practice, empathy is unimportant compared to understanding a person's actions. Whether or not one likes the subjects has little relevance to gathering informative data about their behavior. Instead, good research results from researchers participating in the assumptions their subjects make about reality. The reasons why people see values and purposes rather than objects and causes should be the focus of attention.

This sort of sensitivity is not necessarily forthcoming from technical competence. The reason for this is that technology is not reflexive, or self-critical.[52] Hence the presuppositions that are built into a methodological technique go unscrutinized. In fact, positivists avoid anything that is not related to procedural issues. In this way, the reality of a subject is not questioned, and is made to conform to mandates that are methodologically imposed. Methodological purity is thus guaranteed. Nonetheless, without raising the question of reality, a subject's "life-world" may never be understood. On the other hand, postmodernists require that researchers be self-critical, and that they work at what Lyotard calls the "horizon" of their methodological, or linguistic, assumptions.[53] As a result, researchers can begin to recognize the limitations of their language game, thereby enabling them to enter the worldview of those who are studied. According to postmodernists, gaining access to someone's linguistic world can occur only through communicative competence. Researchers are communicatively competent when they comprehend the "linguistic pragmatics" of their subjects.

Communicative competence is not forthcoming from the state of "double contingency," for example, described by Parsons.[54] Because all roles are constructed according to a single style of reason, persons are thought to communicate with one another simply by fulfilling their role requirements. Also, "taking the role of the other," as outlined by G. H. Mead, does not necessarily culminate in competent interaction, for the "other" may be treated as a projection of the self, or, equally insidious, as an abstract alter.[55] In each case, Lyotard notes correctly that the other is not approached as someone who is unique, a "norm-giving subject."[56] Rather than a "Thou," the other is transformed into an "It," to use the terms made famous by Martin Buber. Postmodernists such as de Man contend that only through "double rapport" is communicative competence achieved.[57] While summarizing the thrust of communicative competence, Barthes declares that "we should read as people write."[58]

This form of dialogue can be fully appreciated only if the postmodern view of the subject is explained. Michel Foucault, for example, caused quite an uproar among literary critics when he pronounced the author, or subject, to be an illusion.[59] In a slightly less provocative way, Barthes writes that the "I is nothing other than the instance of saying I."[60] Authors, that is, make themselves through their work. The subject is in doubt because postmodernists believe there is no transcendental ego that can be invoked to verify an author's intentions. According to Lacan, the so-called subject is also a product of language.[61] A person's identity does not subtend speech, but is established gradually as a result of performing a variety of actions. Rather than an extension of some deeper realm, such as the unconscious, motives are coterminous with linguistic acts. Gajo Petrović expresses this sentiment nicely when he writes: *"man is a being of praxis."*[62] The upshot of this view is that the self is "indefinite," or indeterminate, yet intelligible.

As described by Benjamin, a person's actions are purposeful, although they are not necessarily guided by a telos or purpose.[63] The artist is a *flâneur*, a solitary wanderer and not someone who loves a crowd. Kant's position on aesthetics is relevant at this point, specifically his idea that art has a purpose but is not sustained by utilitarian values. Persons, accordingly, are not prompted into action by social or psychological stimuli. In fact, human intentions supply stimuli with meaning. Action precedes stimulation; motivation exists prior to motives.

A researcher, therefore, must not search for a "self" to understand, a persona that is temporarily hidden from view. For a psychological, or sociological, foundation is unavailable to rationalize behavior. Norms are not denotative but linguistic, suggests de Man. Only from within the "sociolect" that constitutes both the self and the context of a person can in sight be gained into the motivation for an action.[64] In terms of double rapport, the identities of interlocutors are transparent, and thus dialogue does not proceed with respect to preconceived notions about normalcy. Instead, double rapport depends on the willingness of persons to entertain the idea that reality is linguistically manufactured, while recognizing that every language game has rules its players take seriously. Rather than evaluating a patient's illness according to the "sick role," for instance, a researcher must investigate the interpretive significance of illness. In point of fact, recent research suggests that clinical "risk" has little to do with biological, environmental, or other so-called natural factors.[65] How a community interprets and responds to a behavior is instrumental in determining the clinical career of a person. Motivation, simply put, is socially constituted.

Some critics claim that the "death of man" has resulted from the postmodern view that humans are translucent.[66] In a particular sense, this charge is accurate. Yet contrary to the thesis advanced by structuralists and other anti-humanists, the importance of the self is not diminished because the perpetuation of reality is not incumbent on human action. Actually, postmodernists discount the relevance of the self because they argue it cannot be found. A social role, therefore, represents a self that is invented, rather than social or natural tendencies. The self is what Barthes refers to as a "linguistic I."[67] Interpersonal discourse, accordingly, requires that persons treat one another as fickle lovers who are understandable, yet not always predictable.

Postmodern social analysts are uninterested in assessing whether or not behavior is normal. On this point, Derrida writes: "Although it is not a commentary, our reading must be intrinsic and remain within the text."[68] In order to explain what is written, analysis must not extend beyond the language of the text. Most important, therefore, are the speech acts that delimit the parameters of normalcy. Some interpretations are more powerful than others, because more of a text's meaning is understood. Stated differently, a better attempt is made to enter the linguistic world of the author. Contrary to the claims made by their critics, no postmodernist would agree that all interpretations are equal. Accurate interpretations are socially (linguistically) relevant.

A "schizo-analyst" ignores the traditional standards of reason, in order to envision the linguistic fate of events. Overcoming the limits of reason to reveal what is linguistically rational is the aim of postmodern scientists. Accordingly, the stability of measurements is rejected as leading automatically to truth. The "little narrative," or "minor literature" according to Deleuze and Guattari, is the focus of postmodern research.[69] For the story that is told about truth in a specific location reveals reality. Benjamin, however, laments the passage of this sort of storytelling, due to the bureaucratization of the modern mind. Nonetheless, due to the ubiquity of language, historical narration holds the key to reality and truth.

Because minor literature is focus of postmodernist research, it is not surprising that positivists and other realists deny legitimacy to postmodern science. Narratives are usually believed to be mythical, and anything but scientific. Yet postmodernists illustrate that positivism is actually another form of narrative. How can one narrative indisputably cancel another? Because there is no *symbole zéro*, reality is accessible only through stories. Postmodernists, accordingly, are good listeners and recognize that truth emerges gradually from the passion expressed by a speaker.[70] Facts, simply put, are expressive and elusive. Postmodernists agree with Nietzsche that a "gay science" is most effective, one that is not mired in objectivity and reified by methodological demands. How can passion be attracted by the seriousness of measurement? The seriousness of science intimidates interpretation. Postmodern science, therefore, recognizes the story that is told and retold by data. Truth is conjured through a well-told story.

POSTMODERNISM AND THE
HERMENEUTIC TRADITION

Postmodernists reject positivism in favor of a more socially sensitive approach to knowledge acquisition. Facts are not assertive, a positive presence, but represent a sort of absence—an ever-changing body of interpretation. Nonetheless, postmodernists have been less than enthusiastic about hermeneutics. This revelation might at first sound odd, for hermeneutics is also usually understood to be anathema to positivism. Yet postmodernists consider hermeneutics insufficiently radical. This conclusion is based on their belief that those often identified with the hermeneutic tradition have not abandoned realism.

Central to the postmodern critique of modern hermeneutics is that an interpretive ideal is retained, against which texts and other cultural phenomena are judged.[71] Admittedly, this sort of conservatism was witnessed in the early interpreters of the Bible, yet this flaw supposedly has been corrected by current writers. Postmodernists, however, contend that this change has not occurred, or, at minimum, is not as far reaching as is usually thought. They claim that the distinction made originally by Plato between reality and appearance, which has been essential to traditional biblical and legal hermeneutics, is still operative. Typically the aim of an interpreter of the Bible, for example, has been to clear away the residue of history, so as to reveal the true or divinely inspired meaning of the text. While modern hermeneutics is not as blatantly dogmatic, postmodernists believe the tendency remains for texts to be examined with respect to criteria that are non-interpretive. The subject-object dichotomy, in other words, is found in hermeneutics.

Lyotard criticizes advocates of modern hermeneutics because of their apparent desire to unlock the secret meanings of texts.[72] This concern implies that due to procedural difficulties or situational exigencies, the meaning of many texts is able to elude researchers. The interpretation of documents or behavior, therefore, is assumed to be primarily an epistemological exercise. Accordingly, hermeneutics is merely a matter of unlocking the doors that prevent readers from entering into a text. Knowledge is there to be found, if the proper methods are used. In opposition to this inclination, Derrida refers to language use as a "game without security."[73] What he means is that even a perfect methodology will not expose an indubitable foundation of knowledge. Nonetheless, the naiveté of realists has infiltrated hermeneutics, thereby encouraging the "normative discourse" that de Man claims influences the way texts are currently studied.[74] Poetic expression is thus crushed by procedural demands. How the reader enters a text is dictated by methodology. Most problematic, mainstream literary critics and other social researchers who are influenced by hermaneutics seem to be harboring the hope of encountering pure Being. Of course, this faith rests on the success of modern methodological and technical developments. Improved technical competence, in short, will lead to truth.

This newest form of dualism can be traced to the *Methodenstreit* that took place in Europe in the late nineteenth and early twentieth century.[75] Central to this debate was whether or not the social and physical sciences are basically different. Many writers believed that the methods used by the physical sciences are inappropriate for studying humans. The rationale for this differentiation was that social life is interpreted, while nature is not. Inadvertently, however, this bifurcation reified the distinction previously made between subjectivity and objectivity, in addition to suggesting that social scientists can overcome the limitations attendant on opinion. If only social scientists could be as methodologically rigorous as physicists or biologists; even Dilthey, a pioneer in the effort to establish history as one of several *Geisteswissenschaften*, never abandoned hope that universal psychological laws would be eventually formulated.[76]

Although dualism at this time was much more subtle than it had been in earlier centuries, the belief that unadulterated truth exists still persisted. Max Weber, for example, vacillated on the issue of value-freedom, while advocating the use of "ideal types" as methodological tools.[77] These so-called pure examples were retained to allow cross-cultural comparisons to be made, because these concepts are static and ahistorical. Therefore, Weber's rejection of natural or explanatory science is not thought to have been complete. Certainly Karl Mannheim was not a supporter of positivism, yet he was often inconsistent and, like Weber, he seemed to exempt natural science from social determination.[78] Postmodernists are also troubled by Gadamer's hermeneutics, for they believe that he was searching for the primordial conditions of all understanding. For example, they believe that he retained the standard definition of "objectivity."[79] Furthermore, because he distinguished between false and true prejudices, he apparently acknowledged the possibility of gaining unbiased knowledge. And similar to Habermas' critique of Gadamer, postmodernists believe that Gadamer did not subject culture to serious review, but instead treated it as universal. Gadamer, accordingly, is assumed to have been searching for an ahistorical standard to sustain judgments, something he referred to as the "right horizon of enquiry," which leads to a "higher universality."[80]

The postmodern critique of hermeneutics is similar to Derrida's assault on Husserl's work and on phenomenology. Derrida argues that the onset of phenomenology does not represent a break with Western metaphysics, despite the protestations to the contrary made by Husserl and Sartre. The usual search for external essences has not ended, Derrida claims, but has intensified. Phenomenology allegedly proposes a methodology that "brackets" everyday life—the "natural attitude"—so that pure vision is attained. Husserl's use of ancient terminology supplied a surfeit of ammunition for Derrida. Accordingly, Heidegger's attempt to resurrect Being, even in the disguise of *Dasein*, does not earn kudos from Derrida. The focus of the charges levelled by postmodernists is that Dilthey, Mannheim, Weber, and Gadamer, along with phenomenologists, are enamored of the prospect of discovering knowledge unadulterated by the excesses of language use. Terms and concepts are adopted that suggest the pursuit of ideal knowledge has not abated.

In sum, these contributors to modern hermeneutics are chided by postmodernists for trying to resurrect "timeless Reason" as a measure of interpretation.[81] Postmodernists suggest that criteria can be provided to insure the best possible reading of a text—although these rules should not be uncritically accepted. Their fear is that the aim of hermeneutics is merely to improve the accuracy of interpretation, rather than to raise questions related to the existential character of a text or any other phenomenon. Postmodernists are concerned that such an obsession with accuracy or economy—the essence of the outmoded "performativity principle"—unduly truncates the range of possible discourse.[82] Accuracy results from eliminating "noise" or unwanted elements from an interpretation. But postmodernists insist that accuracy cannot be improved without paying attention to the linguistic texture of a manuscript. Because the optimization of the ratio of input to output is the thrust of economic analysis, technical skills rather than reflexivity become most important when analyzing an event. Yet, to continue the economic theme, there is no "idle capacity" in language, but, instead, "persistent inflation." Almost by definition, therefore, critical inquiry is unrelated to technical or procedural considerations. In fact, reflexivity destroys the closed system required for an economic assessment of a linguistic performance. And when interpretation is unsubstantiated by the broad philosophical questions posed by postmodernists, hermeneutics becomes simply a technical enterprise.

CONCLUSION: RESEARCH AND
THE PUBLIC INTEREST

Postmodern research is conducted in the public interest.[83] The terms interest and public are very important and need to be clarified. Interest relates to the Latin *interesse*. Suggested by this etymology is that human involvement extends to the core of reality ("*inter-esse*"). Researchers should be concerned not only with the political or economic agenda of a community, for example, but with the interpretive fabric of order. Although many researchers recognize that a community may exhibit a particular political disposition, they regularly ignore the knowledge base that holds persons together. Accordingly, the public cannot be envisioned as a uniform mass, or something that constrains persons.[84] A community is not organized around structural or logical imperatives, simply because these factors cannot be sustained theoretically any longer.

The position on knowledge and science advanced by postmodernists suggests that the usual version of order should not be utilized. For if knowledge originates from language use, laws, facts, and related social phenomena can not be derived from order. The reason for this is quite simple: order is not divorced from human action, and thus autonomous. Because society is mediated by language, postmodernists refer to order as embodied. Rather than a "collective consciousness," society must be approached as if it constitutes "collective praxis."[85] Order is something more than an idealized form. Hence society is not studied, but rather the modalities of discourse that allow order to prevail. Because order emerges from between persons, research must be directed to a realm many social scientists erroneously believe to be intangible.[86]

While discourse is not necessarily obtrusive, access to language games is not impossible. Yet contrary to traditional wisdom, every research instrument that is adopted must be viewed as a means to engage subjects in dialogue. Clearly, this postmodern approach to research is more difficult than emphasizing methodological or procedural refinement. If discourse is central to the maintenance of order, then only communicative competence on the part of researchers will generate facts. But the aim of methodological discourse is not consensus, but understanding. Therefore, rather than value-freedom, the recognition of values should be encouraged through research. Researchers must begin to appreciate how scientific values may distort the reality constructed by their subjects. Through the recognition of value differences valid knowledge can be acquired, according to postmodernists.[87]

Gathering knowledge is thus an intersubjective process. Postmodernists, nonetheless, are careful to distance themselves from the standard empirical rendition of intersubjectivity. For them, intersubjectivity is not determined by facts, but grows out of praxis. Additionally, as opposed to Gadamer, understanding does not reflect a "fusion" of interpretive horizons.[88] This portrayal of how knowledge is transmitted is simply too static and simplistic for postmodernists. Interpersonal discourse, the heart of the research act, occurs when people confirm each other's definition of reality; when, as suggested by de Man, rules that cannot claim the status of reality become real for both researchers and their subjects.[89] According to postmodernism, research consists of reaffirming the public's reality. Most important, attempting to formalize this sort of dialogue will undoubtedly result in frustration on the part of researchers. Real dialogue occurs despite fluctuations in language, and not because interpretation is artificially removed from speech. Moreover, postmodern research depends on a commitment to protect the fragile, evanescent character of the public's linguistically inscribed identity.

In this regard, reflexivity is imperative. Because language is not structural, speech is malleable and susceptible to self-interrogation. A key consequence of this process is that talk about language is possible. Institutionalizing this spirit of self-criticism as part of research is difficult, but necessary if the linguistic identity of data is to be protected. Traditionally, learning specific techniques has been considered the cornerstone of research. Mimicry and questioning, however, are polar opposites. In order for research to be valuable, self-interrogation must be built into the planning of a research project. Both theoretical and procedural assumptions can thus be examined, so that the social meaning of data is not distorted. Rather than being anti-methodological, postmodernists place research in a context that transforms techniques into media for communication. Techniques do not dictate discourse, because they are adjusted to the patterns of interaction that constitute a society. Surely this is the aim of research: to be responsive to reality. What postmodernists revise is the nature of reality and how it should be studied.

NOTES

1. Lyotard, *The Postmodern Condition*, p. 17.

2. Paul de Man, *Blindness and Insight* (Minneapolis: University of Minnesota Press, 1983), p. 2–35.

3. Emile Durkheim, *The Rules of Sociological Method* (New York: The Free Press, 1965), p. xiii.

4. Ibid., p. 30.

5. Jean Baudrillard, *In the Shadow of the Silent Majorities* (New York: Semiotext(e), 1983), pp. 30–36.

6. Durkheim, *Rules of Sociological Method*, p. 20.

7. Hans Albert, "The Myth of Total Reason: Dialectical Claims in the Light of Undialectical Criticism," in *Positivism and Sociology*, ed. Anthony Giddens (London: Heineman, 1978), pp. 157–194.

8. Félix Guattari, *Molecular Revolution* (New York: Penguin Books, 1984), pp. 86–87.

9. Lyotard, *The Postmodern Condition*, p. 44.

10. John W. Murphy, "Phenomenological Social Science: Research in the Public Interest," *Social Science Journal* 23.3 (1986), pp. 327–343.

11. *Aspects of Sociology* (Boston: Beacon Press, 1972), pp. 1–15.

12. Parsons, *Societies: Evolutionary and Comparative*, p. 29.

13. Albrecht Wellmer, *Critical Theory of Society* (New York: Herder and Herder, 1971), pp. 9–30.

14. Murphy, "Phenomenological Social Science," pp. 332–334.

15. Deleuze, *Proust and Signs*, p. 90.

16. Theodore Thass-Theinemann, *The Interpretation of Language*, vol. 1 (New York: Jason Aronson, 1973), p. 82.

17. Jacques Derrida, *Writing and Difference*, pp. 211–281.

18. Barthes, *Criticism and Truth*, p. 40.

19. Jean-Paul Sartre, *What is Literature?* (New York: Philosophical Library, 1949), p. 208.

20. Jacques Derrida, "Structure, Sign, and Play in the Discourse of the Human Sciences," *The Structuralist Controversy*, ed. Richard Macksey and Eugenio Danto (Baltimore: Johns Hopkins University Press, 1979), pp. 247–272.

21. Lyotard, *The Postmodern Condition*, p. 5.

22. Jean-François Lyotard, *Driftworks* (New York: Semiotext(e), 1984), p. 35.

23. Martin Heidegger, *Being and Time*, p. 262.

24. Barthes, *The Rustle of Language*, p. 331.

25. Derrida, *Of Grammatology*, p. 61.

26. J. Hillis Miller, "Stephen's Rock and Criticism as Cure," *Georgia Review* 30.1 (1976), pp. 5–31.

27. Derrida, *Of Grammatology*, p. 47.

28. Lyotard, *The Postmodern Condition*, p. 36.

29. Durkheim, *Pragmatism and Sociology*, p. 97.

30. Barthes, *The Rustle of Language*, p. 5.

31. Frank Lentricchia, *After the New Criticism* (Chicago: University of Chicago Press, 1980), pp. 3–26.

32. Guattari, *Molecular Revolution*, p. 84.

33. Roland Barthes, *The Pleasure of the Text* (New York: Hill and Wang, 1975), p. 4.

34. De Man, *The Resistance to Theory*, p. 32; see also Barthes, *The Rustle of Language*, p. 54.

35. De Man, *Blindness and Insight*, pp. 60–78.

36. William Gass, *Fiction and Figures of Life* (New York: Vintage, 1972), p. 8.

37. Barthes, *The Rustle of Language*, p. 151.

38. Edmund Husserl, *Ideas* (New York: Collier, 1972), pp. 45–71.

39. Barthes, *The Rustle of Language*, p. 242.

40. Lacan, *Ecrits*, p. 282.

41. Jacques Derrida, *The Archaeology of the Frivolous: Reading Condillac* (Pittsburgh: Duquesne University Press, 1980), p. 48.

42. Barthes, *Criticism and Truth*, p. 90.

43. Gilles Deleuze and Félix Guattari, *Anti-Oedipus* (New York: Viking Press, 1977), pp. 272–382.

44. Guattari, *Molecular Revolution*, p. 77.

45. Ibid., p. 168.

46. Ibid., p. 77.

47. Derrida, *Writing and Difference*, pp. 31–68.

48. Barthes, *The Pleasure of the Text*, p. 53.

49. Deleuze, *Proust and Signs*, p. 91.

50. Kristeva, *Revolution in Poetic Language*, p. 17.

51. Murphy, "Phenomenological Social Science."

52. John W. Murphy, Algis Mickunas, and Joseph J. Pilotta, "Conclusion: Fundamentals of a Responsible Technology," in *The Underside of High-tech*, ed. John W. Murphy, Algis Mickunas, and Joseph J. Pilotta (Westport, Conn.: Greenwood Press, 1986), pp. 191–205.

53. Lyotard and Thébaud, *Just Gaming*, p. 64.

54. Parsons, *The Social System*, pp. 34ff.

55. George H. Mead, *Mind, Self, and Society* (Chicago: University of Chicago Press, 1967), pp. 144–164.

56. Lyotard and Thébaud, *Just Gaming*, p. 23.

57. De Man, *Allegories of Reading*, p. 264.

58. Barthes, *Criticism and Truth*, p. 69.

59. Michel Foucault, "What is an Author?" in *Textual Strategies*, ed. Josué V. Harari (Ithaca, N.Y.: Cornell University Press, 1979), pp. 141–160.

60. Barthes, *Image-Music-Text*, p. 145.

61. Lacan, *Ecrits*, p. 181.

62. Gajo Petrović, *Marx in the Mid-Twentieth Century* (Garden City, N.Y.: Doubleday, 1967), p. 116.

63. Walter Benjamin, "On Some Motifs in Bandelaire," *Illuminations* (New York: Schocken, 1969), pp. 167ff.; see also Martin Jay, *The Dialectical Imagination* (Boston: Little, Brown, 1973), pp. 206–212.

64. Barthes, *The Rustle of Language*, p. 119.

65. John W. Murphy and Joseph J. Pilotta, "Research Note: Identifying 'At Risk' Persons in Community Based Research" *Sociology of Health and Illness* 9.1 (1987), pp. 62–75.

66. John W. Murphy, "Foucault's Ground of History," *International Philosophical Quarterly* 24.2 (1984), pp. 189–196.

67. Barthes, *The Rustle of Language*, p. 16.

68. Derrida, *Of Grammatology*, p. 159.

69. Gilles Deleuze and Félix Guattari, *Kafka: Toward a Minor Literature* (Minneapolis: University of Minnesota Press, 1986).

70. Barthes, *Image-Music-Text*, p. 56.

70. De Man, *The Resistance to Theory*, pp. 55–56, 114.

72. Lyotard, *The Postmodern Condition*, p. 35.

73. Derrida, "Structure, Sign, Play," pp. 247–272.

74. De Man, *The Resistance to Theory*, p. 114.

75. Theodor W. Adorno, et al., *The Positivist Dispute in German Sociology* (London: Heinemann, 1974); see also Martin Jay, *The Dialectical Imagination* (Boston: Little, Brown, 1973), pp. 219–252.

76. H. A. Hodges, *The Philosophy of Wilhelm Dilthey* (Westport, Conn.: Greenwood Press, 1976), pp. 196–224.

77. Max Weber, *Economy and Society*, vol. 1, pp. 20–22.

78. Susan J. Hekman, *Hermeneutics and the Sociology of Knowledge* (Notre Dame, Ind.: University of Notre Dame Press, 1986), pp. 50–90.

79. Hans-Georg Gadamer, *Truth and Method* (New York: Crossroad, 1982), p. 408.

80. Ibid., pp. 269–272.

81. Hekman, *Hermeneutics and the Sociology of Knowledge*, pp. 4–12.

82. Lyotard, *The Postmodern Condition*, pp. 41–53.

83. Murphy, "Phenomenological Social Science"; see also John W. Murphy, "Postmodernism and Social Research," *Social Epistemology* 2.1 (1988), pp. 83–91.

84. Perelman, *The New Rhetoric and the Humanities*, pp. 48–50.

85. Jean-Paul Sartre, *Critique of Dialectical Reason* (Atlantic Highlands, N.J.: Humanities Press, 1979), pp. 505–524.

86. John W. Murphy, *The Social Philosophy of Martin Buber* (Washington, D.C.: University Press of America, 1983), pp. 35–68.

87. Niklas Luhmann, *The Differentiation of Society* (New York: Columbia University Press, 1982), pp. 353–355.

88. Gadamer, *Truth and Method*, pp. 273–274.

89. De Man, *The Resistance to Theory*, pp. 97–98.

4

Order and Discourse

CARTESIANISM AND SOCIETY

The traditional renditions of order have not been immune to Cartesianism. Order is portrayed in a dualistic manner by both classical and a host of modern theorists. Similar to Descartes' search for an indubitable ground of certainty, most sociologists view order as emanating from an inviolable source. Because subjectivity, or human action, is believed to be capricious, a basis for order is sought that is untrammeled by interpretation. In other words, standards must be available that are unaffected by personal motives, or society will devolve into what Deleuze calls "associative chains and non-communicating viewpoints."[1] A type of Newtonian "oasis"—an absolute foundation—is believed to be required for society to survive. A perfect spatial domain is reserved as a basis of order.

As a result of this Cartesian influence, Niklas Luhmann writes that sociologists have exhibited a propensity for conceptualizing order as "centered."[2] By this he means that a single, intractable referent is invoked to legitimize norms. When the common present required for interaction is established in accordance with the assumptions of dualism, order is guaranteed. Consistent with Cartesianism, the knowledge used to organize society is touted as the antithesis of subjectivity, and thus order is associated automatically with reason. In a manner of speaking, society embodies reason, while persons are passionate, misguided, and continuously threaten order. Reality, therefore, is not subject to definition, but represents a comprehensive system that is able to control individuals. When passion is juxtaposed to reason in this way, Herbert Marcuse argues, society becomes invulnerable.[3] After all, how can useless passion have any significant impact on reason? Reason, in fact, is given the power to suppress passion.

When conceived dualistically, society is provided with indisputable justification. For if persons are to act rationally, conventional wisdom suggests, they must look outside of themselves to find guidance. Society, accordingly, is the only source from which this guidance can originate. Durkheim writes that morality is possible only on the "condition that society be always considered as being qualitatively different from the individuals that compose it."[4] In effect, self-denial becomes a prerequisite for order, as individuals are rendered subservient to an idealized version of society. Morality, as Durkheim states, must be free from "sentimental subjectivism."[5] Yet with individuals so thoroughly impoverished, how can norms ever be seriously challenged? Mounting a protest would involve persons in criticizing the source of their identity. This sort of activity, however, requires the autonomy individuals are denied. Because persons are immured by norms, with regard to orthodox portrayals of order, postmodernists charge that traditional social science is very repressive.[6] Society, simply put, is nothing but an agent of control. As imagined by Hobbes, social reality is a grand intimidator.[7] Reality constitutes a "collective force."[8]

MODERN RENDITIONS OF ORDER

Two approaches have traditionally been adopted to conceptualize social reality. Using medieval terminology, these are usually referred to as ontological nominalism and realism. Realists, sometimes called holists, contend that society has its own existence, removed categorically from the realm occupied by individuals.[9] Society, stated differently, is greater than the sum of its parts. In terms of modern sociology, Durkheim declared that society constitutes a *"reality sui generis."* Auguste Comte made a similar point when he argued that through the use of positive science, a universal body of knowledge, dubbed "public opinion," could be established to sustain order. Moreover, Herbert Spencer adopted an organismic analogy, while Talcott Parsons introduced the concept of the social system. In each case, order was said to stem from a source that is disassociated from interpretation. As Durkheim remarked, society represents truth that is irrepressible.[10]

Additionally, according to realism individuals obtain their identity from the social whole. As described by writers such as Spencer and Parsons, for example, individuals are merely components of a much larger social system. Each person, moreover, is assigned a job that contributes to the survival of society. A person's raison d'être, therefore, is determined by the social system. Questions pertaining to the meaning of life are answered in terms of how well individuals perform their duties. Deviance, health, and illness reflect standards associated with various institutions, rather than personal or collective judgments. Actually, the strictures imposed by society delimit the boundaries of reality. Yet realists such as Durkheim applaud this view, because social order cannot be jeopardized by psychological idiosyncracies.

Nominalists, on the other hand, claim that only individuals are real and that society is fictitious.[11] They reject the existence of a so-called macro level of order. Key to this position is the claim that individuals are free to pursue their own aims, and that as a result of this activity, order emerges. Nominalists believe that order can be established on the basis of individualized preferences. Throughout the history of social thought, however, justifying society in this manner has been viewed as dubious, even by nominalists. According to Deleuze, the nominalist viewpoint treats persons as "sealed vessels." Moreover, it is quite a leap of faith to assume that individual greed will enhance the common weal.[12] After describing individuals as monads, for example, Leibniz introduced the notion of "pre-established harmony" to explain how they are organized. In a similar vein, chaos is averted at the marketplace, according to Adam Smith, through the intervention of an "invisible hand." Modern supply-side economists acknowledge that something they refer to generally as the market regulates trading. In each instance a non sequitur is made. Specifically, a force that is superior to the individual is given the latitude to control behavior; the perpetuation of reality is again taken out of human hands.

As with realism, individuals are not responsible for their destiny. Instead of a "reality *sui generis*," a style of reason or logic nominalists accept unquestioningly as valid underpins cognitive activity and, ultimately, interaction. Those who depart from this ideal, as might be suspected, are labelled as aberrant. Social mores are not a topic for debate, for these rules serve to differentiate reason from madness. Besides, how can the principles that make order possible be suspended? Without the insight imparted by reason, interaction would at best be undisciplined, and at worst completely disorganized. Economic exchange, for example, would be highly volatile, unless price signals are evaluated similarly by traders. Nonetheless, as should be seen, nominalists also deprive persons of autonomy.

As Buber has pointed out, moral order has been considered a product of either individual or collective demands. Yet morality is depersonalized in each case, in that both personal autonomy and social responsibility are undermined. In nominalism, individuals who are absolutely reasonable are the focus of attention, while social concerns are of secondary importance. According to realists, individuals are associated intimately with the collective, yet the element of personal choice is undermined. In neither approach are human action and social order united. The implication, then, is that moral order and freedom are incompatible. Postmodernists maintain that this conclusion is very problematic, since order inevitably becomes inhospitable:

the needs of society are satisfied, regardless of the desires voiced by individuals.

Luhmann charges that society is typically assumed to be centered. Lyotard reviles the work of Spencer, Comte, and Parsons, because they describe society to be a "unicity."[13] These thinkers consider society to be a natural fact or object, waiting to be discovered by anyone who is sufficiently scientific. Accordingly, readers should not be surprised that the use of structural metaphors is so prevalent among mainstream sociologists. For the separation of consciousness, or subjectivity, from the knowledge base of society is thought to be entirely justified. Doubtless, Descartes set the precedent for this gambit by distinguishing *res cogitans* from *res extensa*. Although order can be secured in this way, postmodernists contend that it reifies society. Thus, contrary to traditional imagery, they compare society to a "rhizome."[14]

THE POSTMODERN CRITIQUE OF
THE "CENTERED" SOCIETY

In terms of Western metaphysics, existence has often been compared to a tree with deep roots. The metaphor implies that because these roots are deeply buried and removed from everyday events, society has a firm foundation. A rhizome, on the other hand, appears to grow in an almost unlimited number of directions, and thus has no center. The point Guattari and Deleuze are raising by adopting this imagery is quite simple. They are questioning the appropriateness of Cartesianism for conceptualizing any phenomena, particularly society. Can the belief be sustained that order extends from a single locus, unaffected by situational contingencies? By using the rhizome as an example, the implication is that order emerges from within itself, rather than from principles that are protected from scrutiny. According to Gebser, the center of society in the postmodern world is everywhere.[15] Derrida reaffirms this point when he declares that philosophers are consigned to working at the periphery (or "margins"), instead of in the core of reality.[16] Social existence is thus decentered by postmodernists. The source of order, contends Derrida, must be a "noncenter."[17]

Further, postmodernists charge that the speculative social ontologies perennially used can no longer be theoretically supported. Simply stated, the success of Cartesianism depends on a defunct philosophical démarche. How can persons leap beyond the realm occupied by interpretation, in order to discover the pure knowledge coveted by Descartes? For if knowledge is mediated by language games, how can the impersonal truth, sought by Descartes and modern social philosophers such as Durkheim, possibly be

captured? Rather than constrain persons, speech acts establish order. Institutions, accordingly, are not the pillars of society, but embody the interpretive process they are supposed to repress.

Implicating institutions in language use marks a noteworthy departure
from the past. Usually institutions have been portrayed as unencumbered
by opinions, or by any other situational factor that would limit the ap-
plicability of norms. Institutions have been divorced from persons for a
simple reason—to maintain social control. Institutions are given almost
unlimited authority; this is accomplished by restricting symbolism to
specific areas of society. "Symbolic energy," as Barthes labels it, is not permitted to flow freely throughout a culture.[18] Symbolism is defined as
something personal, while social organizations are public. Insisting on
maintaining this dichotomy provides institutions with the freedom from
restraint required to enforce norms. Symbols are privatized and unable to
affect reality.

With institutions mired in language, critics of postmodernism argue,
society is plunged into anarchy. For example, René Wellek contends that
postmodernism poses a serious threat to institutional and pedagogical practice. Traditionalists believe this philosophy encourages "apocalyptic irra-
tionalism," "cognitive atheism," and "dogmatic relativism."[19] Clearly,
mainstream social philosophers and sociologists have reason to fear the
thesis advanced by postmodernists. Deprived of an ahistorical framework,
theories such as functionalism, structuralism, and cybernetics, for example,
lose their appeal. And if social theorists are unable to employ structural
metaphors, their status as scientists may be jeopardized. Nonetheless, does
the loss of an ultimate $arch\bar{e}$ mean that society must be inevitably
destroyed? Because order must stand in the midst of language, are social
relationships impossible to establish and perpetuate? As a result of emphasizing the "undecidables" indigenous to language use, opponents of
postmodernism contend that culture is eviscerated. Indeed, postmodernists
are thought to delight in undermining society. Yet is Terry Eagleton correct
when he states that only Justice can be forthcoming from a society based on
postmodern philosophy?[20]

This charge, however, is not difficult to understand. As might be expected,
postmodernists do not accept the centered version of society. Such impetu-
ousness worries realists. Nonetheless, Lyotard goes further: he announces
that consensus is an outmoded concept, and that social laws are impossible to
know.[21] What is the uninitiated reader to make of such pronouncements? The
conclusion reached by many critics is that postmodernism collapses under
its own demands. For if social contracts cannot be enacted, laws cannot be
enforced. Order is not only impossible, the ideas expressed by postmodernists can be neither comprehended nor implemented. Idiosyncracies, these

critics charge, are simply not sufficient to sustain a community. Therefore, advocates of postmodernism are thought to court political disaster.

Advocates of realism and nominalism contend that no other conclusion is warranted. With the element of interpretation given such importance, they claim, all standards of culture must be abandoned. If one interpretation of events is as good as any other, reality vanishes. Nothing is available to dictate when particular actions are appropriate and others are not. Relativity reigns, thus creating chaos. If every behavior rests on a value judgment, anything is possible at any time. Considering this a dismal state of affairs, critics sometimes label postmodernism as nihilistic. Reminiscent of the early critiques of Nietzsche, postmodernists are thought to invite the degeneration of morality. A never ending cycle of re-evaluation culminates in personal immobility and a complete lack of social direction.

POSTMODERN SOCIAL IMAGERY

In order to understand the postmodern conception of society, a couple of key ideas must be remembered. First, Lyotard was a member of the "Socialisme ou barbarie" movement, while various other postmodernists are advocates of what has come to be called Western Marxism.[22] These writers are not necessarily calling for the complete elimination of order; they merely reject the view that a bureaucratic state is a rational form of social organization. What they are criticizing specifically is the reification of society inaugurated by Stalin. Consistent with what Claude Lefort has to say on this issue, postmodernists understand bureaucracy to be a philosophy and not simply a form of management.[23] Bureaucracy creates the illusion that certain social arrangements are "ahistorical," and thus invulnerable to critique. As a result, society is thought to operate according to rules that are scientific and fair. Vast amounts of information and persons can be processed efficiently and with expediency; yet dehumanization becomes prevalent.

Bureaucratization requires the separation of substantive and formal rationality, notes Weber. With intepretation removed to the periphery of an organization, the illusion is created that decisions can be made without bias. In order to enforce this belief, behavior is standardized, communication is regulated, authority patterns are explicitly defined, and the type of knowledge that is introduced into the decision making process is extremely restricted. Rather than simply an increase in organizational size, the key to bureaucratization is formalization. Every activity is accomplished by mastering a particular technique, while decisions become increasingly mechanistic. The aim of formalization, as might be expected, is to allow organizations to be scientifically designed and operated. In fact, developing bureaucracies was thought to be a rational approach to eliminating waste and corruption. This original appraisal, however, has proven to be extremely naive.

The end product of bureaucratization is a symbol-free *mise en scène*, where judgments are made on the basis of facts, without interference from extraneous influences. To use the example provided by Benjamin, the "aura" is stripped from any phenomenon that is encountered.[24] Because knowledge is materialized, events can be easily manipulated. Hence managers become technophiles, who rely mostly on analytical methods when evaluating policy options. In point of fact, so-called "soft" data, such as those derived from direct experience, are often cited as promoting faulty reasoning. Primacy is given unquestioningly to "calculative rationality." Yet this uncritical acceptance of instrumental reason has dire consequences. Most important, the way knowledge is conceptualized may alter irreparably the organization of society.

With the logic of an organization standardized, efficiency will almost certainly increase, at least initially. Politically, however, the bureaucratization of society is disastrous. Power becomes extremely concentrated, usually in the hands of a few technocrats.[25] These functionaries are believed to possess the education and skills required to make scientific or rational decisions. Because knowledge is not widely disseminated, the political process begins to collapse. The average citizen is unable to make informed choices, while those who have knowledge become increasingly indispensable. What some Marxists call "etatism" is the eventual result of bureaucratization. In other words, society is transformed into a elitist system, which is monolithic and impenetrable. Foucault remarks that when a society is bureaucratized, power no longer assumes the form of brute force.[26] Actually, this sort of display seems almost infantile. Power is exerted, instead, through the use of classificatory schemes and criteria for judging behavior that are believed to be thoroughly rational. A management science that is unquestioned, for example, contributes to the disenfranchisement of citizens. Accordingly, the political process becomes nothing more than administration. Persons may actually request to be assessed by these standards, as is the case when they volunteer for psychiatric or medical examinations. To counter this terrorism, Lyotard calls for the development of "flat" organizations.[27]

Second, researchers must appreciate that Lyotard was influenced by Martin Buber and Emmanuel Lévinas, in addition to the Hasidic masters. The paradoxical statements made by Lyotard will most likely be misconstrued, unless the role played by these authors in the formation of postmodernism is recognized. While making reference to Hasidism, Lyotard is loath to base society on a set of prescriptions.[28] Also consistent with his critique of bureaucracy, establishing rubrics that differentiate absolutely reality from illusion will surely lead to trouble, especially if personal freedom is valued. Lyotard's statement that laws cannot be discovered simply means that no imperious authority can be introduced to legitimize order. Because the claim is not justified that particular standards are ultimately rational while others are irrational, conformity need not be the result of apprehending reality. Order is not necessarily jettisoned, but merely the social imagery whereby normalcy is equated with adjustments to societal expectations.

Most relevant about Hasidism in this context is that knowledge is believed to reside within language and truth is sought among everyday activities. According to Hasidic teachings, salvation is associated with social justice. God is thoroughly worldly, and thus religious escapism is discouraged. Moreover, Buber describes the development of society as synonymous with linguistic invention. In general, like postmodernists, the Hasidim oppose realism. Ultimate principles, in short, are thought to dwarf the human side of reality. Yet the realm of the interhuman is where life unfolds. The Hasidim argue that ignorance of this dimension can destroy what is sacred about society. Life should not be transformed into a lifeless Golem, as a consequence of worshiping idols and eternal truths. Institutions exist between persons, write the Hasidim. With knowledge tied to experience, how can absolute political proposals be given credence? The Hasidim, in short, consider a hierarchy to be absurd.

As noted earlier, Lyotard recommends the formation of "flat" organizations. His point is that social institutions should not be approached as if they are autonomous, and thus condition human experience. Due to the pervasiveness of language, organizations must be viewed as primordially linguistic. Instead of specifying the parameters of reality, institutions are a product of the pragmatic impetus of language. This is why some postmodernists refer to society as an embodied polity.[29] Order cannot be severed from the human presence, because social life is held together by the desire persons exhibit to make their lives meaningful. In short, an abstract universal cannot be derived from interaction.

With their corporeal social ontology, postmodernists want to avoid "totalizing" society.[30] For when this is the case, they argue, spontaneity is replaced by security. Society, in a manner of speaking, becomes a straitjacket that insures uniformity among persons. De Man, for example, uses Kleist's *Marionettentheater* to characterize modern society.[31] Persons, he writes, have become mere puppets, tethered to a political and economic system that they no longer understand. As in the castle described by Kafka, the source of authority cannot be found, yet laws are everywhere. In order to enliven social life, postmodernists claim that order emerges from the realm obscured by both nominalists and realists. Buber, for instance, calls this place the "in between," a domain devoid of the highs and lows of traditional metaphysics.[32] Recently, another author referred to this place as the "dialogical region."[33]

What nominalists and realists overlook is the space between persons. Because this region is obviously replete with interpretation, traditionalists warn that society could not possibly be erected on such a flimsy foundation. Buber utilized appropriate imagery when he called this area the "narrow ridge."[34] He suggested that winds whirl around anyone who resides there, thus limiting a person's vision. This is not to say that certainty cannot be obtained, but that knowledge must be extricated from the flotsam left behind by history. Rather than being immaculately conceived, order emerges from the maelstrom of claims that compete to dominate everyday life. Truth, in other words, is buried deep within social concerns. Lyotard, therefore, writes that society is comprised of institutional "patches." Described in this way, postmoderns feel, order is no longer ominous.

Lyotard uses Plato's ontology to exemplify what he wants to avoid. Like the Hasidim, Lyotard believes that Plato envisioned society as an eternal idea.[35] Once this version of order is given credence, everyday life is eliminated as a source of ethical and moral values. Plato, along with most Western philosophers, had little positive to say about opinion. Yet as Buber recalls, fleeing from daily experience and repairing to a cloistered environment renders life meaningless.[36] Striving to fulfill the requirements of abstract laws may provide an individual with the promise of security, yet the resulting behavior occurs in a vacuum. The price paid for this salvation consists of the values, sentiments, and commitments that serve to organize a person's existence. Further, as Erich Fromm remarks, ethereal ideals tend to undermine the human condition.[37] The more expansive these ideals become, the relevance of human action becomes less important. What could be more alienating?

Again like the Hasidim, Lyotard wants to sanctify the world of everyday activities. To use Paul Tillich's terminology, what "concerns" persons "ultimately" is assumed to exist within the dialogical region.[38] Because of the emphasis that has been placed on identifying structural imperatives, this simple idea has been overlooked. The "in between" is no longer thought to be holy, because the mystery of how order is established is currently obscured by technical operations. For example, merely formalizing relationships is believed to optimize interaction. In a bureaucracy, explicit lines of interaction and clearly defined rules of logic are identified as leading naturally to improved communication. Technical competence is thus deemed sufficient to guarantee the success of discourse. Rather than being a set of technical procedures, postmodernists maintain, language gives rise to society. Communicative, instead of technical, proficiency is central to the survival of order.[39] As in postmodern epistemology, the key to a postmodern social ontology is intersubjectivity, more accurately known as linguistic pragmatics.

ORDER AND DISCOURSE

Postmodernists recognize that successful communication does not necessarily result from mastering the form or structure of language. Instead, linguistic pragmatics sustain order. The language game that people play must be grasped, before their intentions can be anticipated with any regularity. De Man uses the phrase "double rapport" to describe this mode of engagement.[40] As noted in Chapter 3, linguistic comprehension occurs when a reader enters the world deployed by an author's use of language. Clearly, grammar and logic miss this side of communication. Interpersonal discourse is possible only when the "polysemic" nature of language is realized.[41] In other words, once a person appreciates that a sign may convey a variety of meanings simultaneously, the need to preserve a person's world through interaction can be demonstrated. Interlocutors can begin to live at the boundary of their respective interpretations of reality, so that the presence of other linguistic worlds can be recognized.[42] Dialogue demands that persons work "at the limits of what the rules permit," states Lyotard.[43] The linguistic "moves" that constitute one of these new worlds can then be adequately evaluated. Sartre describes this process in terms of reading a book: "Each one [reader and author] trusts the other; each one counts on the other, demands of the other as much as he demands of himself."[44] The social world is thus mediated by the reflexivity inherent to reading.

Obviously this portrayal of order is different from that provided by Parsons, with respect to his notion of "double contingency."[45] He assumes that roles are structurally linked, and thus offer a cohesive and stable system. The reduction of complexity necessary for interaction to succeed results from persons not violating their assigned roles. Moreover, a postmodern order is not the product of persons "taking the role of the other," as described by G. H. Mead and, later, symbolic interactionists.[46] One of Foucault's most controversial claims explains why this cannot be the case. Stated succinctly, Foucault says that there is no self that subtends an author's work or, accordingly, a person's identity. No atavistic or collective psyche, for example, can be found. Foucault's position is that an individual's self-concept is comprised of nothing more than discursive practices that have been internalized. Considering that postmodernists abandon dualism, consciousness is not pure but linguistic. Therefore, adopting the role of the other is impossible.[47] Mutual understanding depends upon the willingness of persons to acknowledge linguistically inscribed identities that may be different from their own. Language must be explored until a common ground is discovered. Only language piled upon itself can serve as the basis of order. The phrase "discourse-figure" best conveys the identity of social reality.[48] In other words, reality is based on discourse that assumes a fragile form.

The resulting order should not be referred to as a system, according to Jean Gebser. When society becomes known as a system, an all-encompassing mechanism is thought to be available to reconcile divergent points of view. Instead, in a postmodern world, order is envisioned to be a "systase."[49] Systasis means that various elements are directly integrated, without an intermediary. No abstraction is involved in this process. Luhmann transforms Gebser's idea into more social terms when he suggests that through the recognition of difference, discourse can be initiated.[50] By this he means that persons who do not adhere to a similar reality can successfully interact. Accordingly, avenues of accessibility must begin to connect realities that were formerly considered to be irreconcilable. This is what Lyotard has in mind when he writes that postmodernism "refines our sensitivity to differences and reinforces our ability to tolerate the incommensurable."[51] Social reality, in this sense, consists of a myriad of differences, none of which is inherently superior to the other.

A concrete universal unites a postmodern society—that is, accessibility to the other. Organized diversity is the hallmark of a society based upon postmodernism. Borrowing from Proust, Deleuze declares that "transversality" allows for order. By this term he means that "unity and totality are established for themselves, without unifying or totalizing objects or subjects."[52] The fundamental moral principle at this juncture is that the integrity of the other—his or her difference—must be guaranteed at all times. Derrida writes: "There is no ethics without the presence of the other."[53] Lévinas refers to this as an ontology without metaphysics, whereby persons encounter one another "face-to-face" in a non-reductionistic manner. Individuals are treated as valuable in themselves, and not as a means for some other end prescribed by either God or the state. Society embodies a whole, but not one that dictates how persons must conduct their affairs. In fact, Lyotard labels those who transgress the language games played by others as "terrorists."[54] Obviously, order is not a consensus, because persons are not necessarily oriented by similar ideals. However, rejecting consensus is not the same as advocating anarchy or nihilism.

Critics of postmodernism are correct when they charge that both God and man are undermined by this philosophy. Yet order is not cast aside, but only the "reality *sui generis*" that is usually retained to legitimize social arrangements. In a sense, postmodernists radicalize contract theory. In addition to certain folkways, they negotiate the entire framework within which discussions about norms are undertaken. Accordingly, fundamental to the maintenance of society are "flexible networks of language games."[55] While criticizing the dogmatism of Parsons and other functionalists, Luhmann observes that reality is sustained by "contingency formulae," rather than by an ultimate reality.[56] The basis of reality is thus "localized." Further, the *sensus communis* resides at the nexus of two or more language games. The social bond, Lyotard observes, consists of a linguistic game "agreed on by its present players and subject to eventual cancellation."[57] Accordingly, social stability results from certain linguistically inscribed meanings coming to be accepted as real. Social order, in other words, is organized in terms of discursive practices that are momentarily not questioned. As Lyotard explains, the "social universe is formed by a plurality of language games without any one of them being able to claim that it can say all to the others."[58]

Nonetheless, the relationship of the "I" to the "other" is not a natural condition. A causal mechanism or some other form of determinism does not unite persons. In fact, the "we" that is a community can be revealed only through choice. Through an authentic act, one that is self-inaugurated, a specific behavior is enacted with respect to other possibilities. Actually, if an act is stimulated by a so-called external source, the horizon of options that accompanies volition is irrelevant. Behavior understood as a response cannot contribute to a sense of community. In other words, without freedom social relations would be impossible to envision. For outside of the implicative structure that sustains choice, the "I" and the "other" cannot be understood to exist.

POSTMODERNISM AND A
RESPONSIBLE SOCIETY

Hence persons are not agents of socialization when they instruct one another about the ways of the world. They speak for no one but themselves; they are not surrogates for some higher reality. Institutions are fragile, because these organizations merely record the choices that have been made pertaining to how society shall operate. Therefore, according to postmodernists, institutions are revealed only through their deformations. This is another way of saying that reality bears the imprint of judgments, and thus no longer has the status required to restrain passion. While alluding to Kant, Benjamin notes that historical institutions have a purpose that is not imposed by structural imperatives.[59] Like a *flâneur*, society meanders according to a self-imposed aim. An order is left behind that is meaningful, yet devoid of dogmatism. Humans are thus "fateless," writes Benjamin, for fate exists in an ahistorical context.[60] For this reason, a postmodern social ontology is one of danger. Obligation is secured through action, rather than necessity. According to de Man, Hölderlin's words are truly relevant: "We are our conversation."[61] In this regard, Lévinas comments that persons encounter one another without intermediary or without achieving communion. There is no solitary individual or absolute We. Persons must risk security constantly to encounter others.

Lyotard refers to this version of order as a "self-managed" society.[62] Self-management is a theme that has become quite popular in recent years in various Marxist societies, particularly in Yugoslavia. Basic to this idea is that jobs are meaningful only when workers are able to establish an intimate relationship with the means of production. This requires far more than allowing workers to participate at opportune times in planning the labor process. More important, the entire organization of work must reflect human needs and desires. The workplace must not regulate work; instead, the producers must design their jobs. As a group of Yugoslavian Marxists note, this requires that factories no longer be viewed as autonomous entities.[63] Rather, the "being" of these organizations must originate from human action. Order is thus legitimized through the "autonomy of interlocutors involved in ethical, social, and political praxis," as described by Lyotard.

A self-managed institution is different from a bureaucracy in several crucial respects. While authority and rules still exist, order is not imposed upon workers. Also, because workers embody the workplace, power is not something that is used, for example, against line staff to secure advantages for a select group of managers. And finally, decisions are not made in secrecy by a few experts. Organizations that are self-managed are sometimes referred to as organic, because they are flexible and responsive to social and not simply managerial concerns.

Conceived in this way, a self-managed society is responsible because order embodies the vox populi, rather than abstract imperatives. How can such an organization ever gain the autonomy necessary for it to turn against and to repress its creators? With the subversion of dualism, institutions can never acquire this much power. There is no justification for assuming that a particular form of reason, body of knowledge, or set of norms is undoubtedly real, and thus deserves to dominate the social scene. For this reason postmodernists depict society as a patchwork of contrasting positions, with the integrity of each one protected. According to Lyotard, society is a process of striving to reach a consensus that is never achieved. He argues that persons are always working at the limits of their language games, thereby constantly reinventing reason and reformulating relationships.[64]

Some writers, such as Hayek, refer to this as a "spontaneous" order.[65] Yet do postmodernists understand the formation of order to be this capricious? Certainly not. Order is not an afterthought, resulting from the accidental confluence of idiosyncrasies. Although order is not contrived, discourse is not random or haphazard. Those who want to interact work within language, through critical reflection and iteration, until a variety of mutually acceptable discursive practices are identified. Once this procedure is satisfactorily completed, a provisional government exists. Although this is a "non-empirical" order, society is not based on chance.[66] Barthes is correct when he remarks that long-forgotten beliefs substantiate both reason and order.

POSTMODERNISM AND LAISSEZ-FAIRE PHILOSOPHY

Critics claim that postmodernists are conservative and promote merely a laissez-faire approach to managing economic and other social affairs. Some writers, such as Jameson, Eagleton, and Said, suggest that postmodernism is compatible with Reaganomics and the trend toward increased deregulation of the marketplace.[67] Yet because they reject the idea that society is an abstract system, does this mean that postmodernists are proponents of the "tooth and claw" morality extolled by Herbert Spencer and most capitalists? Or, in line with Hayek, do postmodernists assume that individualized preferences are somehow brought into harmony because all rational traders are guided by similar motives? If postmodernists could be considered advocates of a laissez-faire outlook, they would probably be closer to Adam Smith than anyone else. And would Smith condone the sort of unrestrained or undisciplined economic activity that has been recently witnessed? The Scottish philosopher was careful to note that unfettered trading could easily result in barbarism, unless certain moral principles were prevalent throughout society. Shared by laissez-faire economics and postmodernism is the belief that social life is underpinned by human action. Nonetheless, these two philosophies part company on many other crucial issues.

In one respect, postmodern thinking is similar to that of Adam Smith. Postmodernists do not consider the formation of order to be ancillary to the pursuit of individual gain. Therefore, postmodernists disagree with supply-siders on a variety of key points. First, postmodernists do not focus on the individual, but on the relationship between persons. Second, rather than being spontaneous, order emerges through discourse. Third, postmodernists make very clear that legitimate discourse is non-repressive or non-coercive. And fourth, abstract factors, such as "market forces," cannot be invoked to explain either aberrations or stability at the marketplace. In general, postmodernists differ from conservative economists with regard to how individuals, or traders, are conceptualized. According to postmodernists, persons are not ahistorical and apolitical; they are not atoms somehow brought into alignment through their desire to interact (that is, to trade).

To counteract the influence of supply-side or conservative economists, Lyotard introduced the idea of "libidinal economics."[68] He suggested that ahistorical equilibrium models are inappropriate for examining economic activity. Trading, instead, should be viewed as corporeal, whereby decisions to buy and sell are understood to reflect the various contexts in which economic actors find themselves. How persons interpret power, reason, and, as Max Weber says, their "life chances" determine the trading gambits they will make. In fact, Lyotard may be considered quite radical, for he recognizes these crucial elements of economic exchange that supply-siders choose to ignore. What could be more rarefied and stifling than a model of trade that excludes the situational exigencies noted by Lyotard, which relate to class interests?

THE SOLIPSISM OF POSTMODERNISM?

Fredric Jameson declares that subsequent to the onset of postmodernism, "Alliance Politics" is no longer possible.[69] His point is that collective action is precluded, due to the emphasis postmodernists place on individualism. This is the same criticism that is lodged against sociologists who concentrate on studying how symbolism shapes reality. These writers are referred to unaffectionately as "micro-theorists" and are assumed to be incredibly naive. Allegedly, they are oblivious to the social factors any competent analyst must concede influence daily life, such as power. Yet are persons characterized as solipsistic or asocial by postmodernists? Is the individual depicted as only remotely connected to social considerations?

If postmodernists were Cartesian in their orientation, a collective response to a problem would be impossible. The dualism attendant on Descartes' position prevents persons from coming into contact with anyone outside of themselves. Moreover, are individuals the "windowless monads" described by Leibniz, who are indirectly related to one another? According to Lyotard, "even before he is born, the human child is already positioned as the referent in the story recounted by those around him, in relation to which he will inevitably chart his course."[70] Persons face each other immediately, in other words, as "addressee" and "referent." For "no self is an island," writes Lyotard.[71] What Lyotard, and postmodernists in general, argue is that subjectivity is simultaneously intersubjectivity. Essential to postmodernism is that persons are recognized as open to the world, or, as Buber suggests, as always acting in the presence of others. In point of fact, language games are not described as self-contained, for any move influences how other gambits are planned.[72]

For postmodernists, as with Wittgenstein, private language games are impossible. Every linguistic maneuver presupposes the existence of others that are not immediately visible. Nonetheless, each move has a countermove. And as anyone knows who has ever played a game, an adequate defense cannot be formulated when offensive strategies are randomly generated. Moreover, plans that are merely reactive, according to Lyotard, are easily integrated into the future gambits of an aggressor. Pre-emptive actions are necessary to thwart an attack. In order to make a surprise move, however, the realm of possibility imagined by the offense must be understood. What is needed to describe social interaction, claims Lyotard, is a "theory of games which accepts agonistics as a founding principle."[73] Persons who pursue their own goals, and happen to come into contact with one another, are not playing a game. According to postmodernists, a game is an interactive endeavor.

Clearly, postmodernists are not advocates of solipsism. They are holistic, without reifying patterns of social discourse. Foucault and Derrida, therefore, are able to discuss the exercise of power, even class relations, while refusing to speak in systemic terms. They argue that systems do not cause repression, but rather discursive formations that are treated as absolute. Only on rare occasions nowadays are entire systems witnessed attacking their inhabitants. As Foucault suggests, such an officious mode of social control tends to antagonize persons.[74] A more efficient means of regulating citizens is to convince them that they are all part of a comprehensive system, which is well integrated, fair, and created to benefit everyone. Further, this system is rational, while all challenges to it are irrational. If the members of one class are able to manipulate symbolism in this manner, any attempt to undermine their hegemony can be easily diffused. This does not mean simply that certain persons have access to information while others do not. More important, through the use of language, those who are in power can implode reality in such a way that their position is viewed as justified, and even necessary.

Postmodernists abandon the view that power is metaphysical, or derived from history or the property owned by a particular class. Rather, power is enacted through discourse that occurs between persons, whereby one group is able to "inferiorize" another.[75] Stated differently, primacy is given to a specific form of reason, which is then accepted as distinguishing normal from abnormal social relations. "Dominant significations," according to Guattari, ravage the soul of the masses and transform these persons into sycophants, who gladly implement the policies of their oppressors.[76] Thus social control does not have to be manifestly violent or spectacular. On the other hand, however, liberation does not result from equally abstract causes, such as a zeitgeist, or professional revolutionaries. Activists must expose the limits of reason, so that the symbolism adopted by an unpopular government can no longer stifle thinking and revolt. Emancipation occurs when persons are not intimidated by their own use of language; when the excesses of language are not repressed. Accordingly, the range of discourse will not be prematurely truncated, simply because a course of action is classified as deviant by scientists or other professionals who represent the state. Once reason is not limited to a specific segment of society, or style of language use, experimental modalities of discourse can proliferate. In sum, postmodernism is not solipsistic and thus should not be viewed as apolitical.

POSTMODERN ETHICS?

Is ethical action defunct, in view of the outlook espoused by postmodernists? Traditionally, correct action is presumed to be deduced from non-contingent standards. The early Greeks thought that Justice was a cosmological principle. In the manner recommended by Durkheim and later, functionalists, ahistorical structures are essential to insure that interaction among persons is fair and just. Nonetheless, recourse is blocked to these imperatives, because of the ubiquity of language. Due to the unavailability of a reality *sui generis*, a framework for ethics is thought to be missing from postmodernism. While it is true that postmodernists have not as yet developed a system of ethics, fragments of a theory are available.

Again, it must be remembered that postmodernists reject Cartesianism. Their concern with maintaining the integrity of praxis, therefore, does not mean that social life is obscured. Indeed, as mentioned earlier, language games intersect, thus preventing solipsism. This is what Derrida means when he says that a postmodern ethics is based on the other. As a result of recognizing intersubjective pragmatics, postmodernists have at their disposal a context for analyzing ethical behavior. What critics must mean when they assert that postmodernists consider ethics unimportant, is that behavioral mandates are not proposed. Actually, postmodernists loathe prescriptions. Yet as in all other facets of social existence, postmodernists explain ethical action with reference to the "in between." And ethical absolutes cannot be propagated within this domain.

Consistent with Buber, postmodernists argue for an ethic based on interpersonal respect.[77] Because language games are finite, no game can legitimately dominate others. In fact, according to postmodernism, repression results from the belief that select games are infinite, and thus can rob others of their integrity. Frantz Fanon, for example, explains that this is exactly how colonization is enforced.[78] Specifically, the linguistic or cultural game of those who are oppressed is disallowed. In this way, social control is maintained. What can justify this sort of "symbolic violence"?[79] With all forms of knowledge originating from interpretation, domination such as this is not legitimate. Persons, instead, must approach one another as "I and Thou." Because others are not necessarily ancillary to a person's actions, and there simply to be manipulated, their desires must be considered when the impact of a behavior is evaluated. As Buber writes, a person is neither the individual described by Kierkegaard nor a member of a mass society.[80] Rather, persons always act in the face of real persons, who must be recognized.

Postmodernists alter Kant's maxim slightly when they suggest that only universal propositions should be given serious consideration.[81] As opposed to Kant, however, they are not referring to abstract standards, but are maintaining that acts which impugn or transgress the language games of others are invalid. Universal, in this sense, means transsubjective, rather than ahistorical. Due to the linguistic nature of reality, behavioral demands must be issued between persons, whereby the "I" and "other" are co-constituted. Barthes, for example, claims that readers are immoral when they fail to take into account the world conveyed by an author in a text.[82] Likewise, persons act irresponsibly when they make plans without recognizing the presence of others. Lyotard, accordingly, writes that justice consists of "preserving the purity of each [language] game."[83] In a postmodern world, behavior is ethical when the linguistic realm of others is recognized and preserved. Proposals that do not include the "Other" as a "Thou" are, by definition, illegitimate.

Justice, therefore, is not an eternal principle that integrates competing claims. According to postmodernists, a society is just if it fosters pluralism. In order to realize this aim, however, discourse that both protects and refutes oppositional views must be encouraged. In this sense, postmodernists are quite radical: they do not stress individualism, ignore power, or assume that order is a product of nature or some other abstract force. Because the self and the other are intimately related, this association must be integral when planning behavior, and not simply an afterthought. Therefore, justice transpires interpersonally, or within the dialogical region, and nowhere else. While their ideas are far from complete, postmodernists have embarked on a trek that demands a grounded or embodied view of ethics. Yet as should be recognized, postmodernists do not give persons a license to do whatever they please—contrary to the opinions of opponents of this philosophy. Only behavior that is sustained intersubjectively is legitimate. Therefore, postmodern philosophy disallows the rapaciousness that motivates behavior in the modern world.

POSTMODERNISM AND CORPOREAL INSTITUTIONS

As should be noted, institutions are not necessarily anathema to post-modernism. Postmodernists are not restricted to addressing simply "micro" issues, related to the pursuit of personal pleasure. Mechanisms for insuring long-term interaction among persons can also be proposed and analyzed. These institutional arrangements, nonetheless, cannot reflect so-called "aggregate demands," or be legitimized by metaphysical principles such as "social forces."[84] Typically, institutions have been viewed as satisfying deep seated needs based in human nature or society. In either case, personal or collective praxis is usually superseded by institutional requirements. The locus of order is thus externalized, in the form of what Parsons calls functional prerequisites. Institutions, accordingly, serve merely to perpetuate the rules they enforce. Stated differently, institutions are concerned primarily with their own survival.

As might be suspected, when self-preservation is of primary importance to managers, the resulting organizations gradually become socially insensitive. Modern bureaucracy is currently cited as the epitome of this trend toward more rational, yet unresponsive, institutions. Questions related to format, technique, and procedure overshadow more substantive concerns. For example, debates over the relevance of institutions are treated as disruptive. According to postmodernists, however, organizations cannot be divorced from language games. To ignore the pragmatic thrust of an institution represents a serious, possibly fatal, mistake. For bureaucracies, as will be shown in Chapter 5, stifle creativity and innovation. As a result, productivity suffers.

Postmodernists contend that technical changes alone will not remedy the flawed structure of a bureaucracy. Much more important, these institutions must be provided with a human ground. Postmodernists suggest that institutions should be established in terms of the dialogue that unites persons. In this way, a workplace, for example, can never be reified to the extent that it dictates how a job shall be undertaken. A variety of attempts have been made recently to conceptualize and to implement "self-managed" institutions that are consistent with the intent of postmodernism. These can be characterized as "organizations without control," for their purpose is not to regulate behavior, but to respond quickly and effectively to human desires.

What postmodernists want to reform is the view that social existence inherently constitutes an abstraction. They insist that society is not an impersonal body, governed by eternal laws. Rather, social relations originate from dialogue, although in the modern world this claim has come to be trivialized. In today's "Corporate Society" persons are commodities, while morals are nothing more than platitudes expounded by crooked politicians or television evangelists. For too long, according to Jean Baudrillard, persons have been envisioned as a "silent majority," fulfilling the demands of society.[85] In fact, virtue has come to be identified with acting in ways that are socially prescribed. Yet postmodernists demonstrate that persons can forge their own identity, without sacrificing society. Personal desire, in other words, can be united with the common weal.

Postmodernists work well within the tradition of the French *moralistes*. The issue of "moral order" is paramount to both groups. Postmodernists, nonetheless, do not create a system of absolutes to guarantee the perpetuation of society. A postmodern order is predicated on openness, rather than the denial of liberty. According to postmodernists, freedom is not a threat to order. Even more to the point, postmodernists argue that freedom and order must somehow be united in a non-repressive manner, or society will only deteriorate further.

NOTES

1. Deleuze, *Proust and Signs*, pp. 98–101.

2. Luhmann, *The Differentiation of Society*, pp. 353–355.

3. Herbert Marcuse, "The Affirmative Character of Culture," in *Negations* (Boston: Beacon Press, 1968), pp. 88–133.

4. Durkheim, *Sociology and Philosophy*, p. 37.

5. Ibid., p. 67.

6. Lyotard, *The Postmodern Condition*, p. 11; see also Guattari, *Molecular Revolution*, pp. 24–44.

7. Michael Oakeshott, *Hobbes on Civil Association* (Berkeley: University of California Press, 1975), pp. 75–131.

8. Durkheim, *Sociology and Philosophy*, p. 55.

9. Werner Stark, *The Fundamental Forms of Social Thought* (New York: Fordham University Press, 1963), pp. 4–5.

10. Durkheim, *Pragmatism and Sociology*, pp. 86–88.

11. Stark, *The Fundamental Forms*, p. 2.

12. John W. Murphy, "The Centered Society and the Sacrifice of Human Freedom," *E.T.C.* 42.2 (1985), pp. 109–118.

13. Lyotard, *The Postmodern Condition*, p. 12.

14. Gilles Deleuze, and Félix Guattari, *On the Line* (New York: Semiotext(e), 1983), pp. 10–20.

15. Gebser, *The Ever-Present Origin*, p. 544.

16. Vincent Descombs, *Modern French Philosophy* (Cambridge: Cambridge University Press, 1980), pp. 136–167.

17. Derrida, "Structure, Sign, Play," p. 264.

18. Barthes, *Image-Music-Text*, p. 158.

19. Howard Felperin, *Beyond Deconstruction* (Oxford: Clarendon Press, 1985), pp. 110–115.

20. Terry Eagleton, *Walter Benjamin or Towards a Revolutionary Criticism* (London: NLB, 1981), p. 134.

21. Lyotard and Thébaud, *Just Gaming*, pp. 81, 91; see also Lyotard, *The Postmodern Condition*, p. 60.

22. Mark Poster, *Existential Marxism in Postwar France* (Princeton, N.J.: Princeton University Press, 1975), pp. 203-205.

23. Claude Lefort, *The Political Forms of Modern Society* (Cambridge, Mass.: MIT Press, 1986), pp. 181-236.

24. Walter Benjamin, "The Work of Art in the Age of Mechanical Reproduction," in *Illuminations* (New York: Schocken, 1969), pp. 217-251.

25. Jean Meynaud, *Technocracy* (New York: The Free Press, 1969).

26. Michel Foucault, *Power/Knowledge* (New York: Pantheon, 1980), pp. 109-145.

27. Lyotard, *The Postmodern Condition*, p. 39.

28. Lyotard and Thébaud, *Just Gaming*, p. 97.

29. Lefort, *The Political Forms of Modern Society*, p. 151.

30. Lyotard, *The Postmodern Condition*, p. 12.

31. De Man, *The Rhetoric of Romanticism*, pp. 263-290.

32. Maurice Friedman, *Martin Buber: The Life of Dialogue* (New York: Harper and Row, 1960), pp. 57-61; see also Martin Buber, *Between Man and Man* (New York: Macmillan, 1965), pp. 202-205.

33. Algis Mickunas, "The Dialogical Region," in *Phenomenology and the Understanding of Human Destiny*, ed. Stephen Skousgaard (Washington, D.C.: University Press of America, 1981), pp. 153-167.

34. Friedman, *Martin Buber*, pp. 3-10.

35. Lyotard and Thébaud, *Just Gaming*, pp. 19-21.

36. Martin Buber, *Meetings* (LaSalle, Ill.: Open Court Publishing, 1973), pp. 59-61.

37. Erich Fromm, *The Sane Society* (New York: Rinehart and Company, 1955), pp. 120-152.

38. Paul Tillich, *Systematic Theology*, vol. 1 (Chicago: University of Chicago Press, 1951), pp. 12-13.

39. Jürgen Habermas, "Toward a Theory of Communicative Competence," in *Recent Sociology*, vol. 2, ed. Hans Peter Dreitzel (New York: Macmillan, 1970), pp. 115-148.

40. De Man, *Allegories of Reading*, pp. 246-277.

41. Michel Foucault, *The Archaeology of Knowledge* (New York: Harper and Row, 1972), p. 110.

42. Lyotard and Thébaud, *Just Gaming*, p. 100; see also Roland Barthes, *Writing Degree Zero* (New York: Hill and Wang, 1968), p. 13.

43. Lyotard and Thébaud, *Just Gaming*, p. 100.

44. Sartre, *What is Literature?*, p. 55.

45. Parsons, *The Social System*, pp. 36ff.

46. Mead, *Mind, Self, and Society*, p. 254.

47. Niklas Luhmann, *Trust and Power* (New York: Wiley, 1979), p. 21.

48. Jean-François Lyotard, "Presentations," in *Philosophy in France Today*, ed. Alan Montefiore (London: Cambridge University Press, 1983), pp. 116-135.

49. Gebser, *The Ever-Present Origin*, pp. 309–310.
50. Luhmann, *The Differentiation of Society*, pp. 353–355.
51. Lyotard, *The Postmodern Condition*, p. xxv.
52. Deleuze, *Proust and Signs*, p. 150.
53. Derrida, *Of Grammatology*, pp. 139–140.
54. Lyotard and Thébaud, *Just Gaming*, p. 98.
55. Lyotard, *The Postmodern Condition*, p. 17.
56. Niklas Luhmann, *Rechtssystem und Rechtsdogmatic* (Stuttgart: Kohlmammer, 1974), p. 58.
57. Lyotard, *The Postmodern Condition*, p. 66.
58. Lyotard and Thébaud, *Just Gaming*, p. 58.
59. Walter Benjamin, *Reflections* (New York: Harcourt Brace Jovanovich, 1978), pp. 304–311.
60. Ibid., pp. 304–311.
61. De Man, *The Resistance to Theory*, p. 110.
62. Lyotard, *The Postmodern Condition*, p. 35.
63. Svetozar Stojanović, *Between Ideals and Reality* (New York: Oxford University Press, 1973), pp. 115–134.
64. Lyotard and Thébaud, *Just Gaming*, p. 94.
65. John W. Murphy, "An Examination of Hayek's Theory of Social Order," *Journal of Interdisciplinary Economics* 1.1 (1985), pp. 5–17.
66. Derrida, *Of Grammatology*, pp. 267–268.
67. Eagleton, *Walter Benjamin*, p. 138; see also Christopher Norris, *The Contest of Faculties: Philosophy and Theory after Deconstruction* (London: Methuen, 1985), pp. 19–46.
68. Alphonso Lingis, *Libido* (Bloomington: Indiana University Press, 1986).
69. Fredric Jameson, *The Political Unconsciousness* (Ithaca, N.Y.: Cornell University Press, 1981), p. 54.
70. Lyotard, *The Postmodern Condition*, p. 15.
71. Ibid., p. 15.
72. Ibid., p. 16.
73. Ibid.
74. Michel Foucault, *Discipline and Punish* (New York: Pantheon, 1979).
75. Barry D. Adam, *The Survival of Domination* (New York: Elsevier, 1978), p. 6.
76. Guattari, *Molecular Revolution*, p. 68.
77. Murphy, *The Philosophy of Martin Buber*, pp. 93–114; see also Lyotard and Thébaud, *Just Gaming*, p. 66.
78. Emmanuel Hansen, *Frantz Fanon: Social and Political Thought* (Columbus: Ohio State University Press, 1977), pp. 71–114.
79. John B. Thompson, *Studies in the Theory of Ideology* (Berkeley: University of California Press, 1984), pp. 42–72.
80. Martin Buber, *Between Man and Man*, pp. 177ff.
81. Lyotard and Thébaud, *Just Gaming*, pp. 57–58.
82. Barthes, *The Rustle of Language*, p. 30.
83. Lyotard and Thébaud, *Just Gaming*, p. 96.
84. Roscoe C. Hinkle, *Founding Theory of American Sociology, 1881–1915* (London: Routledge and Kegan Paul, 1981).
85. Baudrillard, *In the Shadow of the Silent Majorities*, pp. 1–61.

5

Socially Responsible Institutions

INTRODUCTION: AGAINST BUREAUCRACY

Max Weber made the claim quite some time ago that the primary form of organization in the modern world is the bureaucracy.[1] While he was no advocate of bureaucracy, he recognized that benefits could be derived from this approach to management. When Weber was writing at the turn of the twentieth century, great faith was placed in science. Many commentators believed that most societal ills could be remedied through the application of scientific practices. Managers were no exception. The management of large factories, they believed, could be improved greatly as a result of transforming these organizations into bureaucracies. In short, the stability that was missing from society could be provided through increased bureaucratization.

It should be noted that Weber was writing when the fate of the German empire appeared to be uncertain. The working class was immature, while members of the aristocracy were concerned mostly with advancing their own interests. No group or class was able to assume the value-free stance necessary to represent society as a whole. Reminiscent of Hegel, Weber asserted that bureaucrats constitute a universal class, and thus can be trusted to foster the common good. Because the future of bureaucrats is tied directly to the survival of the state, they work diligently to quell dissent or uncertainty. As shown by Foucault, due to the special status granted to bureaucrats, these functionaries are able to create the illusion that policies are not capricious, or directed against a particular segment of society.[2] Policies are thus provided with a patina of objectivity. For bureaucracies are allegedly unaffected by power and other corrupting influences. Bureaucrats, in short, are assumed to be scientific and motivated to act on the basis of facts.

Weber's concerns are still very relevant today. Rationality and efficiency are unmistakably associated with science. Therefore, bureaucracy is championed by a large contingent of managers as a model of rationality. Computers and systems design, moreover, have reinforced this belief. Although modern techno-bureaucracies are relatively new, the desire to formalize and thus rationalize organizations has a long history. And developing a science of management is still thought to have many advantages, despite calls by politicians to eliminate bureaucracies.

Examples of this faith in science can be found throughout the history of management philosophy in the United States and Europe. Most conspicuous is "scientific management," which is modeled after the views of Frederick Taylor.[3] The popularity of Taylorism peaked circa 1915, although elements of this theory are still widely adopted. Like Weber, Taylor was writing during a period of turmoil, when the "*pétite* shop" was gradually being abandoned in favor of the factory. This change, however, required management practices that were practically non-existent. As a consequence of his training as an engineer, Taylor argued that the laws of physics could be used to regulate the workplace. What he produced is a rendition of functional management, also known as the "scalar chain" division of labor, that is present today in a variety of organizations. In France, Henri Fayol expanded on and perfected Taylor's understanding of the workplace. Yet like Fayol, Taylor believed that a factory is analogous to a living body, and thus each worker should be assigned a unique task that contributes to the survival of this organism. Job design, accordingly, is determined by organizational requirements and the laws of nature. It is possible to discover the "one best way" to structure a job, according to supporters of Taylorism. Science, of course, is at the basis of this plan.

Giving primacy to the organization, rather than human needs, is not confined to Taylorism. While human relations theorists were not sympathetic to scientific management and tried to introduce the "human quotient" into the workplace, they were basically unwilling to challenge the prerogative of management.[4] In other words, the image of the workplace as an abstract system, albeit one that is social, was retained. With the advent of cybernetics, during the 1950s, along with "management by objectives," the human side of work was obscured further by organizational prerequisites.[5] Even writers such as Herzberg, Maslow, and McGregor, the core of the so-called humanistic management theorists, treated work as something psychological, and therefore the traditional structure of work was never seriously questioned.[6] Each of these humanists proposed schemes in order to adjust workers to their jobs, without disrupting the logic of the workplace. For they assumed the organization to be the seat of reason and control.

Despite the scientific legacy of bureaucracy, many writers are currently questioning the wisdom of bureaucratization.[7] Bureaucracies are being criticized by a number of managers and workers. Inefficiency and an overall decline in creativity and initiative are said to stem from bureaucratization. Moreover, politicians of almost every stripe contend that the economic problems facing the entire world can be overcome by eliminating bureaucracies. Yet have these critics really understood the thrust of bureaucracy? Postmodernists claim they have not. Usually this desire to arrest the growth of bureaucracy is confined to attempts to reduce the size of organizations. Weber, in addition to a plethora of newer authors, suggests that this association between organizational size and bureaucratization is spurious. The philosophy that justifies bureaucracies, instead, is identified as responsible for producing the irrationality that accompanies these organizations.

As mentioned in Chapter 4, bureaucracies are based on the separation of substantive from formal rationality.[8] This schism allows behavior to be thoroughly rationalized. Substantive or interpretive action is viewed as frivolous, or subjective, and consigned to informal affairs within an organization. Bureaucratic decision making, on the contrary, is sustained by formal logic, which is designed to appear "de-territorialized," or unaffected by situational exigencies.[9] In other words, because formal reasoning is deduced from principles that are assumed to be universal, this style of logic is touted as accurate and unquestioningly valid. With the exercise of subjectivity restricted in organizations, citizens are easily convinced that management decisions are rule-based. Guattari refers to this process of formalization as the "normalization of the libido," in that passion is ostensibly removed from the management process.[10] Presumably scientific managers are value-free.

Once personal judgments are identified as a source of error, no wonder bureaucrats strive to formalize behavior. The more standardized, codified, and quantified rules become, managers are thought to become increasingly rational. This "increasing rationalization," as Weber calls it, is believed to lead unfailingly to improved management.[11] Managers are suddenly given credibility, because sound criteria are believed to underpin their recommendations. In fact, Lefort writes that bureaucracies transform organizational life into "mytho-history."[12] The aim of bureaucracy, stated differently, is to restore faith in a "society without history," where leaders are encouraged to act as if rationality is not implicated in politics or affected by other social factors.[13] Following the repression of interpretation, a vast amount of information can be processed, for data are made to conform to explicit guidelines. The classification of input and the creation of output is thoroughly streamlined, thus allowing precise policy statements to be produced. As Guattari remarks, bureaucracy denies the political side of truth. The focus of this sort of organization, in short, is "bureaucratic meta-languages."[14] The aim of these symbols is to universalize the workplace and any other institution. Therefore, according to Guattari, bureaucracies are "organless bodies."

Although policy development and implementation are certainly refined by bureaucratization, various specious procedures are followed as part of developing organizations in this way. First, primacy is given to a very restrictive mode of conceptualizing knowledge: only "subjectless" or empirical information is considered to have significant utility.[15] Second, because this sort of information is presumed to be objective, the implementation or application of this knowledge proceeds in a routine manner. And third, usually those who are highly specialized and who glorify the benefits of science are thought to be the most competent planners and managers. In general, bureaucracies become inefficient because irrelevant knowledge is used to justify decisions, the implementation of information is socially insensitive, and because technical experts are invited to establish priorities and to guide the formation of policies. Bureaucracies operate as if the social world is comprised of "ideal persons."[16] What Foucault means by this is that an esoteric image of society surreptitiously supports bureaucracies, and that the purpose of these organizations is to operate according to equally abstract standards. Consequently, in a manner of speaking, the needs of citizens are created by the bureaucrat, for bureaucratic rules are treated as if they reflect the most advanced state of human development. The "People-as-One" is the phrase used by Lefort to describe the uninformed view bureaucrats have of social life.[17] Hence bureaucracies are inhumane, or insensitive to extenuating circumstances.

Postmodernists contend that a bureaucratic rendition of society conceals its human core. Life, simply put, is reified under a bureaucracy, for desire is sublimated into particular categories of reason and action. Merely reducing the size of organizations or creating "appropriate technologies," à la Schumacher, is insufficient to remedy this condition. Instead, institutions must be grounded in praxis and made socially responsible. In this way, "enabling" organizations are possible, those that assist persons to fulfill their ambitions, rather than ones that simply perpetuate the existence of certain rules. Consistent with the postmodern theme of self-management, a variety of institutions have emerged recently that respect human enthusiasm. At this juncture, it must be remembered that postmodern institutions operate "without rules in order to formulate rules of what *will have been done*."[18] Rules, in other words, have utility for solving social problems, and nothing more. As a result, non-bureaucratic organizations reflect instead of stifle human needs. Social processes are thus subordinated to the "power of united individuals," writes Stojanović.[19] When this is the case, organizations are not anathema to social life. Organizations "with organs" are spawned.

COMMUNITY-BASED MENTAL HEALTH

The history of mental illness, according to Foucalt, has a Cartesian bias.[20] As a result, madness has been transformed into an object, divorced from interpretation. Madness, in other words, is said to have natural causes that can be isolated and studied. Thomas Szasz, for example, claims that this position fosters what he calls the "myth of mental illness."[21] Mental illness comes to be viewed as a thing or fact to be attacked.

Typically, the "medical model" has been used to analyze mental illness. This means that madness is treated as a disease that infects and debilitates the mind. Specifically, illness is conceptualized and diagnosed as if it were a physiological problem. Medical personnel are assigned primary responsibility for identifying and treating madness. And finally, therapy consists overwhelmingly of altering psychic processes, or controlling outbursts that are believed to have a biological basis. Ivan Illich, for example, refers to this approach to therapy as the "medicalization" of a social issue.[22]

Realists believe that through the efforts of trained scientists the causes of madness can be identified, examined, and, if possible, eliminated. In the spirit of Cartesianism, because science is supposedly value-free, the facts related to the onset of this malady can be revealed. Nonetheless, this strategy for treating madness has proven to be quite myopic. Particularly disconcerting is that disease is imagined to attack and invade its host; human biology is the focus of attention, and pathological behavior is believed to be indicative of a malfunctioning and, most likely, moribund mind. Two aspects of this approach are important to note. First, the social context of health and illness is ignored. All that is emphasized is the analysis of natural events, which are assumed to be out of balance. Questions related to the social meaning of insanity are deemed irrelevant. And second, because this illness signals a psycho-physiological breakdown, madness is equated with a deficiency or an absence of rationality. Mental illness, therefore, supposedly needs to be controlled, rather than understood.

Persons who are mad have been considered human oddities, and thus have been probed, included in bizarre experiments, and even tortured. The rationale for these hideous rituals is that if the body can be rendered uninhabitable, a person's psychic functions will return to normal and madness will subside. The demons within a person must be exorcised. In more modern terms, through the use of surgery, electroshock, or drugs, physiological harmony may be restored. Of course, if these approaches are unsuccessful, confinement is always possible. After all, madness must be kept from spreading throughout the remainder of society, which is believed to be rational.

At the core of the traditional view of insanity is the separation of unreason from reason.[23] It is assumed that persons are fundamentally normal, until they come into contact with the factors that cause them to act irrationally. And once difference is equated with madness, a science of madness is certainly justified. According to Foucault, the science of psychiatry made discourse on abnormality possible.[24] Value-free judgments could be made without recriminations by patients; patients could be assessed without political implications. Likewise, because society is considered rational, at no time is it suspected to be a source of madness. Madness was a value-free determination.

Toward the end of the 1950s, a variety of persons began to question the efficacy of the medical model of mental illness.[25] The very idea of the "mental hospital" was called into question. Psychosurgery was criticized as inhumane, while drug therapy became known as a "psychological straitjacket." Yet patients were tranquilized through the use of Thorazine, symptoms were masked, hospital wards were transformed into warehouses, and the adoption of creative and innovative therapies was curtailed. Therapy became associated with receiving injections of this drug or the prescription of other "meds" (medicine). Many critics even began to argue that state hospitals were the worst places to refer a client. Research illustrated that persons actually develop "institutional neurosis" if they are confined on a psychiatric ward for a substantial period.[26] In other words, clients adapted so successfully to hospital life that they could not function outside of this institution.

The Community Mental Health Centers Act was enacted in late 1963, in response to the criticism mounting against the state hospital system in the United States. This piece of legislation, in fact, was referred to by President Kennedy as a "bold new approach" to dealing with mental illness. The thrust of this bill was to reduce dramatically the number of clients incarcerated in residential facilities. Patients were now to be treated in a more socially respectable manner. Stated simply, clients were to be involved in their treatment. Issues such as sanity, madness, and successful rehabilitation were to be understood to have social, and not merely medical, significance.

Calls for reform are not new. Pinel for instance, argued during the latter part of the eighteenth century that custodial care has little rehabilitative value. At different times during the next one hundred years Dix and Beers would make the same point. The key shortcoming of these writers is that they were not theoretically sophisticated. In fact, many early reformers were proponents of the medical model, because they were influenced by the

Enlightenment. Undoubtedly science is better than demonology or alchemy, yet, as postmodernists point out, madness is understood solely in terms of the methods available to modern psychologists and psychiatrists. Insanity, in other words, is still described with respect to the evolution of reason. Madness is "crushed beneath psychiatry," according to Derrida, and prevented from speaking for itself.[27] This activity constitutes "symbolic violence," according to Pierre Bourdieu, because the language of psychiatry is allowed to eviscerate all other ways of speaking.[28] Hence what has been studied traditionally is madness as it has been construed by professionals, armed with their diagnostic nomenclature and apothecaries full of drugs. Due to their reliance on dualism, the experiential basis of madness has not usually been the focus of concern, at least until the advent of anti-psychiatry.

Anti-psychiatry has a postmodern orientation because madness is understood to occur within language. If this is the case, the diagnostic questions that are asked should not pertain to normalcy, but the actual behavior exhibited by persons. By making this distinction, Ludwig Binswanger is suggesting that a priori definitions of madness are inappropriate.[29] The reason for this conclusion is apparent, according to Shoshana Felman, because to "speak about madness is to speak about the differences between languages."[30] Therefore, while paraphrasing Felman, madness in one language may be sanity in another. While agreeing with Mallarmé, postmodernists contend that the mad simply transgress prohibitions. Derrida summarizes this outlook nicely when he writes: "madness is therefore, in every sense of the word, only one *case* of thought (*within* thought)."[31] As opposed to an agent that attacks reason and induces delirium, madness is merely a modality of speech. In more social terms, madness should be considered indicative of a response to events that violates how symbols are typically used. According to postmodernists, this portrayal of madness is certainly justified, because no phenomenon, even those which appear to be irrational, can be expelled from language. When persons are defined linguistically, or "decentered," there should be no discussion of inherent tendencies to become mad. Instead the interpersonal character of pathology should be of paramount importance. Language use, rather than disposition, supplies the rationale for behavior, including madness. When definitions about reality are transgressed, according to postmodernists, madness occurs.

With madness lodged within language, the usual "monologue of Reason about madness" is no longer sufficient to sustain a diagnosis.[32] Reason does not have the autonomy necessary to carry on this charade. Accordingly, the language game indicative of madness must be deciphered, if those who are mad are to be effectively treated. Clinicians must no longer be perpetrators of symbolic violence, as a result of concealing the contextual significance of their clients' actions. Therefore, according to Foucault, the social ideology of the medical profession should not be allowed to delimit the parameters of madness.[33] Contrary to using solely medical criteria, reference should be made to a community's standards, for example, when attempting to distinguish madness from sanity. "Citizen participation," in other words, is central to postmodern psychiatry. Social competence, therefore, should not be determined by medical professionals alone. Further, treatment should be administered within communities, so patients are able to continue to live with their friends and neighbors. Under the Community Mental Health Centers Act, persons are supposed to be cared for in the "least restrictive environment," rather than within institutional settings. Consistent with Szasz's declaration that mental illness is "manufactured," madness should be viewed as an issue related to interaction, as opposed to a medical problem.

Re-establishing a dialogue between patients and the residents of their communities is, accordingly, the purpose of treatment. This does not mean that conformity is stressed, whereby the mad learn to adjust to collective ideas about normalcy. Institutions other than state hospitals, therefore, had to be developed, for their purpose was to promote social control rather than interactional competence. Accordingly, the therapeutic community was created to foster rapprochement between those who are mad and those who are sane. As opposed to hospitals, in a therapeutic community patients do not live in a rigidly controlled setting, are not governed by a hierarchy of authority, and are not treated primarily by specialists. According to Maxwell Jones, the originator of the therapeutic community, a client's entire milieu should promote constructive behavior.[34] Otherwise the type of bureaucratic "total institution" described by Goffman begins to exist, whereby clients are confined, manipulated, and thus inadvertently encouraged to avoid contact with their peers and therapists.[35] As a result of this mistreatment, clients are cajoled into withdrawal, thereby further undermining their social competence. The gap that is assumed to be present between sanity and insanity is only widened. According to theories of community-based treatment, an open space rather than a totalized institution is where treatment should be undertaken.

Most different about therapeutic communities is that clients are given the responsibility to operate these facilities. If the floors are to be cleaned, the food purchased, and the bills paid, clients must complete these and other tasks. Self-control and responsibility are stressed, rather than the ritualization of behavior. As clients interact with their fellow patients, administrators, and other personnel, interactional competence is improved on the part of all parties. Patients and so-called normal persons learn to accommodate one another, instead of engaging in a discourse designed to degrade the mad.[36] Rather than having their interpretation of reality dismissed as unimportant, clients are challenged to make decisions about the type of life style they desire. The aim of a therapeutic community, in short, is to illustrate that madness transpires between persons and can only be remedied through constructive dialogue. Because madness is not simply a biological problem, medical or similar technical solutions are de-emphasized. Likewise, repressive practices are believed to be inappropriate for "restoring adequate social functioning."[37] Unlike a bureaucracy, a therapeutic community does not restrict communication. The purpose of this organization is to give clients some control over their lives.

Readers should not assume that community mental health programs, along with their European counterparts, are not without faults. Medication is still often used, staff persons are underskilled, and clients' civil liberties are sometimes abridged.[38] Nonetheless, the symbolism associated with the community mental health movement is important. Strongly suggested is that consumers should be allowed to play a significant role in their treatment. Empowering clients in this way is believed to be productive in the long run, for self-control and critical reflection have desirable political implications in a democratic society.

Advocates of community mental health impugn the symbolism usually associated with madness. They reject the idea that mental illness represents a "break with reality," and thus is incomprehensible. And because reality is not violated by those who are mad, confinement is not believed to lead to their rehabilitation. Anti-psychiatrists contend that madness is indicative of communicative inadequacy. Persons use symbols differently to such an extent that discourse between them ruptures. Therefore, in order to remedy this condition, interpersonal sensitivity must be developed on the part of both therapists and clients, so that their respective ranges of interpersonal competence are increased. In this way, behaviors that were once viewed as irrational can be understood. Community-based agencies stress the acquisition of communicative competence, rather than conformity to idealized norms. For this reason, subsequent to 1963, treatment and personal freedom are not supposed to come into conflict.

WORKPLACE DEMOCRATIZATION

Until recently, formalizing the organization of work was thought to be a good management practice. "Job design," accordingly, consisted of establishing a rigid division of labor.[39] For example, Taylor compared the workplace to a machine, and imagined workers to constitute a "train of gear wheels." While relying on the work of Pareto, theorists associated with the Human Relations School believed that only a managerial élite could operate successfully a factory. In the 1950s, advocates of cybernetics argued that the scientific knowledge possessed by managers is most effective for regulating the work process. And with the onset of the Corporate Society during this period, management specialists proliferated at an unprecedented rate. Even throughout the 1960s and 1970s, when so-called humanism was de rigueur, the distinction was maintained between jobs appropriate for managers and those for rank and file workers.

In short, a clear distinction has traditionally been made between managers and workers. The rationale for this démarche is quite simple: the owners of factories want to control their employees.[40] With knowledge centrally located and disseminated along channels manipulated by managers, workers can be supervised without much difficulty. Furthermore, managers are assumed to be scientific, while workers are thought to be unable to generalize beyond their individual experience. Workers are at a disadvantage because they cannot comprehend the intricacies of the workplace, and thus are dependent on managers for direction. At best, workers are believed to benefit from technical training, and are merely socialized to follow instructions. Given the comprehensive view of the workplace possessed by managers, they are in the most favorable position to dictate the pace and rate of production.

Many contemporary critics contend that this fragmentation of the labor process has reached a point of diminishing returns.[41] Because workers are informed only about their respective roles in the division of labor, they tend to lose sight of the final product. Therefore, workers become bored, because they are relegated to performing mundane tasks in a mechanistic manner. Further, due to their narrow focus, workers' skills begin to atrophy. Thorstein Veblen called this reduction in ability "trained incapacity." How can increased productivity be expected from this sort of workplace? At one time, managers thought that productivity would be unlimited, if a worker's routine could be restricted to a few simple movements. The labor power of unskilled workers could be utilized very effectively, thus rendering expensive craftsmen obsolete. All that would be needed are robots who asked for minimum wages. With the cost of labor depressed and technicians regulating the flow of work, no wonder managers were optimistic that productivity could reach new levels. Nonetheless, there was a major flaw in this formula—workers are not machines. Cost-benefit analysis, in short, does not address the essential elements of human motivation.

The discovery that workers do not respond automatically to material incentives, such as improved working conditions and wages, is not new. Since the 1920s and the Hawthorne experiments, the human side of work has been acknowledged as important.[42] It has been shown that workers want to exert control over the labor process and expand their skills and responsibilities. Nonetheless, in the past managers have responded to these requests in a manner that enabled them to adjust workers effectively to the standard division of labor. In order to calm their anger, line employees were given palliatives, such as allowing them to attend various management meetings and thus feel important. Only minimal concessions were ever made, however, toward altering the roles occupied traditionally by these workers. They were simply supplied with increasingly sophisticated measures to assist them to cope with the demands issued by managers. Yet postmodernists charge that this tactic is insufficient to improve the morale, and thus the productivity, of workers.

In order to facilitate cooperation between managers and workers, some writers contend that a contractual relationship should be established between these two groups. This maneuver implies that through negotiation, workers will be able to improve their position at the workplace. Critics of this approach agree that unless the basic social relationships present in the workplace are altered, management will determine the terms of any contract. Without reconceptualizing the workplace, why should workers believe they will ever have the ability to challenge those who have power? Conventional social imagery, after all, conveys the idea that workers have limited understanding and abilities. Work must be regulated by something more than a contract, claim postmodernists, before the traditional bureaucracy will be undermined.

Postmodernists argue that there is no longer any justification for separating formal from substantive reason. Using structures is thus inappropriate for conceptualizing the workplace. Accordingly, a pattern of work organized around traditional roles can certainly be called into question. For subsequent to the linguistic epistemology advanced by postmodernists, every type of order must emerge from experience. The so-called basic nature of a workplace is, therefore, indeterminate. A variety of Marxists, who share with postmodernists a distaste for metanarratives, declare that organizations should be based on praxis. Humane organizations, at least, are planned in this manner. Instead of the metadiscourse, or reified communication, inherent to bureaucracies, a workplace should be established in terms of direct dialogue among workers. Otherwise, the actualization of workers will be ancillary to structural imperatives. Job design, accordingly, will not respect the abilities and desires of employees. As a result, workers will become alienated from their work and themselves, as their existence is systematically objectified.

Marxists associated with the Arguments Group in France, and the Praxis Group in Yugoslavia, for example, claim that dismantling bureaucracy at the workplace is essential, if a society is to be democratic and productive.[43]

Their primary adversary is Stalin and the bureaucratic apparatus he installed. Even prominent Communist Party officials have commented recently that Stalin's attempt to bureaucratize Soviet society was both economically and politically disastrous. These newer Marxists question the wisdom of his collectivization policies, along with the accompanying etatism. Stalin's form of ontological realism is now viewed as repressive, as well as illegitimate; creative human action should mediate knowledge.[44] Consistent with postmodernism, the natural laws assumed to underpin a strict or bureaucratic division of labor are not given any credence. The reason for this is that natural laws are believed to be historical, or a result of social convention.

Like Lyotard, these Marxists are advocates of "self-management." To them this means that the needs of producers dictate the pace and flow of work, rather than the production targets outlined by bureaucrats. Because the value of workers is elevated in importance, key aspects of bureaucracy are undermined. First, scientific knowledge loses some of its appeal. Science is thought to be merely one source of information among others. Second, the seignorial status accorded technocrats is reduced, for their skills are now understood to have limited utility. And third, the structural barriers that have been used traditionally to sequester managers from workers are shown to be fatuous. As a result, the social imagery that is vital to maintaining a bureaucracy collapses. The stage is thus set for workers to shape their own destiny, simply because they need not be intimidated by organizations.

Self-management represents significantly more than job rotation, as defined by humanistic managers such as Maslow or Herzberg, whereby workers and managers exchange positions temporarily in an organization. Much more important, the symbolism associated traditionally with the workplace is altered. Specifically, to use Marxist terminology employed by Lyotard, "use value" determines relationships at the workplace, as opposed to "exchange value."[45] This means that situational considerations are paramount when organizing a work group. For example, leaders are permitted to emerge spontaneously, in terms of the skills that are needed to complete a particular task. While patterns of authority may be established, the resulting roles do not exist *sui generis*. Interpretive (situationally relevant) factors are crucial in specifying the worth of work, the method of production, and the style of association among workers. Self-management means production is guided by the aesthetic, environmental, and political values that producers believe are vital. Economic considerations are thus no longer paramount.

According to Svetozar Stojanović, a self-managed organization is an "integral" social system, whereby all its parts operate "as a whole."[46] Every segment of a workplace contributes to the production process. Most important, all plans emerge from this collaborative effort; they are not influenced by so-called economic realities, which these producers do not recognize as salient. Both horizontally and vertically, the organization is decentralized. In actual practice, workers own factories, decisions are made by employee councils, job expansion and education are extensive, and knowledge about technical and theoretical concerns flows freely throughout a workplace. Even when specialists are authorized to direct a particular project, these individuals are accountable to the collective. Lyotard refers to these as "flat" organizations, for they are integrated at the level of experience, rather than by a reality *sui generis*. Stated differently, these organizations are integrated with respect to praxis.[47] Work and the workplace are not differentiated.

Substantiating self-management is the simple notion that persons are not ensnared within an economic system. Self-management, according to Branko Horvat, is a direct association of producers, who determine economic reality.[48] Economic forces, in other words, are not autonomous and do not affect willy-nilly the course of history. The economy consists, instead, of nothing more than persons generating the goods and services necessary to meet their needs. Mihailo Marković makes a cogent observation when he states that self-management is "self-determination."[49] Self-management is not simply management, but, something much more significant, a philosophy that democratizes social reality. Workers serve as the basis of a workplace, rather than merely participants in the operation of this organization. In short, self-management is the "self-grounding of freedom."[50]

COMMUNITY JUSTICE

Like many other facets of social life, law has become unfaithful to the citizenry. Practically every day in the media someone charges that the judicial system is faltering and laws are unjust. In fact, recent debates in the United States Congress suggest that the enforcement of law depends on the members of the Supreme Court.[51] Citizens react to this debacle by worrying that their legal system is falling into the hands of charlatans. A more important point, however, is regularly overlooked. That is, the judiciary has become a closed system, with lawyers and other specialists searching for the "original intent" of statutes to rationalize how these laws are applied. Seldom is the social world consulted to determine whether or not laws are relevant. In fact, laws may be unjust simply because the judicial system has become abstract. An obsession with legal precedents has all but obscured the issue of social relevance. Postmodernists suggest that persons must live with their neighbors, rather than a set of legal codes.

A discipline referred to as critical legal studies has become an important outgrowth of postmodernism. Because law is understood to be mediated by interpretation, the only valid basis for legal standards is the community. As Barthes might say, this is not a community of origin but practice. In other words, the legal community is manufactured through collective action. The members of a legal community share a future that is formulated and implemented through the choices that they make to adhere to a particular code of decorum. Hence courts must operate in terms of precedents that reflect human concerns instead of procedural mandates. A "correct" verdict is socially informed. Law is thus flexible and tentatively legitimate.

Postmodernists contend that the legal system has become bureaucratized. Precedents and legal technicalities have become the focus of attention. The practice of law, accordingly, is exceedingly formalistic. Concern is focused on the letter of the law and not on the opinions citizens have about their legal system. Methods of law enforcement are deduced from social axioms, while extenuating circumstances are overlooked. In general, the centerpiece of the judicial system has become the application of exceedingly esoteric law.

Only after an introduction to the history of law can the attack levelled by postmodernists be appreciated.[52] As with order in general, law has been viewed as a non-contingent source of justice. In ancient Rome, law was thought to be based on *ratio*. Medieval philosophers popularized natural law, along with the idea that legal principles are legitimized by God. Following the medieval period, a unique combination of positivism and natural law was proposed by Austin, Bentham, and the members of the Italian School. And the modern world, according to Weber, is governed by "rational-legal authority."[53] In other words, laws are believed to be valid if they are codified, or formalized, and if they appear to be impersonal. Because legal decisions adhere to technical guidelines, justice is allegedly depoliticized.

Gradually removing laws from situational exigencies was assumed to ensure that they would be applied fairly. This was the point made by Foucault in his book, *Discipline and Punish*. Indeed, Talcott Parsons argued that only if laws are treated as ahistorical, can advanced industrial societies be expected to survive.[54] The fragmentation indigenous to these societies cannot be overcome without the assistance of objective legal standards. Laws, in point of fact, contribute significantly to the "latent pattern maintenance" that is vital to averting anarchy. Yet as a society becomes more differentiated, laws must be couched at increasing levels of abstraction. In this way, the interests of society are protected, rather than simply the claims made by certain persons. Ostensibly, laws that are judged to be advantageous to a particular economic class or ethnic group are unjust. Pretending that laws are value-free, however, is not bereft of adverse consequences. Particularly problematic, laws have become oriented toward what Chaim Perelman calls a "universal audience."[55]

As laws are removed systematically from local control, the assumption is made that all citizens conduct their affairs according to similar principles of logic and reason. Society, therefore, becomes a "universal audience," comprised of individuals who are similarly informed about the rules of order and the politics of enforcement. Discretion or the exercise of power, furthermore, is not believed to affect the judicial system, because interpretation has nothing to do with how the law is implemented. The judicial system, in a manner of speaking, constitutes a utopia. Many citizens find this conception of law to be ineffective. Due to this rarefied image of legal order, the actual practice of law may begin to offend individuals. Justice may become elusive: once laws become insensitive to community issues, law enforcement begins to violate the culture in neighborhoods and legal experts are given primary access to the judiciary. Centralizing law in this way may result in verdicts that are legally exact, but socially disruptive. Law becomes one of the many "machines" described by Deleuze and Guattari in their book, *Anti-Oedipus*.[56] Accordingly, the social issues related to justice are ignored. For this reason, postmodernists suggest that justice is possible only when legal decisions are mediated by the litigants involved.

In terms of theory, postmodernists require that law be reconceptualized. Luhmann exemplifies this shift when he writes that laws should be envisioned to be nothing more than "contingency formulae."[57] Legal sanctions, accordingly, reduce societal complexity to a manageable level, so that persons can interact effortlessly. Laws, in other words, outline provisional rules for discourse. Rather than binding citizens together, as Parsons believes, laws embody the assumptions individuals make that enable them to interact in concert. Any abridgement of these precepts is a breach of trust. Additionally, legal mandates that disregard the fragile, interpretive nature of the social bond will not necessarily reunite persons. The reason for this is quite simple. An abstract interpretation of law is not value-free, but is likely to represent sentiments that a community may resent. Thus persons may become polarized as a result of a verdict, because one group appears to be favored over another. Such divisiveness may encourage future decisions to be made along political lines, and thus law may exacerbate social conflict.

A socially responsible legal system is based on a simple idea: Nothing should be interjected into the nexus of self and other that is not already present. To avoid causing aggression between claimants, Foucault recommends trying "popular justice."[58] Justice is popular when the legal system reflects the commitments that bind a group together. The exercise of law, accordingly, must reconcile claims, rather than force citizens to comply with abstract and, many times, irrelevant rules. Actually, law enforcement will not promote social solidarity until the criminal justice system is socially sensitive. Advocates of popular justice have called attention to the benefits of community justice centers, block watch programs, and police-citizen patrols.[59] In each case, the point is to create a liaison between citizens and police officials. The belief is that if these two groups can be encouraged to work together, each other's needs will be better understood. In general, law must become the means whereby persons govern themselves, claim postmodernists, or law will be oppressive.

Community justice centers, for example, are agencies that are used to settle disputes between neighbors. The actual buildings used to house these courts are located within the communities which they serve, and thus are easily accessible. Further, the arbitrators are neighborhood members, rather than legal experts. The purpose of utilizing these persons is to insure that verdicts are reasonable rather than rational, recalling Perelman's distinction. Decisions, simply put, are made with respect to local rules of social decorum, the impact they may have on the quality of life in a community, and the political climate.[60] The proceedings are purged of bureaucratic impediments, as persons simply tell their stories to a jury of their peers. Some critics argue that community justice verges on vigilantism. This charge is untrue, for justice is not dispensed under the cloak of darkness or by a few thugs. All courtrooms are open to the public, while every issue is subject to debate. Persons may be "taking justice into their own hands," yet this is always the case, even when traditional law enforcement is undertaken. Are not the police supposed to represent communities? The significance of community justice is that the "inner morality" of law, as Lon Fuller calls it, guides the adjudication process.[61] Rather than formalized statutes, community sentiment is given a prominent place in the legal system.

Community justice, however, does not occur in a vacuum. Introduced simultaneously are democratic principles, such as tolerance for unpopular views. In fact, this approach to justice is supported by a belief in democracy, which is further developed by citizens participating directly in the formulation and enforcement of laws. Law is not an object of adoration, but something that must solve problems effectively. Social harmony is not guaranteed by abstract laws, since only persons who are able to discuss their differences can bring about this end. Therefore, law should facilitate dialogue, according to postmodernists. Indeed, Luhmann contends that relevant laws increase social cohesiveness.[62]

In a sense, maybe Eagleton is correct when he states that postmodernists are advocates of Justice. The early Greeks believed that Justice (*dikē*) was an all-encompassing steering mechanism, which served to unite the various component parts of the cosmos. Law, in other words, was cosmological. Postmodernists treat this view as fatuous, for any metaphysical factor such as Justice is believed to be dubious. As with order, postmodernists charge that justice occurs between persons. Justice is the result of persons respecting one another, so that uninhibited discourse between them is possible. Community justice centers are created to foster this sort of group cohesion. Persons reconcile their differences while trying to take into account each other's values, beliefs, and experiences. In this way, laws are enacted within a framework of social relevance. Litigants react to one another, rather than legal mandates. Law, therefore, integrates persons.

THE DEATH OF GOD AND RELIGION

Nietzsche's announcement that "God is dead" is the hallmark of postmodern religion.[63] However, emphasis has been placed traditionally on the vertical dimension of religion, otherwise known as the transcendent domain occupied by God. Durkheim, for example, calls this the "sacred," while Rudolf Otto favors the term "holy."[64] Their concern is that God should be known as an ultimate reality, which gives meaning and direction to history. Furthermore, morality receives its raison d' être from this divine source. With God presumed to be infinite and separated from daily life, an omniscient judge of behavior is available. Yet Nietzsche remarks that this God is defunct, or devoid of merit. Does this claim plunge society into nihilism, as critics of Nietzsche argue? For without God, persons would be on their own and have to decide their fate.

Why is God dead? God's heavenly home is undermined, because according to Nietzsche values sustain reality. Tarnished by values, the power of God is appreciably reduced. If the Divine does not transcend the world, then the sacred must be articulated within experience. In postmodern terms, God can no longer retain the status of a metanarrative. Therefore, the so-called theological problem is suddenly a social or historical issue. Although nihilism does not result automatically from God becoming a value base, after the demise of the traditionally conceived view of the sacred, social control must be self-imposed. That is, if God is dead, all things are possible. Surely, at minimum, traditional religion must be conceptualized anew. Theological questions cannot be directed to or resolved by an infinite, ineffable Being. Nietzsche calls for the end of this sort of metaphysics.[65]

This "end of metaphysics" is revealed in Nietzsche's notion of the "eternal return." Because values sustain all phenomena, everything returns to the same origin. Rather than a speculative referent, however, this basis is simply another value. History does not begin or end; a value-free base of judgments is a chimera. History is merely a compilation of values. What this suggests is that history always returns to the human present. The symbolism of the circle is significant. Usually development is depicted to be a line, moving in a unidirectional manner. This implies that growth has a preordained end, which is autonomous. When imagined as a circle, on the other hand, movement is thought to be frivolous. Nietzsche's point is that nothing justifies growth, but growth itself. The human value of development is thus the only source of legitimacy for change. Accordingly, history always returns to itself. Because the terminal point of values cannot be reached, no one can leap outside of the circle proposed by Nietzsche.

Following the devaluation of God, all that is left is the earth. Only the so-called horizontal dimension of religion, therefore, can be given serious consideration. Is the denouement of this change of outlook nihilism? Not necessarily, although religion must be viewed as a human invention intended to solve social problems. In this vein, Buber writes that religious enthusiasm is a collective phenomenon that occurs within the nexus of human relationships, rather than an experience that catapults persons outside of their daily existence, as is suggested by Durkheim.[66] Confining religion to worldly affairs, however, is not all bad, for the traditional image of God tends to dwarf humans—history is the product of a divine plan. Critics of Nietzsche and postmodern religion are accurate in one respect. Nietzsche's "dancing god," who is wordly, cannot offer solace to persons or legitimize their existence. All religion provides is an image of society that citizens can inaugurate, if they have the courage.

Associating religion with everyday affairs does not necessarily culminate in chaos. Max Horkheimer, for example, offers a postmodern view when he argues that a grounded version of religion represents a desire for justice, in the midst of a world that seems to be on the brink of barbarism.[67] Religion is a call for the establishment of a community, where virtues such as peace, love, and charity prevail. Many Death of God theologians go so far as to say that religion is liberation politics, in that a truly religious person should not tolerate social injustice. Hope is offered to the oppressed, while their oppressors are chastised. Theodor Adorno suggests that through religion persons are given an opportunity to transcend their limitations, but not their responsibility to their fellow citizens.[68] Salvation, accordingly, is not personal but social. In a sense, persons are able to extricate themselves from a life of alienation, thereby restoring their integrity. Religion interjects inspiration into a world that is often rife with hate and despair. Yet, according to postmodernists, traditional churches are not conveying this message of hope.

The appeals made for love, charity, and justice by postmodern religions are not inspired by an ultimate godhead. If these ideals are to have any meaning, their significance must be drawn from intersubjectivity. In view of Nietzsche's claims and the epistemology proposed by postmodernists, only an interpersonal cosmology can be assumed to exist. The confluence of the "I" and the "other" is reality, and thus religious values can be manifested only within this domain. Love and hate, for example, must be directed toward the "other," rather than an eternal being. And because the "I" and "other" are inextricably linked, how can an impersonal morality be justified? Postmodernists recognize, therefore, that religion is interpersonal. As Buber says, the embodiment of religion is the "Eternal Thou"—the realization that God exists at the juncture of person and world.[69]

Yet, as Thomas O'Dea illustrates, most churches are currently bureaucracies.[70] The priestly role of religion is given primacy over the prophetic. Church leaders are more concerned with increasing the number of their parishioners and insuring a correct reading of the Bible, than with addressing relevant economic and political issues. Worldly proposals, in short, are eschewed. For example, concern for the poor has vanished, while corporate religions flourish. Gone is the social gospel, along with the attendant critique of society. Religion has become a private affair, as individuals shop around for the most palatable scriptures, rituals, and services. In point of fact, Jeffrey K. Hadden documents that mainstream congregations expect their religious practices to be routine—that is, uninspired—and church officials predictable.[71] The charisma and activism of the founders of these churches are clearly not appreciated. Still, many persons of all ages find this style of religion to be stifling and search elsewhere for inspiration. This exodus from mainstream churches has prompted Thomas Luckmann to state that an "invisible," or non-bureaucratic, religion has begun to evolve.[72]

Harvey Cox writes that this postmodern religion is emerging from the "bottom and edges" of conventional churches.[73] This opposition has been manifested in the form of "base communities." These groups are appearing mostly in Latin America, although they are not restricted to that area. Base communities meet in the homes of their members. Sometimes priests and other official ministers are present, yet their input is not viewed as crucial. The Bible is read regularly and discussed in conjunction with pertinent political and economic news. These communities are designed to dissolve the traditional church hierarchy, which is believed to be conservative and repressive. Moreover, the Bible is treated as a foundation for action, aimed at correcting social injustice. Practice and moral philosophy are thus joined. For these reasons, some theologians declare that these base organizations pose a serious challenge to established churches, similar to the Reformation. Religion is not sequestered from the world, but unleashed as a moral force. Rather than being simply an organization, a church is transformed into a community that exemplifies universal solidarity.

Postmodern religion recognizes Rudolf Bultmann's contention that religious proposals originate from the *Fragestellung*, or, literally, the point from which a question about the meaning of existence is asked. Religious institutions that do not operate around this vital point are criticized as ir-relevant. In the postmodern view, in other words, a religion must be respon-sive to the social concerns that are within the purview of this institution. A religion should not be self-consumed, as is the case with a bureaucracy. Consistent with writers such as Metz and Moltmann, religion must provide the conscience for social policies.[74] Religion must not only presuppose, but solidify the social bond.

CONCLUSION

Postmodernists introduce revolutionary social imagery, as a result of call-ing for the adoption of non-hierarchical organizations.[75] Usually, however, this demand is met with skepticism, for a bureaucracy is supposed to be the harbinger of reason and order. Left to their own devices, the belief is that persons will surely create turmoil. Yet, as noted by postmodernists, the dualism that justifies externalizing control in this manner has lost its legitimacy. According to Sartre, this means that persons are "condemned to be free," even if they choose to bury themselves under bureaucratic regula-tions.[76] The bureaucrat's acquiescence to rules and authority, accordingly, does not relieve persons of their radical freedom. Neither are organizations exempt from their social responsibility. Postmodernism requires that per-sons understand that organizations do not absolve them of their duty to create rules of order.

The institutions described in this chapter operate on a postmodern princi-ple: order is possible without control. Because a person has no other alter-native but to invent rules and treat them as if they are necessary, no institu-tion can issue mandates. This view of organizations requires courage on the part of individuals, who must recognize that their needs are simultaneously relevant and irrelevant. Nothing, in other words, legitimizes any particular institutional arrangement. Persons must be able to tolerate ambiguity, while modifying their organizations to meet the expectations presupposed by new discursive practices. In fact, organizational change is nothing more than one modality of discourse being eclipsed by another.

As noted above, however, the intent of a bureaucracy is to enforce con-trol. Postmodern organizations have a different purpose, for the dualism implied by control is unjustifiable. Simply put, a postmodern institution empowers individuals. A workplace, for example, is merely a means to fur-ther the autonomy of workers. In fact, as preliminary research suggests, en-trepreneurship will probably not flourish until workers and managers are not inhibited by the organizations which they create.[77] Organizations such as the workplace should not be viewed as anything more than a collective mode of wish fulfillment. As a reminder of the past, institutions provide merely a concise summary of previous commitments. Instead of administering behavior, these organizations represent a decision not to question a particular rendition of discourse. And once decisions lose their relevance, making new ones cannot be avoided. Hence even conformity is non-conformity, and sublimation is desublimation, for social adjustment is nothing more than persons adhering to their own demands. Is self-control the same as conformity? Postmodernists answer No.

Obviously, a postmodern understanding of society has significant cultural and political repercussions. In repressive societies, organizations such as the workplace are used to "inferiorize" their inhabitants.[78] With organizations representing reason, an almost inviolable source is available to suppress dissent, which is identified as irrational. Such intimidation is no longer effective, claim postmodernists, simply because organizations are stripped of their oedipal, or authoritarian, stature.[79] Those who aspire to positions of power through manipulation cannot justify their desires by recourse to an unquestioned source of wisdom. All claims must stand naked, so to speak. Power, as postmodernists like to state, is thus "unmasked." Surely this finding is liberating. Yet this process of opening the world will undoubtedly incense those who want to determine the destiny of others.

NOTES

1. Max Weber, *Economy and Society*, vol. 2, pp. 956–990.

2. Michel Foucault, *The Birth of the Clinic* (New York: Vintage, 1975), pp. 22–37.

3. Karen A. Callaghan and John W. Murphy, "Changes in Technological Social Control: Theory and Implications for the Workplace," in *The Underside of Hightech*, pp. 15–28.

4. Henry A. Landesberger, *Hawthorne Revisited* (Ithaca, N.Y.: Cornell University Press, 1958); Paul Blumberg, *Industrial Democracy: The Sociology of Participation* (London: Constable, 1968).

5. George S. Odiorne, *Management by Objectives* (New York: Pitman, 1965); Stafford Beer, *Cybernetics and Management* (New York: Wiley, 1959); Kenneth E. Boulding, "General Systems Theory—The Skeleton of Science," *Management Science* (1956), pp. 197–208.

6. John W. Murphy, "Critical Theory and Social Organization," *Diogenes* 117 (Spring 1982), pp. 93–111.

7. John W. Murphy, "Organizational Issues in Worker Ownership," *American Journal of Economics and Sociology* 43.3 (1984), pp. 287–299.

8. Weber, *Economy and Society*, vol. 1, pp. 225–226.

9. Guattari, *Molecular Revolution*, p. 98.

10. Ibid., p. 77.

11. Weber, *Economy and Society*, vol. 2, pp. 809–815.

12. Lefort, *The Political Forms*, p. 220.

13. Ibid., p. 222.

14. Guattari, *Molecular Revolution*, p. 145.

15. Ibid., pp. 135–143.

16. Foucault, *The Birth of the Clinic*, p. 34.

17. Lefort, *The Political Forms*, p. 297.

18. Lyotard, *The Postmodern Condition*, p. 81.

19. Stojanović, *Between Ideals and Reality*, p. 118.

20. Michel Foucault, *Madness and Civilization* (New York: Random House, 1965), pp. 38–64.

21. Thomas Szasz, *The Myth of Mental Illness* (New York: Harper and Row, 1961).

22. Ivan Illich, *Limits to Medicine* (New York: Penguin Books, 1977), pp. 47–130.

23. Foucault, *Madness and Civilization*, p. 107.

24. Ibid., pp. 199–220.

25. Anthony Brandt, *Reality Police* (New York: William Morrow, 1975); Peter Sedgwick, *Psycho-Politics* (New York: Harper and Row, 1982).

26. David Ingleby, "Understanding 'Mental Illness'," in *Critical Psychiatry*, ed. David Ingleby (New York: Pantheon Books, 1980), pp. 23–71.

27. Derrida, *Writing and Difference*, p. 34.

28. John B. Thompson, *Studies in the Theory of Ideology* (Berkeley: University of California Press, 1984), pp. 42–72.

29. Erwin Straus, "Psychiatry and Philosophy," in Erwin Straus, Maurice Natanson, and Henri Ey, *Psychiatry and Philosophy* (New York: Springer Verlag, 1969), pp. 1–83.

30. Shoshana Felman, *Writing and Madness* (Ithaca, N.Y.: Cornell University Press, 1985), p. 19.

31. Derrida, *Writing and Difference*, p. 56.

32. Foucault, *Madness and Civilization*, p. xi.

33. Foucault, *The Birth of the Clinic*, pp. 107–123.

34. Maxwell Jones, *The Therapeutic Community* (New York: Basic Books, 1953).

35. Erving Goffman, *Asylums* (Chicago: Aldine, 1961).

36. Lisa Callahan and Dennis R. Longmire, "The Role of Reason in the Social Control of Mental Illness," in *The Underside of High-tech*, pp. 51–65.

37. Naomi Weisstein, "Psychology Constructs the Female," in *Radical Psychology*, ed. Phil Brown (New York: Harper and Row, 1973), pp. 390–420.

38. Sherry Turkle, "French Anti-Psychiatry," in *Critical Psychiatry*, pp. 150–183.

39. Bengt Abrahamsson, *Bureaucracy or Participation* (Beverly Hills: Sage, 1977), pp. 85–100.

40. Harry Braverman, *Labor and Monopoly Capital* (New York: Monthly Review Press, 1974), pp. 59–123.

41. Murphy, "Organizational Issues in Worker Ownership," pp. 287–299.

42. Rosabeth Moss Kanter, *The Change Masters* (New York: Simon and Schuster, 1983), pp. 69–126.

43. Edward Ball, "The Great Sideshow of the Situationist International," *Yale French Studies* 73 (1987), pp. 21–37; see also Poster, *Existential Marxism in Postwar*

France, pp. 361–398; John W. Murphy, "Yugoslav Self-Management and Social Ontology," *East European Quarterly* 20.1 (1986), pp. 75–89.

44. John W. Murphy, "Yugoslavian (Praxis) Marxism," in *Current Perspectives in Social Theory*, vol. 3, ed. Scott G. McNall (Greenwich, Conn.: JAI Press, 1982), pp. 189–205.

45. Lyotard, *The Postmodern Condition*, p. 5ff.

46. Stojanović, *Between Ideals and Reality*, p. 121.

47. Lyotard, *The Postmodern Condition*, pp. 17, 39.

48. Branko Horvat, *The Political Economy of Socialism* (Armonk, N.Y.: M. E. Sharp, 1982), pp. 235–367.

49. Mihailo Marković, *The Contemporary Marx* (Nottingham, England: Spokesman Books, 1974), p. 209; see also Petrović, *Marx in the Mid-Twentieth Century*, pp. 125–127.

50. Lyotard, *The Postmodern Condition*, p. 35.

51. This statement refers to the debate over the proposed appointment of Judge Robert Bork to the Supreme Court in October 1987.

52. John W. Murphy, "Social Ontology and Responsive Law," in *Practical Reasoning in Human Affairs*, ed. James L. Golden and Joseph J. Pilotta (Dordrecht, Netherlands: D. Reidel, 1986), pp. 341–355.

53. Weber, *Economy and Society*, vol. 1, pp. 217–223.

54. Parsons, *Societies: Evolutionary and Comparative*, p. 26.

55. Perelman, *The New Rhetoric and the Humanities*, pp. 48–50.

56. Deleuze and Guattari, *Anti-Oedipus*.

57. John W. Murphy, "Niklas Luhmann: His Contribution to the Sociology of Religion," *International Sociology* 9.2 (1987), pp. 205–213.

58. Foucault, *Power/Knowledge*, pp. 1–36.

59. Dan A. Lewis, "Design Problems in Public Policy Development: The Case of the Anti-crime Program," *Criminology* 17.2 (1979), pp. 172–183.

60. Perelman, *The New Rhetoric and the Humanities*, pp. 17–23; see also Philippe Nonet and Phillip Selznick, *Law and Society in Transition: Towards a Responsive Law* (New York: Harper and Row, 1978).

61. Lon Fuller, *The Morality of Law* (New Haven: Yale University Press, 1964).

62. John W. Murphy, "Niklas Luhmann and His View of the Social Function of Law," *Human Studies* 7 (1984), pp. 23–38.

63. John Robinson, *Honest to God* (London: SCM Press, 1963).

64. Emile Durkheim, *The Elementary Forms of the Religious Life* (London: George Allen & Unwin, 1926), pp. 36–38; Rudolf Otto, *The Idea of the Holy* (London: Oxford University Press, 1923).

65. Martin Heidegger, *Nietzsche*, vol. 1 (New York: Harper and Row, 1979), pp. 200–210.

66. Durkheim, *The Elementary Forms*, p. 38.

67. Siebert, *The Critical Theory of Religion*, p. 157.

68. Ibid., pp. 131–132.

69. Martin Buber, *I and Thou* (New York: Charles Scribner's Sons, 1970), p. 123.

70. Thomas O'Dea, *Sociology and the Study of Religion* (New York: Basic Books, 1970), pp. 240–255.

71. Jeffrey K. Hadden, *The Gathering Storm in the Churches* (Garden City, N.Y.: Doubleday, 1969).

72. Thomas Luckmann, *The Invisible Religion* (New York: Macmillan, 1967).

73. Cox, *Religion in the Secular City*, p. 175.

74. Johann B. Metz, *The Emergent Church* (New York: Crossroad, 1981); Jürgen Moltmann, *The Theology of Hope* (New York: Harper and Row, 1976).

75. John W. Murphy, "Manifestations of Postmodern Culture," *Philosophy Today* 30.4 (1986), pp. 346–353.

76. Jean-Paul Sartre, *Being and Nothingness* (New York: Philosophical Library, 1956), p. 439.

77. Kanter, *The Change Masters*, pp. 156–179.

78. Barry D. Adam, *The Survival of Domination* (New York: Elsevier, 1978), pp. 6ff.

79. Guattari, *Molecular Revolution*, p. 38.

6

Dimensions of Postmodern Culture

INTRODUCTION

The epistemology advanced by postmodernists clearly has cultural significance. Culture is no longer a system of prescriptions that antedates the appearance of action. Contrary to the claims made by Freud, for example, culture does not defend against sudden eruptions of the libido. Given the intimate association of language and reality, culture is not free from the influence of passion. The unstable, spontaneous aspects of social life are also thoroughly cultural. Accordingly, because culture and language arrive together, civilization is tenuous. Nothing prevents the onset of chaos but the promise of civility. As has been suggested, however, this way of viewing culture is relatively new.

Typically, culture is thought to provide security for a society. Stability is certainly worthwhile, yet how has this been understood to occur? The justification for stasis is important to postmodernists. A standard definition of culture contains elements such as "shared values," a "collective purpose," or a "common reality."[1] Naturally, beliefs, emotional sentiments, and commitments are vital to preserving these ideals. Most important about culture is that ideas are expected to be disseminated, inculcated, and thus shared. Supposedly underpining everyday affairs are principles that must be internalized, or humans will be no different from animals. Raymond Williams states that an "informing spirit" must begin to influence all persons, according to the traditional rendition of culture.[2] This description suggests the acceptance of Cartesian dualism. Apparently culture makes persons human, as a result of insuring that their behavior conforms to "regular patterns," or roles. Central to culture, in other words, is constraint. Herbert Marcuse refers to this as "Affirmative Culture," an "independent realm of value that is also considered superior to civilization."[3] Once persons channel their energy appropriately, they are identified as acculturated. Regularity and dependability are considered to be the hallmark of culture. Yet how are these virtues instilled?

Acquiring culture is a process whereby persons are refined and abandon their natural state.[4] Through enculturation, persons are instructed how to realize their potential and how to approximate an ideal. As part of their educational regimen, persons must begin to overcome the limitations imposed by daily living, if this exalted state is to be achieved. Maybe even more disconcerting, involvement in quotidian chores is thought to distract persons from reaching perfection or fulfillment. In Plato, for example, philosophy leads to insight, yet emerging from the shadows of illusion indigenous to everyday existence is not easy. A lifetime of dedication and sacrifice is imperative. The highest achievement for any person, according to Aristotle, is contemplation, which can culminate in pure perception, or *theoria*. During the medieval period, monasteries provided refuge for those who sought the solitude necessary to know the will of God. And finally, following the Enlightenment, a new style of asceticism became popular, commonly known as science. The point of this brief exposé is to illustrate that the price of perfection is very high, for persons must jettison their human foibles. Through meditation, the scientific method, and other mendicant practices the strength of the will is increased, thus allowing persons to improve their character.

In terms of modern sociology, Talcott Parsons describes how culture keeps society from deteriorating. He believes that any rational society must be based on universal symbols. These signs convey values that are necessary for any society to survive. "Shared values," as might be suspected, are required for the maintenance of order. The transmission of this information, however, can take place in a variety of ways, one of which is direct dialogue. Yet Parsons does not opt for this method. Instead, he prefers to portray culture to be an "independent system," divorced from psychology, biology, and other mundane aspects of life.[5] The contribution made by culture, therefore, is more valuable than personality, in terms of preserving social order. Actually, without the information supplied by culture persons would not have an orientation, and could only wander aimlessly. Out of necessity, writes Parsons, individuals must submit to the values that are imposed by culture. Further, once this internalization process is complete, the legitimacy of social laws and other mores are guaranteed.

Parsons relies on systems theory, and thus assumes that information controls energy.[6] Culture, accordingly, is high in information, while the psyche is merely a source of energy. And energy without the direction given by information the mind is presumed to be ineffectual. Although he is far removed from the early Greeks, Parsons does not deviate from their views. Particularly, in a manner similar to Aristotle, persons are still imagined to be imbued with pathos that needs guidance. Parsons requires that the psyche be subordinate to culture, or else norms will, at best, be ephemeral. Also influenced by Freud, Parsons requires that role structures be the focus of cathexis. Roles, in other words, serve to outline the parameters of the "reality principle."[7] Culture is thus presumed to be a precondition for rational demeanor, for otherwise regular patterns of behavior are believed to be difficult to sustain.

Culture appears to be the outgrowth of an abstract spirit, and thus is believed to consist of various objective forces. Divorced from the contingencies of everyday life, culture serves as a universal backdrop for social activities.[8] Hence civilization comes to be synonymous with humanity. A common nature unites those who are rational and attuned to their basic needs. Cultural mandates are the focus of sublimation, while human energy is turned into something that is usable. In this sense, the human essence is reflected in culture.

In a postmodern fashion, Marcuse challenges this rendition of culture.[9] Simply put, he regards this interpretation of culture as leading to a society based on "dominance." Culture becomes synonymous with necessity (*ananke̅*), although Parsons does not apologize for holding this dismal viewpoint. In effect, persons cannot provide the government with legitimacy, for example, because this agency saves them from ruin. Because the appetitive desire of persons is rendered functional by culture, the agents of socialization are very powerful. These officials are given the latitude to dictate the principles of reason. Hence personal pleasure is sublimated easily into socially acceptable forms. A rational person, furthermore, understands the common good to take precedence over personal responsibility. In other words, the message conveyed is that the common good is not enhanced as a result of seeking personal freedom. Civilization is "inspired by culture," rather than by good works and virtuous behavior, for an independent or autonomous realm is thought to be the origin of *arête.*[10] Anxiety about which action is most appropriate in a particular setting should subside, because uncertainty is anathema to culture. Culture, in this respect, brings into harmony the particular and general interests. Again, similar to what the early Greeks intended, culture instills a respect for beauty—an appreciation for balance and measure.

Culture, in sum, is traditionally conceived to be purged of passion, and thus is able to reconcile disparate interests. One is reminded of Hegel at this juncture, for culture weighs heavy on the human spirit. In this respect, culture becomes an object of veneration. Culture is treated as something alien, the adversary of creative acts. In a sense, culture is treated as a sort of "graven idol," thereby perverting socialization. Specifically, a person's source of identity is externalized, in that the rules of normative behavior are specified by culture. Persons can only reflect reality, similar to the way in which their image is reflected in a mirror. This rendition of socialization results in what the Stoics called *apatheia*, as individuals almost cower in the face of their destiny. Internal motivation is impossible, because the person is a chimera, a faint image of reality. Why attempt to change something that is beyond human control? Persons are not apathetic due to psychological reasons, but because their actions are rendered irrelevant by reality.

In effect, this rendition of culture requires that society become a classificatory scheme, according to Deleuze.[11] Social utility, therefore, specifies the worth of an activity. Does an action—a behavior or policy—foster social stability? Aesthetic and other non-utilitarian values are diminished in importance, for they appear to be devoid of purpose. What good can possibly be forthcoming from such irreverence? The "aesthetic dimension," as Marcuse calls it, lacks seriousness and emphasizes play.[12] In contrast to utilitarian definitions, play is believed to be a "waste of time" or simply provide an opportunity for "energy release." Nonetheless, like Nietzsche, Derrida believes that "free play" is continuous recreation, with no *Aufhebung*, or final termination. Play, in other words, is "genetic indetermination and [a] seminal adventure of the trace."[13] Necessity is defied by play, because spontaneity and innovation are stressed. Rules are not superimposed on a person's actions, but are part of the play that is enacted. Aesthetics is the embodiment of pleasure, the act of confusing frivolity with gravity. However, this spirit of lightness resides traditionally at the periphery of culture, where reason has no special status. Yet Sartre laments that seriousness pervades culture once the worth of behavior is determined by functional prerequisites. Sanctioned purposelessness is simply intolerable.

Sensuousness is thus repressed by reason, thereby depriving the world of its soul. Society becomes a hollow space, into which persons are inserted. Configurations of objects, pathways, and functionaries constitute daily life. Additionally, relationships between these entities are causal and mechanical. Directions are clear and distances obvious, because the space according to which order is calculated is undisturbed by quantum fluctuations. A self-contained domain is posited, wherein choices about the meaning of a person's existence are senseless. After all, space surrounds the body and serves to insulate persons from fear. The future is certain, yet not very challenging. The element of planning that makes life interesting is simply irrelevant. Reason is clear, but not necessarily exciting—conclusions follow nicely from premises. The intelligent person merely figures out what ought to be done logically in any situation. Imagination, simply put, is ancillary to logic and analysis.

Postmodernists reject this treatment of imagination. In the postmodern world, emphasis is placed on the ability to fantasize. Actually, imagination and reality arrive together. The explanation for this is as follows: reason does not exist outside of imagination, for dualism is abandoned. Rather than being juxtaposed, as is usually the case, these two capacities interpenetrate one another. As a result, culture is not the guardian of reason, but simply imaginary. A specific culture represents a modality of imagination.

According to postmodernists, the culture of dominance that has been accepted throughout Western philosophy is no longer justified. Implied by dominance are the dualism and hierarchy that postmodernists reject. For this reason, postmodern society spawns a "culture of immanence"—a style of culture that embodies human inspiration. Hence society must be self-legitimating, because culture is not autonomous. In direct opposition to Parsons and other realists, culture is not accorded the status of an independent system. Culture delimits what was considered to be possible in the past.

ELEMENTS OF POSTMODERN CULTURE

A. Reason

Postmodernists are often accused of undermining reason. Lyotard's praise of René Thom and his Catastrophe Theory suggests that mathematically exact probability statements are passé.[14] Championing the cause of Gödel also implies that formal systems are dubious and not to be trusted. Further, de Man is constantly illustrating the shortcomings of knowledge that is empirical and readily quantified.[15] Along with the postmodern rejection of computerization is its criticism of binaries, which are the cornerstone of formal logic. With the emphasis placed on uncertainty and undecidability, postmodernism creates the impression that reason is unimportant, even counterproductive. In point of fact, associating logic with prescriptive statements, as does Lyotard, would seem to destroy reason altogether.

Clearly the relevance of formal or axiomatic logic is challenged by postmodernism. Yet does this mean that reason per se is abandoned? Upon close examination, however, all that is rejected is a mechanistic conception of logic. Postmodernists deny that logic constitutes a unified system. Accordingly, they contend that reasoning consists of far more than drawing conclusions from premises. This sort of logic, they say, lacks a key component: learning.[16] Reason is decontextualized and described as if logic and judgments are unrelated. Yet is reason pristine and activated in a vacuum? Or are actions undertaken in situ, and thus rationalized with regard to a number of limiting conditions? Postmodernists believe that reason is not innocent, but has social consequences. In other words, the fundamentals of reason must be acquired, thus suggesting that they are not universal. For example, a person's judgments may or may not have any situational relevance. Either way, reason is not innocuous. Reasoning is similar to a wager, because no one can know in advance the outcome of a particular gambit. Whether or not an action is perceived as rational has little to do with induction or deduction. The impact of reason is not this predictable.

What is reason? To paraphrase Derrida, reason begins and ends with conceptualization.[17] By this he means that at the basis of logic are judgments, which are not derived from any format that may be used for making decisions. The choices that make specific assumptions thematic establish the framework for reasoning. As opposed to Aristotle, for example, Derrida believes that the beginning of logic is difficult to pin down.[18] Reasoning does not consist of merely identifying, processing, and analyzing information, with the aim of reaffirming certain beliefs about reality. Instead, reason provides its own justification in the form of special commitments. Reason is uncertain, therefore, because no judgment is indispensable. Derrida writes, nonetheless, that praxis is the only source of stability for reason.[19] Human action, in other words, is a presupposition of rational behavior.

Have postmodernists spurned reason? Absolutely not, they simply refuse to allow reason to control its creators. Persons are still able to classify and explain events, and accordingly to generalize their findings. But now, this process is understood to be predicated on judgments that need social corroboration, if decisions are to be known as rational. As Derrida writes, "reason is declared at the moment of speech."[20] The linguistic "world" that subtends logic, in other words, holds the key to comprehending rationality. Accordingly, logic must be disseminated before it can have any social relevance. This does not simply mean that the effort must be made to make fundamental axioms accessible to the public. Much more important, a commitment must be made to specific values, so that reason may appear to be reasonable. Reason is not value-free.

This is where learning enters the picture. Reasoning is not simply the ability to reach correct conclusions from premises. Acquiring reason is much more involved, at least from a postmodern perspective. Reason and logic are thought to be symbolic, but not in the manner suggested by logical positivists. Positivists exclude the element of interpretation postmodernists claim is central to reasoning. This understanding that reason is socially manufactured should be of interest to social scientists. First, it implies that premises are value-based, and thus are not necessarily universal. Second, because premises are assumptions, an interpretation of reality must be stabilized long enough for these factors to become widely known. Therefore, persons must begin to appreciate how particular interpretations come to be recognized as real. And third, reason is understood to be based on priorities that are volatile, due to their symbolic nature. What all this means to postmodernists is that rationality originates from a process that antedates the construction of axioms and the solution of logic problems. Reason and judgments are intertwined. But as far as formal logicians are concerned, this means that logic is compromised. Yet because postmodernists recognize that rationality is context-bound, they should not be accused of destroying reason.

B. Space

In a somewhat difficult statement, Derrida suggests that space is neither spatial nor temporal.[21] What this suggests is that space does not have a spatial basis. If this contention were true, Derrida would be at odds with the Western tradition, particularly subsequent to Newton. In a Newtonian universe, the spatial relations that are experienced in everyday life are underpinned by a much more fundamental dimension, which has been referred to as the *"sensorium Dei."*[22] Space, in other words, is conceived as an almost divine receptacle, in which objects reside undisturbed. This domain is assumed to have absolute dimensions, because they extend to infinity. The exact location of each entity can thus be pinpointed, according to a system of coordinates that reaches to the boundaries of space. Hence space serves an unquestioned frame of reference for charting the movement of objects, as well as of persons. Space, in other words, is an absolute dimension.

Yet Derrida maintains that Newton's rendition of homogeneous space is misleading. Contrary to Newton, he argues that there are no "blank spaces," "zero points," or "lacunae."[23] There are no privileged points, around which social or natural phenomena can be neatly ordered. The reason for this is that space does not have a uniform density. Coincident with the movement of objects, space is bent or folded in various ways. Stated simply, a spatial context is carried along with the movement of an object. Something moving fast creates "thin" space, whereas space becomes increasingly dense as the speed of an object decreases. Postmodernists argue that space rather than being an envelope, is an expressive medium. The dimensions of space relate to localized movement, instead of eternity.

Postmodern space is Riemannian. That is, space is altered by desire. Or, as Lyotard illustrates, postmodern space is not plastic. Space, instead, is political—a practical construct. As opposed to the realm imagined by Newton, space invites change, innovation, and risk taking. Nothing is offered by space but an arena for commitments to be made. Stability is not spatial, but a product of volition. Spatiality is not restricted by space.

Space is not infinite because it exists within language, writes Derrida.[24] The character of speech, therefore, determines the relationship between objects. Space is the experience of proximity. As postmodernists comment, relations are internal rather than external. And because the identity of objects is conceptual, their location is determined as a result of comparing them to one another. A Newtonian "oasis" cannot be preserved through language use, because speech is not pristine. According to Derrida, speech does not have empty spaces. Therefore, space cannot be viewed as a vacuum. Derrida argues, instead, that space is *différance.*"[25] In this case, his neologism means that emptiness is a matter of vacancy and not a natural condition. In other words, a space that is not utilized is open rather than empty, for absolute emptiness—that is, nothingness—is impossible. De Man makes this point when he contrasts Newtonian with literary space.[26] Literary space is unoccupied when its meaning is understood to be insignificant. As opposed to an empirical *topos*, literary space is inscribed in terms of its meaning. Again, emptiness is an existential condition and not a cosmological state.

In terms of social analysis, what is the significance of giving primacy to literary space? Succinctly put, space is the site of a linguistic performance. More concretely, space is a *Lebensraum*, or living space, and not an autonomous realm.[27] As a result, a context can no longer be treated simply as an environment. Material surroundings, for example, are inadequate to explain an event. Before these empirical indices can be properly understood, their conceptual milieu must be given serious attention. A context, therefore, is not a backdrop, something latent, but a prerequisite for understanding an event. With reference to Gadamer, a context is a "prejudgment"—a prejudice or presupposition that prescribes the boundary of reality.[28]

According to postmodernists, persons do not respond to objects within an environment. The reason for this is quite simple: human movement cuts an arc that establishes the framework used for locating events. Thus, objects and movement coexist. Analysis that disregards this association holds little hope for understanding social existence. The nature of the encounter persons have with an object depends on their frame of movement. In this regard, persons lend meaning to objects prior to responding to these phenomena. The moral of this story for social analysts should be that a context is not a causal but an interpretive factor. As opposed to the view of space advanced by Durkheim, space is not impersonal. Assessing the context of an action is useless, unless the dimensions of this domain are recognized to have a human origin. In the view of postmodernism, space is nothing more or less than an interpretive category.

Referring to space as a "living world" is significant. The empirical world, claim postmodernists, is nothing more than a wasteland of empirical indicators, and thus is dead. In actuality, however, spatial distance is a matter of commitment. Establishing and maintaining a friendship, for example, cannot be predicted on the basis of spatial proximity, contrary to the opinions held by social psychologists. During the 1950s and 1960s, social scientists believed that close proximity would lead to increased interaction and would culminate in social solidarity.[29] Space, in this sense, was a causal variable. Nonetheless, the relationship between propinquity and friendship was not at all clear. For space proved to be mediated by various social factors. This finding does not surprise postmodernists. For as Heidegger suggests, space shrinks when interpersonal attraction is strong. Space, in other words, is dependent on human action and does not cause anything to occur.[30]

Space is a landscape that obeys the laws of beauty, not form. Gadamer's definition of beauty is most appropriate: "The beautiful is that in the vision of which desire comes to rest."[31] Vision and beauty are inseparable. Space is thus not an immovable being, but a dimension shaped by prophesy. Since the God of space is questioned, society is not destined for tragedy. Human behavior does not have to be understood as limited by space. Reflecting Bachelard's work, space is "poetic" and consists of an essential tension between belief and disbelief, fact and fantasy, and an individual's world and the public good.[32]

C. Time

Jacques Lacan, for example, questions the legitimacy of Huygen's clock, in addition to the mathematization of time proposed by Galileo.[33] Time, in each case, is a measure of distance, with temporalization equated with an infinite number of moments placed side by side. Accordingly, the present resides between the past and the future. G. H. Mead referred to this as the "knife edge present." As movement occurs along this timeline, present after present comes to fruition. Each moment is self-contained, and thus should not be mistaken for any other. Further, no more than one present can exist at any instant. Every present, therefore, is universal.

This image of time is socially important, for several reasons. First, events can be arranged in a neat causal sequence, for the past always precedes the present. And second, because each present is universal, a temporal basis is available to justify social order. For example, when persons arrive at a similar present, their actions are assumed to be synchronized. This linear conception of time is socially very functional. Events can be explained and organized with relative ease. Nonetheless, postmodernists such as Deleuze and Lacan believe that when time is described as linear, temporalization is misrepresented.

Deleuze brorrows from Bergson in order to illustrate the passage of time. As with Bergson, Deleuze argues that time is *durée*.[34] Instead of a measure of space, the movement of time represents shifts in conscious attention. The past, in other words, is not something that disappears behind a time horizon, but a present that has lost some of its importance. Rather than being a line, time consists of a collage of significant periods. All of these moments exist in what might be called the "expansive present," and thus any one of them can become thematic. According to Luhmann, along with a host of other writers generally referred to as existentialists, time consists of the past-present, present-present, and future-present.[35] Each moment of time is underpinned by the understanding of temporal movement.

For Lacan, too, time is not linear. He suggests that temporalization consists of a continual renewal of the present.[36] For him, the *"temps pour comprendre"* is different from the *"moment de conclure."* Hence temporal coordination depends on persons reaching an agreement about time, rather than them simply arriving at an identical present. For postmodernists, the present must be made, or maintained in spite of other competing possibilities. Time is the *"représentation du présent,"* writes de Man.[37] The present does not exist, but must be brought to presence. Punctuality does not relate merely to meeting someone at a prearranged time, but, more important, depends on a common perception of temporality.

Temporality is thus the experience of time. "Time is precisely the transversal of all possible spaces, including the space of time," writes Deleuze.[38] In short, he adds, time is the "ultimate interpreter, ultimate act of interpretation." Moments do not pass away, but are arranged according to their relevance. In a period of crisis, for instance, the temporal horizon collapses, for a person's attention is centered on immediate concerns. During a period of leisure activity, the present expands. Postmodernists contend that the parameters of time change according to shifts in consciousness. Time may either stretch or shrink. Upper-class persons tend to expand time, because they live in the far future. These individuals delay gratification, in the hope of reaping long-term benefits. Working-class persons, on the other hand, do not wait to consume goods, for their future is uncertain. Yet if a researcher is to predict accurately the behavior of every group, their respective conceptions of the future must be grasped. Edward T. Hall, for example, illustrates how time differs across cultures.[39] Therefore, as Husserl suggests, the passage of time must be approached as alterations in the "lived experiences of time," rather than cosmic changes.[40]

Numerous sociological concepts must be refurbished due to this shift in conceptualizing time. Causality cannot be viewed as a sequence of events. Before A can be assumed to lead to B, these two factors must be experientially, or temporally, related. This means that A must have meaning that is significant to the existence of B. Two realms of meaning can be associated only if they have a common theme, or share a similar experiential domain.

A does not spawn B, as is suggested by the early Greek understanding of cause. Additionally, order cannot be predicated on an eternal present. The communal present presupposed by order, instead, emerges as a result of persons coordinating their respective experiences of time. Through discourse a span of relevance—or history—can be established among persons. Individuals' past-presents or future-presents must become present-presents. Alfred Schutz, for example, refers to this activity as "growing old together" and "tuning in."[41] Persons are thus able to make reference to similar themes. Rather than being a mechanical association of events, a span of time embodies experiences that are consciously united. The present on which causality and order are based is a moment that has interpersonal relevance. Before A can cause B, A and B must be experientially related.

D. History

Critics of postmodernism, particularly Marxists, charge that this theory undermines historical continuity. This claim, however, has only limited validity. Clearly the two most popular views of history cannot be adopted, yet does the notion of progress lose its meaning altogether? Is a course or pattern of events impossible to envision?

Idealism and materialism are the theories most often invoked to justify history.[42] For example, Plato, most medieval thinkers, and Hegel are typically known as idealists. According to these philosophers, historical development is brought about through the effort of an eternal form, which reconciles or integrates conflicting positions. Materialists, such as Aristotle, Comte, and Parsons, have regularly identified evolutionary laws as performing this function. Although materialists and idealists are assumed to be diametrically opposed, with respect to portraying history they share a similar outlook. Specifically, both attribute to history guidance by an ahistorical apparatus. The meaning or purpose of an event is discovered, according to Lyotard, by merely ascertaining its place on the "itinerary of the Spirit."[43] His attack on Hegel is intended to discredit these speculative renditions of history. For postmodernists, history has nothing to do with the spirit or the movement of matter.

The purpose of history emerges neither above nor below the historical process. According to postmodernists, there is no substratum to history. All that exists are events, which somehow must be organized into a meaningful pattern. This meaning, however, resides within history. This is what postmodernists mean when they say that history is discontinuous—there is no inherent justification for associating events. A pattern comes into relief because particular occurrences are recognized to have a common denominator. Similar assumptions, in other words, are understood to be operating in different locations. And once certain presuppositions are revealed to have expanded validity, events can be viewed as constituting a general outlook, or *weltanschauung*. Events hang together because their interpretive frameworks interpenetrate.

The idea that humanity is moving implacably in some direction lacks credence, declare postmodernists. Understandably this announcement might arouse the ire of Marxists, for example, such as Perry Anderson, who writes that philosophies like postmodernism destroy historical continuity, because the proletarian revolution Marxists anticipate cannot be guaranteed.[44] For all that exists are persons who must struggle to find meaning for their lives, within an interpretive context. Critical theorists make this point by stating that after Auschwitz metaphysics no longer makes any sense. A revolution, accordingly, must be fomented, rather than planned according to social laws. An interpretation of a government's economic polity, for example, must be exposed as faulty and other options explored. Yet just because persons are not carried along by waves or cycles, does this imply that trends in behavior cannot be noted? Postmodernists assure readers that history is discontinuous, yet still meaningful.

All postmodernists maintain is that history is not a universal metaphysical category. In other words, they deny a realistic version of history. Neither an ideal nor material telos is acceptable, and thus nothing ahistorical preserves the integrity of history.[45] History, instead, is a "subject" imbued with praxis, claims Guattari. He writes: "To me, history—the history made and remembered by human beings—is a subject."[46] History is organized through repetition or memory, rather than by fate or destiny. As opposed to structuralists, for instance, postmodernists claim that individuals are not the bearers but are the instigators of history. Indeed, with regard to Nietzsche, history reflects the eternal recurrence of the same, in the form of humans remaking themselves.[47] A revolution, therefore, is a collective fantasy, rather than something that is justified by evolution. History will not absolve anyone of their deeds, for these actions must be judged on their merits. A particular policy is enticing or repulsive because it makes sense socially, and for no other reason. According to Lacan, something other than prediction is thus required to alter the course of events.[48] The course of events must be transformed.

With the telos of history undermined, how is the resulting discontinuity made meaningful? Quite simply, persons have the ability to recollect and project time. When apprehended to be modalities of *durée*, the past and the future are not forever separated from the present. Luhmann stresses this idea when he states that the present sustains the past, present, and the future.[49] At the center of history, therefore, is memory, which coordinates events and distinguishes possible from impossible actions. Rather than disappear, a particular present simply loses its relevance and becomes a past experience that is used as a benchmark to assess other options. Further, the future is a possibility that has not yet been activated.

History, therefore, represents the convergence of the choices persons have made in order to define their collective experience. Although "total history" vanishes, states Foucault, the regular appearance of events can be documented.[50] A type of historical consciousness can be preserved and transmitted between persons. While history does not emanate from an absolute origin, a community's recollections and beliefs about what is possible or likely to occur can certainly be preserved. With regard to continuity, postmodernists recognize the fragility of history. Revolutions can still happen, only now they must be based on unrealized hopes and unpopular social arrangements. In the absence of depth, surface regularity can be established between occurrences.

Throughout the growth of social science, the desire to record fundamental historical trends has been very important. Most notably, social scientists have thought that if the basis of history could be exposed, universal principles might also be discovered. Comparative methodological standards, in short, might be formulated. Nonetheless, for postmodernists memory is central to history, as opposed to natural or divine laws. In this regard, Deleuze praises Bergson's version of memory, as outlined in *Matter and Memory*.[51] According to Bergson, memory is not a psychological property, stimulated by the present to represent the past; instead, the past is actually recollected, interpreted, and, possibly, altered. Hence the past is directly encountered and (re)made. As a result, Foucault states that only "points of compatibility and incompatibility" are available to judge the development of societies.[52] History is simply a "discursive constellation"—a living order that is sustained by personal preferences. Accordingly, history cannot lend certainty to judgments about progress. These acts of valuation take place within or inside of history, and thus are, at best, provisional.

Thus students of history should be archaeologists of the present: this living dimension has always specified the meaning of both the past and future. The direction of a person's existential commitments in the present has impact on how the past is interpreted and how the future is projected. History springs from the present. This existential present, it should be noted, is not the product of history, although previous interpretations of social possibilities can influence the present. The present is the final arbiter, pro tempore, of the course of history. Historians, therefore, should dwell in the present, rather than inhabit the past. The present that spans time should be their focus of attention, claim postmodernists. For, as argued by Tillich, *kairos* gives meaning to *chronos*.[53] Time brought to fulfillment by desire subtends temporality or history measured by a clock.

E. Personal Identity

At least since circa 1600 and the introduction of the *cogito*, the psyche or self has been given an important position in the history of sociology and psychology. This self has been associated with various phenomena, such as innate ideas, cognitive a prioris, the ego, a stream of consciousness, and so on.[54] In terms of modern sociology, functionalists have equated the self with role characteristics. While borrowing from G. H. Mead, symbolic inactionists have modified slightly the functionalist position. A person's identity is referred to as a "social self," which is constructed through interaction with various socially significant individuals. In all of these examples, the self is conceived as something substantial or real.

The self is a remnant of an era when an indubitable ground of existence was sought. As a core, the self provides a sense of certainty for a person. Everyone, accordingly, has a real self, which must find fulfillment in society. Meeting so-called basic needs is a vital part of this scenario. If these fundamental needs are not satisfied, for example, a therapist will assist patients to achieve their full potential. In fact, assisting persons to discover or "find" themselves has become a multimillion dollar business. What justifies this approach to analyzing and treating persons is a belief in a primordial self. Sanity and insanity, therefore, depend upon the extent to which this identity remains balanced. Likewise, a remedy for madness consists of bringing the self into conformity with a standard psychological or sociological profile.

Yet is this search for an identity proof that a self exists? Deleuze and Guattari say No. These and other postmodernists claim that the self is fictional. Due to this theoretical maneuver, the final source of social or personal security is demolished. In his critique of the concept of the author, Foucault writes that there is no "transcendental anonymity."[55] There is no hidden psyche that can be discovered to support the meaning of a text or everyday existence. Further, Barthes explains that the author is "indefinite," because the "I is linguistic.[56] He argues that the "I is nothing other than saying I." An author is merely the one who writes, rather than someone who expresses, better than other persons, psychological themes that are basic to humanity. Because writing and speaking mediate every presentation of the body, authors create themselves through their work. Barthes calls this activity the "author effect."[57] In a manner of speaking, persons "write themselves," for they bring themselves into existence through their words. Lacan goes so far as to claim that the entire self, even the unconscious, is linguistic. In this respect, Foucault writes that the author is "located in the break that founds a certain discursive construct and its very particular mode of being."[58] He adds that there is no "deep motive," "creative power," or "design" to the self. The self, rather, is invented.

European feminists, such as Hélène Cixous, Luce Irigaray, and Julia Kristeva, have adopted this rendition of the self.[59] Cixous, for example, claims that a woman's identity consists of nothing more than "feminine forms of signification." Contrary to Freudian theory, there is no such thing as "womanhood," which represents a deformed libido. Women, simply put, are not deficient men. Nonetheless, the idea that females are malformed can be found as early as in ancient Greece. Irigaray, therefore, suggests that femininity is a mode of sexuality that is other than male. She asserts that a feminine self is different from but not inferior to the male identity. In this regard, Kristeva declares that being a woman can be defined only in terms that are rejected. Rosalind Coward describes women in her book, *Female Desire*: "our subjectivity and identity are formed in the definition of desire which encircles us."[60] A person's identity, accordingly, is "thetic." Their point is that a woman's self, along with that of men, is linguistically created. The self is a lack that must be filled through creative acts. This is what postmodernists mean when they claim that the self is "decentered." The centrifugal force inaugurated by creativity propels the self in many directions.

In his *Feminine Sexuality*, Lacan argues that the phallus is symbolic, and is given meaning from the web of social relations within which it resides.[61] In the language of Foucault, within particular discursive or epistemological "grids" the phallus has a limited range of meaning. Lacan identifies these "grids" as unconscious. Nonetheless, his point is that women are not natural objects. All human identity, therefore, is related to the *jouissance* of the body. A self-concept is thus as multifaceted and unpredictable as sexual excitement. Using the idiom supplied by Derrida, Lacan writes that there is no such thing as "The" woman, but only "The" woman.[62]

It should be no surprise that postmodernists view the self as a linguistic convention. After all, existence, even the psyche, is mediated fully by speech. This means that the soul is linguistic. Accordingly, reminiscent of Benjamin's discussion of the storyteller, the tales persons spin about themselves provide the substance for their concept of self. In the modern world, however, self-actualization has become a featured attraction. Since the work of Abraham Maslow in the early 1950s, a concern for self-actualization has come to pervade society.[63] Suggested by this concept is that the self will unfold naturally, if this growth is not hampered by social impediments. Similar to Aristotle's description of the acorn growing into an oak tree, the self supposedly has potential to fulfill its destiny. According to postmodernists, this portrayal of the self is wrong. The self does not represent potential, but a range of possibilities that are linguistically outlined. The self is created, rather than being a natural phenomenon.

To suggest that the self is a fiction, does not mean that persons do not strive to maintain their identity. Instead, consistent with what Gabriel

Marcel reveals, individuals do not "have" or "possess" a self.[64] The self, stated simply, is not a thing but something that a person manufactures. Paraphrasing Viktor Frankl, persons must exhibit a "will to meaning" in order to sustain themselves.[65] In line with the postmodern view of language, persons define or speak themselves into existence. This process, of course, is never-ending, for language cannot be exhausted. Because the self resides within language, a search for a so-called real self would be interminable. An identity is not something that is found or rehabilitated, but consists of various modes of action. According to Lacan, persons' questions constitute their existence.[66]

Is the self eliminated as a point of departure for studying and predicting behavior? The answer to this question is No. Nonetheless, the self should not be viewed as a reservoir of needs and drives, or considered to be a part of human nature. A self, instead, reflects assumptions, definitions, and other symbolic practices. As a persona, the self can change dramatically as a person's orientations and commitments shift. This is not to say that others, who may be more powerful politically or economically, cannot manufacture a person's identity. In point of fact, the members of the anti-psychiatry movement demonstrate that this regularly occurs.[67] Yet when this sort of denigration happens, for example, during a psychiatric interview, the resulting identity is still symbolic, rather than natural. The essence of the self is freedom, even under adverse conditions. Accordingly, the cohesiveness of an identity is maintained through a conservation of activity, that is, through the perpetuation of a specific linguistic self-image. Using Foucault's comparison, the self is a document rather than a monument.[68]

An anti-psychiatrist would not search for the self, in order to explain a patient's symptoms. A psychiatric examination, accordingly, would not evolve around instruments used to classify behavior. Instead, an adequate diagnosis can be based only on a person's experience of self. Awareness of a client's self-understanding is essential for the logic of madness to be grasped. This means that making a diagnosis is a political and not merely a scientific endeavor. Client and therapist must enter into a contract, whereby they negotiate the rules to be used during a diagnostic assessment. The boundary that separates, and unites, a client and therapist must be penetrated. In this way, the respective outlooks adopted by these persons are simultaneously questioned and understood. The so-called world of madness can thus be investigated. To a postmodern psychiatrist or psychologist, a diagnosis should not be undertaken within the context of treatment, but of companionship. If this is not the case, a client will most likely be mauled by scientific reason. Only by responding to the invitation conveyed by madness, can the world of the mad be entered and examined. If the mad are merely treated, they are likely to be overtly or covertly manipulated.

F. The Realm of the Interpersonal

Until recently, the problem of "other minds" has always plagued Western philosophy. Perennially the question has been asked: How is discourse between persons possible? At least since the time of Descartes, attention has been paid to the ego. A person is understood to be a point that is differentiated from all other points. Hence the individual is self-contained, independent, and indubitable. For example, Leibniz described the ego as a monad, while more modern writers refer to personhood. With a chasm separating persons, how are they to come into contact with one another? How is knowledge of others to be obtained?

Persons must overcome the limits imposed by the ego, before others can be approached. Yet how is this possible? The parameters of the ego must extend indefinitely, because the *cogito* is severed from everything else. Due to the isolated nature of the ego, solipsism is inevitable. Two tactics have been used to correct this shortcoming. First, all minds are believed to be similar. Minds are assumed to be connected because they function according to uniform physiological or psychological laws. Second, the "other" is thought to be a projection of the self. In this case, knowledge by analogy is presupposed to be valid. Both theories preclude gaining direct insight into the "other," or alter. Specifically, the "other" is not unique, but merely a facsimile of the self. Presumed is that individuals are basically autonomous and only indirectly related to others.

Most troublesome about this position is that individuals are assumed to be naturally isolated. A community, accordingly, results from uniting disparate individuals. Yet the social implications of this conclusion are manifestly derogatory. It is particularly noteworthy that interpersonal commitments are portrayed as optional. Individuals, in short, have no inherent obligations to the collective. Currently this belief is revealed in a variety of ways. For example, the so-called lifeboat ethic has become prominent. This approach to morality suggests that not all persons can survive, because resources are limited. Therefore, encouraged are piecemeal solutions to problems that benefit only specific sectors of society. Another philosophy motivated by egoism is supply-side economics. Instead of stimulating the demand capacity of all citizens, incentives are allocated to those who are wealthy. Supposedly these persons spend their money wisely, and thus promote economic growth throughout society. Their windfall is more valuable than increasing the buying power of the entire population.

Due to the primacy accorded to the ego, the focus of policies is the individual. Persons compete for a few resources, rather than outline a collective plan for production and consumption. In the lifeboat scenario persons are permitted to consume so much that a few passengers must be thrown overboard.

A more equitable solution would be to tolerate only a rate of consumption that would allow all persons to survive as long as possible. Yet such a collective strategy is not likely, due to the emphasis placed on individualism. The welfare of others is simply a concern that is ancillary to self-actualization. The same is true of supply-side economics. Instead of targeting investment in order to stimulate particular parts of the economy, the wealthy are given money to spend as they please. Economic growth, therefore, depends on the whims of these individuals. Moral issues are outlined primarily in terms of personal well-being, which is not necessarily similar to the commonweal. Obviously, the standard of living of a society can be elevated by increasing the wealth of a few persons, while the life style of the rest declines. If the poor are kept out of sight, the illusion can be perpetrated that a society is prosperous. Yet is this the modus vivendi of a just society?

Because dualism is undermined by postmodernism, an individual can no longer be treated as a point or dot. In fact, when emancipated from dualism, a foreground is recognized to be unintelligible without a background. A figure, as Gestaltists showed some time ago, is accompanied by a surrounding field. This is Lyotard's argument when he writes that "no man is an island," because persons are joined at "nodal points."[69] His thesis is that "I" presupposes "Thou," and that these elements are not accidently united. Deleuze and Guattari reach a similar conclusion when they remark that everything is collective.[70] People are not brought together, and then suddenly or miraculously become social. By the fact persons recognize that they are apart, they are related. In this respect, togetherness is presupposed by divergence. Postmodernists claim that a fundamental "We" exists, before the world is divided into "I" and "Thou." This is the "We," according to Derrida, that "makes possible the reduction of the empirical ego and the emergence of the eidos 'ego.' "[71] Similarity and difference are co-determined.

Here, again, is where Buber's notion of the "Eternal Thou" is relevant. Actually, in this case, this phrase might be better rendered "Always Thou." Persons are always open to the world, even when they withdraw from others. In point of fact, presupposed by withdrawal is connectedness. Ontologically, persons are social while they acquire their identity, for the public and private spheres can be differentiated only analytically. All acts occur in the presence of the other, and thus are public. The idea of private morality is not recognized by postmodernists. Or, more accurately, the sphere of the private is socially designated. While all behavior is not, nor should be, subject to collective control, no action is entirely private. An abstract collective does not have the right to control an individual's actions. At worst, persons can agree to keep their views separate. To say "I," notes Buber, implies "Thou," thereby undermining the crude notion of individualism that has come to be associated with modernity.

Technically, a person cannot "take the role of the other," because no space is traversed between persons. Before a person encounters others, the whereabouts of these persons is already suggested. The "other" is merely an alter and not a foreign entity. What this finding requires is that the self never be treated as independent, even though persons may appear to be isolated. No matter how hard they may try, individuals cannot escape from their responsibility to others. Absolute strangeness, in short, could never be imagined in a postmodern world. Anyone who claims to be an individual is simultaneously a consideration for others. Therefore, Lucien Goldmann refers to social relations as "intrasubjective," for association is an event affirmed by its denial.[72]

This basic connectedness between persons never begins or ends. It is at this juncture that postmodernists depart from traditional social philosophers. Typically the view has been that persons who are unsocial—who lack culture and thus reality—can be made civilized. Civilization, accordingly, begins at a particular time in history. Those who existed prior to this moment are asocial, and cannot be trusted and, possibly, should be persecuted. Since no one is asocial, persons who are different are not completely strange or abnormal. These novel individuals merely represent a special modality of otherness. And like every "other," the style of rationality exhibited by a new arrival can be examined and eventually comprehended. The in-group/out-group differentiation is now illegitimate, along with the discrimination that typically accompanies this distinction.

Simply because the "I" and the "alter" cannot be separated, this does not mean that these two persons understand each other. Here norms must be distinguished from community. Persons are involved in community life because the self is always the "other" for someone. Individuals are never anti-social or unrelated. Nonetheless, this fundamental relationship does not automatically grow into mutual appreciation. When individuals act on similar assumptions about themselves, these persons begin to lead a normative existence. Norms are possible when persons hold similar expectations about behavior. Because the internal/external dichotomy is subverted by postmodernists, norms can be erected even between persons who appear initially to be very different. These differences can be explored. Therefore, the absence of explicit norms is not an excuse for antagonism. The "other" does not disappear simply because a social contract has not been finalized. Persons who are ontologically connected cannot disregard this connection, no matter how hard they may try.

CONCLUSION

Intelligent action has particular meaning with respect to the "culture of immanence." Simply put, intelligence is symbolic, and thus is inextricably related to the assumptions persons make about reality. For example, a perceptive person recognizes that judgments sustain reality, logic is prescriptive and not value-free, and a social process is central to establishing criteria for measuring intelligence. Intelligence is indicative of social competence, and not necessarily psychological functioning. The intent of this distinction is to emphasize that intelligence is not a natural condition, but a social construct. Accordingly, someone who is socially competent attends to the values that are operative within a particular interpretation of reality. Rather than being a basic trait, intelligence reflects the ways persons choose to act, or interact, within particular cultures. This is because interpretation—linguistic action—cannot be eliminated from the identification of intelligent behavior, as witnessed by the "Rosenthal effect."[73] This experimental effect shows that the identification of intelligent behavior cannot be separated from the expectations teachers have for their students.

In a particular area of study, usually known as artificial intelligence (AI), this insight has for the most part been ignored. Typically, AI is linked closely with modernity and realism. Accordingly, as Lyotard notes, knowledge is associated with "quantities of information."[74] Leading writers in this field describe knowledge as "context-independent, objective features of the real world."[75] When knowledge is conceived in this way, facts or bits of information can be gathered, stored as a computer's knowledge base, and used to diagnose situations. As information is introduced into a computer, judgments follow concerning a proper course of action. Computers designed in this manner are called "expert systems." Exponents of AI argue programs are available, for example, that can recreate the decision making ability of physicians and psychologists, minus human error.

Yet progress in expert system design has slowed recently, according to some critics. Postmodernists blame a serious oversight in this research: persons do not make decisions in a vacuum, as do computers.[76] Everyday judgments are guided by values that are ignored or, better, eschewed by advocates of computerization. Actually, this sort of standardization is cited to be the strength of computerization. Yet persons act with reference to a linguistic world that cannot be readily computerized. Expert systems, therefore, render precise but sanitized decisions. When computerized, for example, a psychological evaluation becomes synonymous with testing. According to postmodernists this is a serious shortcoming, for overlooked by testing are historical, political, and economic considerations that influence a person's behavior. Computers render "context-free" verdicts that may be accurate, but are often socially nonsensical. This finding does not shock postmodernists, for they argue that positive science, especially its modern variants such as computer modeling, lacks social sensitivity.

Some theorists are attempting to move beyond the impasse that has been reached in the construction of expert systems. These writers contend that work on AI will not advance until the linguistic world inhabited by persons can be built into software. By this they mean that assumptions about reality can no longer be dismissed as unimportant by those who design computer programs. Natural language use, in other words, must be given serious attention by computer engineers. Everyday speech must be rendered programmable. Only when computers process and analyze input on the basis of social priorities can these machines be expected to produce pertinent judgments. Again, the idea is that cognition, and thus intelligence, are context-bound.

In a culture of immanence, every facet of life is socially or linguistically mediated. Reason, logic, and intelligence are imbued with judgments that can be undone. Anyone who neglects this finding is condemned to irrelevance. AI research represents the most recent attempt to abridge this fact. As shown by postmodernists, however, policies and practices that are implemented without regard for the element of interpretation will be intrusive and ineffectual. Because policy makers cannot transcend culture, value-relevance, as opposed to value-freedom, must guide decision making. Therefore, interventions must be community based, or oriented in terms of a particular *Lebenswelt*. Scientific standards, in other words, should be placed in the service of humanity. Planners must not be so enamored of reason that their vision is unduly narrowed.

A case in point is provided by environmentalists.[77] Often these activists resort to using the weapon adopted by their opponents—that is, science. Land developers use science to legitimize their projects, while environmentalists adopt the identical tactic to halt the construction of a new factory or power plant. But because a proposal can be justified scientifically, does this mean that it must be undertaken? According to Ellul, a project is not necessary merely because it is feasible. Likewise, the use of science is not essential to rejecting a plan that is unwanted. Many environmentalists do not appreciate this point. Specifically, why are the values associated with science given primacy in the area of environmental planning? To work within the realm presupposed by science automatically restricts a person's options. Specifically, aesthetic and other less utilitarian concerns may be important in a particular locale. These factors, therefore, should not be disregarded simply because they are not scientific. Postmodernists claim that no justification exists for this maneuver. The culture of immanence demands that values guide action, even if they contravene conventional, scientific wisdom. These values are not universal, but local, and cannot restrict further discourse.

In short, acculturation is not merely a matter of persons achieving an ideal. Instead, they must cultivate their linguistically inscribed world. Persons must learn to dwell comfortably, yet critically, within their linguistic reality. This linguistic milieu is where personal identities and social policies come to fruition. Nowhere else can the elements of culture be found. In this sense, postmodernists contend that culture is a narrative, which persons are constantly rewriting. This is not a Grand Narrative, but literature that represents the interpersonal, or social, constitution of reality. The story persons fabricate is locally determined and transmitted. Hence the attainment of culture occurs when persons are satisfied with the plot that they have conceived. In the culture of immanence, the only restrictions that are justified are the limits persons place on imagination. Invention is the cornerstone of the culture of immanence.[78]

NOTES

1. Robert Wuthrow, James Davidson Hunter, Albert Bergsen, and Edith Kurzweil, *Cultural Analysis* (Boston: Routledge & Kegan Paul, 1984), pp. 1–20; Raymond Williams, *The Sociology of Culture* (New York: Schocken, 1982), pp. 11–32.

2. Williams, *The Sociology of Culture*.

3. Herbert Marcuse, "The Affirmative Culture," in *Negations* (Boston: Beacon Press, 1969), p. 95.

4. A. L. Kroeber and Clyde Kluckhohn, *Culture* (New York: Random House, 1952).

5. Parsons, *Societies: Evolutionary and Comparative*, p. 11.

6. Ibid., p. 28.

7. Talcott Parsons and Robert F. Bales, *Family Socialization and Interaction Process* (Glencoe, Ill.: The Free Press, 1955), pp. 133–186.

8. *Aspects of Sociology*, pp. 89–100; see also Bruce Brown, *Freud, Marx, and the Critique of Everyday Life* (New York: Monthly Review Press, 1973), pp. 38–67.

9. Herbert Marcuse, *Eros and Civilization* (New York: Vintage, 1962), pp. 20–49.

10. Rudolph H. Weingartner, *Experience and Culture* (Middletown, Conn.: Wesleyan University Press, 1962), pp. 70–84.

11. Gilles Deleuze, "Nomad Thought," in *The New Nietzsche*, ed. David B. Allison (New York: Dell, 1977), pp. 142–149.

12. Herbert Marcuse, *The Aesthetic Dimension* (Boston: Beacon Press, 1978).

13. Derrida, "Structure, Sign, and Play," p. 264.

14. Lyotard, *The Postmodern Condition*, pp. 58–59.

15. De Man, *The Resistance to Theory*, p. 13.

16. Daniel Dennett, "Cognitive Wheels: The Frame Problem of AI," in *Minds, Machines, and Evolution*, ed. Christopher Hookway (Cambridge: Cambridge University Press, 1984), pp. 129–151.

17. Jacques Derrida, *Dissemination* (Chicago: University of Chicago Press, 1981), p. 19; Jean-François Lyotard, *The Differend* (Minneapolis: University of Minnesota Press, 1988), pp. 51–58.

18. Ibid., p. 33.

19. Ibid., p. 220.

20. Ibid., p. 115.

21. Jacques Derrida, *Positions* (Chicago: University of Chicago Press, 1981), p. 43.

22. Akhundov, *Conceptions of Space and Time*, pp. 95-98.

23. Derrida, *Positions*, pp. 62, 72. See also Jean-François Lyotard, "Plastic Space and Political Space," *Boundary 2* 14, nos. 1 and 2 (1985-1986), pp. 211-223; Ihab Hassan, *The Postmodern Turn* (Columbus: The Ohio State University Press, 1987), pp. 46-83.

24. Ibid., p. 14.

25. Derrida, *Speech and Phenomena*, pp. 85-86.

26. De Man, "Literary History and Literary Modernity," pp. 255-256.

27. Ludwig Landgrebe, *Major Problems in Contemporary European Philosophy* (New York: Frederick Ungar, 1966), pp. 68ff.

28. Gadamer, *Truth and Method*, pp. 239ff.

29. Muzafer Sherif and Carolyn W. Sherif, *Social Psychology* (New York: Harper and Row, 1969), pp. 135ff.

30. Heidegger, *Being and Time*, pp. 82-83, 138-139.

31. Gadamer, *Truth and Method*, p. 443.

32. Gaston Bachelard, *The Poetics of Space* (New York: The Orion Press, 1964).

33. Lacan, *Ecrits*, pp. 75, 98.

34. Gilles Deleuze, *Cinema 1: The Movement-Image* (Minneapolis: University of Minnesota Press, 1986), *passim*; Deleuze, *Bergsonism* (New York: Zone Books, 1988), pp. 51-72.

35. Luhmann, *Trust and Power*, pp. 10-17.

36. Lacan, *Ecrits*, pp. 44, 48, 75.

37. Paul de Man, "Literary History and Literary Modernity," in *In Search of Literary Theory*, ed. Morton W. Bloomfield (Ithaca, N.Y.: Cornell University Press, 1972), pp. 239-267.

38. Deleuze, *Proust and Signs*, p. 115.

39. Edward T. Hall, *The Silent Language* (Garden City, N.Y.: Doubleday, 1959); see also Edward T. Hall, *The Dance of Life* (Garden City, N.Y.: Doubleday, 1983).

40. Edmund Husserl, *The Phenomenology of Internal Time Consciousness* (Bloomington: Indiana University Press, 1964), p. 28.

41. Alfred Schutz, *Collected Papers*, vol. 1 (The Hague: Nijhoff, 1967), p. 220; vol. 2 (The Hague: Nijhoff, 1964), pp. 159-178.

42. Murphy, *The Social Philosophy of Martin Buber*, pp. 115-135.

43. Lyotard, *The Postmodern Condition*, p. 35.

44. Perry Anderson, *Considerations of Western Marxism* (London: NLB, 1976), pp. 111-121; see also, Perry Anderson, *In the Tracks of Historical Materialism* (Chicago: The University of Chicago Press, 1984), pp. 35-55.

45. Guattari, *Molecular Revolution*, p. 176.

46. Ibid., p. 176.

47. Deleuze and Guattari, *Kafka: Toward a Minor Literature*, pp. 53-62.

48. Lacan, *Ecrits*, pp. 93, 52.

49. Luhmann, *The Differentiation of Society*, pp. 271-288.

50. Foucault, *The Archaeology of Knowledge*, p. 9.

51. Henri Bergson, *Matter and Memory* (London: George Allen & Unwin, 1962).

52. Foucault, *The Archaeology of Knowledge*, p. 65.

53. Paul Tillich, *The Religious Situation* (New York: Henry Holt and Company, 1932), pp. 136-143.

54. James Ogilvy, *Many Dimensional Man* (New York: Harper and Row, 1979), pp. 88-135.

55. Foucault, "What is an Author?" p. 144.

56. Barthes, *The Rustle of Language*, p. 15.

57. Ibid., p. 62; see also Roland Barthes, *Roland Barthes* (New York: Hill and Wang, 1977), p. 56.

58. Foucault, "What is an Author?" p. 148.

59. Rosalind Jones, "Writing the Body: Toward an Understanding of *l'Ecriture Féminine*," in *The New Feminist Criticism*, ed. Elaine Showalter (New York: Pantheon, 1985), pp. 361-377.

60. Rosalind Coward, *Female Desires* (New York: Grove, 1985), p. 16.

61. Jacques Lacan, *Feminine Sexuality* (New York: Norton, 1982).

62. Ibid., pp. 137-148.

63. Abraham Maslow, *Toward a Psychology of Being* (New York: Van Nostrand Reinhold Company, 1968).

64. Gabriel Marcel, *Being and Having* (New York: Harper and Row, 1965), pp. 154-164.

65. Viktor Frankl, *Psychotherapy and Existentialism* (New York: Simon and Schuster, 1967), pp. 5-14.

66. Lacan, *Ecrits*, p. 86.

67. Guattari, *Molecular Revolution*, pp. 45-50.

68. Foucault, *The Archaeology of Knowledge*, p. 7.

69. Lyotard, *The Postmodern Condition*, p. 15.

70. Deleuze and Guattari, *Anti-Oedipus*, p. 280.

71. Jacques Derrida, *Edmund Husserl's Origin of Geometry: An Introduction* (Stony Brook, N.Y.: Nicolas Hays, 1978), p. 61.

72. John W. Murphy, "Lucien Goldman and His Precarious Relationship to Structuralism," *Human Affairs* 6 (Spring 1984), pp. 17-43.

73. Robert Rosenthal and Lenore Jacobson, *Pygmalion in the Classroom* (New York: Holt, Rinehart, and Winston, 1968).

74. Lyotard, *The Postmodern Condition*, p. 4.

75. Hubert L. Dreyfus and Stuart E. Dreyfus, *Mind over Machine* (New York: The Free Press, 1986), p. 53.

76. Ibid, pp. 67-100.

77. John W. Murphy, "A Modern View of the Transfer of Technology," *Science and Public Policy* 12.3 (1985), pp. 144-148.

78. Lyotard, *The Postmodern Condition*, p. 52.

7

The Politics
of Postmodernism

INTRODUCTION

Many social and literary critics consider postmodernism to be, at best, apolitical. Simply put, undecidability is interpreted as indecisiveness. Terry Eagleton, for example, argues that because truth is undermined in postmodernism, standards of justice are sacrificed.[1] In the *Rape of Clarissa*, he declares that Clarissa must be saved from deconstruction by history.[2] This criticism is advanced a step farther by Edward Said, who suggests that along with truth, postmodernism undermines a sense of history.[3] And without criteria for assessing correct action, how can social problems be examined and remedies proposed? Collective solutions, according to Fredric Jameson, are effectively curtailed, if persons are unable to judge the appropriateness of policies.[4] Because truth and history are "deconstructed," postmodernists are assumed to be advocates of a politics of pure negativity. In point of fact, Eagleton wonders whether postmodernists find facts to be tyrannical.[5]

How are persons supposed to secure freedom, if they cannot cast off the yoke of oppression? After all, emancipation is a social process, which requires both individual and collective resistance. Revolutionaries are incensed by injustice and are passionately driven to rectify this situation. Yet without the ability to formulate a position, rally public support, and implement policies, social change will never occur. In order to generate opposition to a régime, in short, persons must be organized. Due to the emphasis they place on relativity, postmodernists are believed to be incapable of translating their theory into a coherent political platform. Is the postmodern political agenda really too subtle? Do postmodernists advocate a business as usual approach to politics?[6]

It is quite perplexing that postmodernism is considered apolitical. For example, Deleuze and Guattari are decidedly anti-capitalistic. Their work in the area of psychiatry is overtly political. Derrida has chided his Yale colleagues for their reticence, while lately he has spoken out on apartheid and nuclear war. Although a cloud has begun to form with respect to his World War II journalistic activity, de Man did recognize that his reliance on Kant supports progressive politics.[7] And clearly, Foucault's analysis of prisons and clinics has political overtones. The problem many critics have with postmodernism is that this philosophy is not manifestly militant. Nietzsche's statement that he would serve as a "rail" but not a "crutch" for persons is instructive. Postmodernists are subtly but powerfully political, in that they offer criticism, but no formulae for liberation. The offer of liberation is made, yet not in the usual way. In short, a political philosophy without prescriptions is provided; postmodernists have not illustrated how governments can be overthrown.

In a manner of speaking, postmodernists believe that emancipation occurs before a revolution, and not at its climax. Persons must have a vision that is denied by the present government, and have the resolve to transform this speculative ideal into reality. Knowledge of a novel way of existence must be available to the revolutionary. Revolutionaries are not discouraged that their vision is considered by most persons, at least initially, to be a fantasy. But because postmodernists do not outline a program of action, guidelines for a political party, or a framework for a government, they are chastised for being hopelessly naive. Moreover, critics ask, how can disorganization possibly lead to anything productive?

Postmodernists are upbraided for not understanding the realpolitik of domination. But surely the most successful approaches to repression are subtle and unobtrusive. As Pierre Bourdieu suggests, "symbolic violence" is much more effective than controlling the populace by directly assaulting persons.[8] It is much more effective, in other words, to convice those who are oppressed that they deserve such treatment; the victims of discrimination are told to review their condition logically and accept their fate. Frantz Fanon, for example, illustrates that those who are subject to colonization eventually begin to detest themselves.[9] Myrdal's classic study, the *American Dilemma*, showed that biological inferiority was accepted by many Americans as adequate justification for enslaving blacks.[10] Consequently, many blacks attempted to forget or conceal their ethnic heritage. And women, following from the "anatomy is destiny" argument, are expected to accept their second-class status as a result of their "wandering womb," or lack of a penis. In short, those who are vanquished are symbolically violated, in that their style of reasoning and personal traits are portrayed as deficient. Repressed persons are provided with allegedly irrefutable evidence to explain their deprivation.

Edward Said has coined the term "orientalism" to describe this sort of inferiorization. Orientalism, he writes, is "a Western style for dominating, restructuring, and having authority over the Orient."[11] Consistent with Foucault's thesis, Said states that this domination is the result of a particular discursive formation. Specifically, a shameful approach to scholarship has resulted in a body of literature that depicts what Said calls "the Orient." Accordingly, orientals have received a negative identity, in terms of traits which Westerners do not value. So-called facts and reason are used to degrade this society. The Orient is thus a negative ideal, created by scientists who are not ostensibly ideological.

As this suggests, power can be retained as a result of perpetuating an illusion. And what better way is there to create the image that one's own position is inviolable than to link it with science? Who is likely to challenge the legitimacy of science, but those who are irrational? Furthermore, in the modern world irrationality can never undermine reason. If those in power can monopolize scientific knowledge, or at least the information associated with science, their opinions can come rapidly to dominate politics. Additionally, if schools accept and reward instructors who teach according to this paradigm, the views held by the powerful may never be challenged. Science, in this respect, is simply ideology. It avoids critical self-inquiry, while it encourages the acceptance of dogma. As predicted by Auguste Comte, the scientist has, to a certain degree, become the high priest of modern society. Scientific questions, in other words, are believed to be most important. And thus science is in a position to legitimize almost any activity.

Writers such as Fanon, Freire, and Sartre, for example, contend that repression is basically metaphysical.[12] That is, a particular group of persons is assigned a station in society in terms of criteria that are supposedly free from values. How can repression be legitimized by particular judgments, which, by definition, reflect mere opinions? Surely depriving an entire race of its rights must be sanctioned by a much higher authority. Further, this must be accomplished surreptitiously, for as Foucault illustrates, blatant displays of power often arouse the ire of the public. Ideally, therefore, repression should assume the form of self-denial, referred to by Nietzsche as "resentment."[13] As a result of oppressors supplying the "truth" about their victims, social control is relatively straightforward. The victims of domination accept this treatment as being consistent with their natural disposition. And once these persons begin to internalize their inferiority, they may begin to act in ways that result in further discrimination. A self-fulfilling prophecy may be inaugurated, whereby definitions lead persons to exhibit behavior that warrants repression, according to those who profit from this sort of activity.

The most staunch opponents of postmodernism, as might be suspected, are Marxists. Marxists argue that wages, profit, and productivity are not static ideas, contrary to orthodox economists, but are indicative of a special social relationship. Specifically, capitalists and workers are involved in an internecine struggle. In the capitalist system, the wage a worker receives is merely another cost the owners of the means of production must incur. Capitalists, therefore, must strive constantly to keep this expense as low as possible. The best method for accomplishing this aim is to convince workers that they are incidental in the production process so that they moderate their wage demands. Accordingly, often workers are portrayed as unintelligent, uninspired, incapable of delaying gratification, and uninterested in issues related to the management of the workplace. The purpose of this campaign is to degrade workers, by illustrating that their jobs require little skill and can be performed by almost anyone. Workers, therefore, are not diminished simply by economic factors but by symbolism. In this regard, the monopolization of language can lead to totalitarianism. Similarly, in his inaugural address at the Collège de France, Barthes suggests that coded language leads to unreflective thinking and thus to repression.[14] Further, he informed his audience that power is expressed in language.

An entire culture has been developed in capitalist societies to reproduce workers who have unenviable characteristics. Schools, movies, and television programs, for instance, all contribute to this negative image of workers. Capitalists have at their disposal a variety of means to convey the message that their description of reality represents the truth about economic life. While capitalists may be set free by this truth, workers are not. As Marxists like to say, reality becomes reified to such a degree that workers believe they have no choice but to relent to the demands issued by capitalists.

Workers must be produced who will not likely challenge their employers. The best way to secure this exploitative relationship is to convince workers that their lives cannot be improved, through political or any other form of change. In Leibniz's words, the capitalist system must be portrayed as the "best of all possible worlds." Or, according to some recent beer commercials, "it doesn't get any better than this." Capitalists, however, are very subtle and manipulative in their attempt to create this illusion. Officious displays are eschewed, which cause workers to be suspicious. Derrida recognizes in "Limited Inc." that those in power can employ language to camouflage their decay.[15] For in democratic societies, no one is supposed to be able to dictate how a class of persons is supposed to act. Instead, workers must believe that any departure from the status quo is indicative of irrationality. And as is usually stated, any system that advances beyond capitalism must surely be a utopia. Although direct coercion is not used, workers' alternatives are clearly truncated. For in a society that stresses utility and efficiency, no reasonable person would want to be labeled as a visionary.

The inferiorization of workers must be enacted unobtrusively, for otherwise capitalists draw unnecessary attention to themselves and discredit their economic system. Power, therefore, must be ubiquitous, rather than confined to capitalists and their agents. This is the lesson taught by Foucault. Power must be manifested in the very fabric of social existence. For example, the reality that benefits capitalists must appear to be neutral and non-partisan. Laws and other means of social control must be perceived as fair and unbiased. The application of the law, in other words, must not be undertaken in a blatantly prejudicial manner. Law must appear to inundate the system. In this way, power is not concentrated, but pervades every recess of society. Normativeness extends to the core of social relations. Standards of fairness are thus ingrained in every citizen. This is not to say that capitalists will not use coercive measures to maintain their social position, but that such action is inefficient, messy, and, in the long run, may interrupt the normal course of events.

Chaim Perelman notes, however, that justice and fairness are not identical.[16] Furthermore, postmodernists contend that justice is far more important than fairness. Fairness is related to whether or not the application of laws favor a particular constituency. Judging favoritism, however, should not be limited to assessing legal protocol, but must encompass broader philosophical questions. These broader issues relate to justice. As opposed to merely logistical concerns, justice pertains to the purpose of law in society. For instance, What social agenda is served by a particular course of legislation? Raising this kind of question, nonetheless, should not be a part of a worker's repertoire of activities. As far as the owners of production are concerned, workers should come to realize that the ideal and real are united in the capitalist system. This mode of economic exchange, therefore, is extolled by capitalists to embody the end of history. From the capitalist's point of view, discussions about justice may eventually become dangerous.

This reification of reality, according to Foucault, is accomplished through the formalization of social relations.[17] Class conflict is occluded by science, technology, and bureaucracy. Job design in a factory, for example, is based on laws of nature, which are ergonomically sound and implemented in terms of a precise division of labor. The aim of management is to adjust workers to a reality that is not questioned. Attention is focused on technical issues, while theoretical and conceptual concerns are avoided. In fact, philosophical, moral, or ethical discussions are treated as disruptive, for the assumptions that underpin reality must never be exposed. All that should be addressed are the problems associated with the maintenance of the prevailing policies. In this sense, instrumental rationality subsumes all other styles of thinking. Efficiency, for example, becomes paramount in any discussion of management practices or debates over policy. And therefore, the survival of the polity becomes a technical operation.

Any social problem that occurs, accordingly, is assumed to be a technical difficulty. If an assembly line proves to be unproductive, engineers are consulted to provide technical correctives. Rarely are alternative methods suggested for manufacturing goods. Actually, once primacy has been given to instrumental rationality, non-technical concerns are seldom viewed as relevant. Workers, therefore, can only strive to improve the system if their proposals are to be viewed as reasonable. "Work within the system" is the usual advice given to those who object to particular social conditions or policies. Implied is that any radical change could never receive serious consideration. Because of the promises that they make, sensible persons can only conclude that revolutionaries are mad. Yet political proposals organized around instrumental rationality can be nothing more than conciliatory, because procedural refinement is the thrust of technical reason. Adjustment is the fundamental focus of technocrats, in order to avoid disrupting the social system.

Yet are postmodernists helpless to challenge this situation? Are postmodernists merely apologists for repression, as some of their critics charge? It is unfortunate that Michael Ryan and Jonathan Arac, who argue that postmodernism has a political dimension, were not as rigorous as they might have been when discussing this issue.[18] Therefore, the practical thrust of postmodern politics has not received attention. In addition to Ryan and Arac, Hayden White suggests that nothing very organized should be expected from postmodernism.[19] Regardless of this misinformation, postmodernists do not stress negativity to the extent that radical politics is impossible. Nonetheless, because of its disdain for hierarchy, absolutes, and coercion, members of traditional political parties find the postmodern program deficient. Yet postmodernists are advocates of human freedom; pluralism is basic to their project.

Marxists are leery of postmodernism because liberation is not thought to follow automatically from economic change. According to postmodernists, traditional Marxists offer a very narrow form of social analysis. Marxists, on the other hand, view postmodernists as superficial and unsophisticated. Yet even Marx, in his examination of the "Jewish question," distinguished between political and social revolutions. Simply stated, he demonstrated that a political revolution could occur without any significant social changes. The reason for this is quite simple: another repressive authority structure could easily be instituted. For this reason, the proletariat was identified as truly revolutionary, because these workers did not have anything to gain from perpetuating capitalism or serving another master. Similarly, postmodernists argue that revolutions must stem from creativity, rather than from economic or any other imperatives. Once creativity is unleashed, any form of repressive authority will be perceived as intolerable. Like Marx, postmodernists do not look for "great men" or a telos to deliver the revolution. Even though postmodernists are no less committed to social change than Marxists, this claim must be outlined in some detail. Up until now, postmodernism has not been given a fair reading with respect to politics.

DEMYSTIFIED KNOWLEDGE

According to Lewis Mumford, the greatest benefit to be derived from instrumental or technical rationality is control. As never before, social processes can be easily regulated.[20] The reason for this is quite simple: judgments are ostensibly removed from any activity. Judgments, in other words, are transformed into technical operations. For example, a statement such as "do not drive too fast in a school zone," might be translated to "do not exceed twenty miles per hour between two and three o'clock on schooldays within the designated area." With subjectivity or interpretation eliminated, a task can be learned without difficulty. All a person has to do is follow a series of step-by-step instructions to complete a job without difficulty. Through the introduction of what is sometimes called a logic tree, explicit instructions are provided for making decisions. This sort of formalization is thought to improve efficiency and effectiveness. How is this démarche justified?

The use of instrumental rationality presupposes a particular "worldview." This outlook is comprised of three items. First, all phenomena are materialized, or assumed to be inert objects. Second, mathematics is considered the most appropriate method for identifying events. And third, the laws of physics are believed to explain both natural and social occurrences. Taken together, these principles objectify reality. Cognition, moreover, is equated with technical functions. An activity is made rational as a result of quantifying procedures, and of writing with precision. Anything that is not initially quantified is rejected or, if possible, transformed into quantifiable terms. In a sense, technological rationality becomes synonymous with reason. Jacques Ellul, however, charges that this gambit culminates in "technological slavery," for cognition is unduly restricted.[21] Imagination, simply put, is merely a variation of technical acuity.

Emphasizing instrumental reason results in what Marcuse calls a "one dimensional" existence.[22] A paramount reality is proposed, against which all others are compared. Imagination, accordingly, is assumed to be comprised of dreams, which by implication are unrealizable. Nonetheless, a person may be creative. Yet creativity consists of merely the ability to apply basic axioms, possibly in untested ways. Creative individuals recognize more intricate relationships, quicker than less imaginative persons. Still, an unquestioned framework for cognition is presupposed, which is derived from the principles of positive science. Convergent creativity is possible, while the judgments associated with thinking and acting are denied.

With values quantified, instrumental rationality seems to be free of bias. It is assumed that following technical prescriptions does not involve judgments, and thus that technological reason is not impaired by human frailties. If a mistake should occur, such an error is corrected through technical improvements. In general, however, performance is thought to improve as a result of rendering decision making mechanistic. Technical instructions are objective, precise, and uniform, and are not influenced by extenuating circumstances.

When the use of instrumental rationality is put into practice, society becomes a technocracy.[23] Those who glorify the benefits of science and technology are treated as very important. In fact, these experts gradually accrue immense power, because they are given the latitude to formulate and implement policies. They rise to this exalted position because of their commitment to science and objectivity, and thus are believed to be best able to guide society. Those who lack a technical education are subtly discouraged from offering their advice, for example, to managers or politicians. When political power is introduced into this scenario, the problems associated with this withdrawal from social affairs is compounded. Specifically, those who possess political power may use science to further enhance their position, as a result of couching their opinions in scientific language. Contrary to the position held by Karl Mannheim, postmodernists do not believe in the existence of a class of "free-floating intellectuals."[24] Indeed, many postmodernists contend that science is the newest means of social control, even though scientifically inspired motives are not ostensibly sinister.

Clearly, this use of science and technology has spawned a social hierarchy, with those in power taking advantage of this imagery. Hardly a day goes by that the insensitivity and corruption of government bureaucrats is not illustrated. Yet these professionals seem to be almost immune to critique. Only rarely are they successfully prosecuted, for their motives are seldom called into question. Furthermore, in a technocracy only particular knowledge can be included in a political debate, and this information is not accessible to everyone. Consequently, a limited number of ideas and proposals dominate the political scene, thus encouraging lassitude and corruption. Postmodernists claim that technocracies are unjustified. Their reasoning is as follows: the strength of science is not that it is scientific, but that persons bet their fate on this form of knowledge.[25] In other words, faith sustains but is concomitantly obscured by science. Persons have decided, although indirectly, not to scrutinize the assumptions of science, and therefore scientific data are given a unique status. Science becomes the premier approach to generating knowledge. But, as shown throughout this book, postmodernists argue that scientific data are no different from any other type of knowledge.

All knowledge represents a modality of interpretation and nothing more. Because every facet of life is fully mediated by language, merely one rendition of reality is provided by science. Although positivists strive to conceal this association, fact and value are not separate in science. According to postmodernists, science is just another style of symbolism or semiotic scheme.

Science, therefore, is not the center of truth.[26] Merely a particular cosmos, as Weber might say, is represented by science. Outside of this realm the relevance of science is debatable. Most important, desire underpins both political and scientific decisions. Also, scientists are guided by the same values that condemns politicians to their lowly status in society. Accordingly, citizens should not be afraid to make their views known, because rationality is not the exclusive right of scientists or other professionals. A suggestion should be judged on its merits, rather than accepted or rejected because it originates from a particular segment of society. While existing within language, no opinion can gain the autonomy necessary to dominate others. The status of facts is not guaranteed by reality; reality has nothing to do with the survival of any form of knowledge. Yet power is exercised when specific symbols are elevated above quotidian concerns and are enforced by scientists. Postmodernists question the legitimacy of this exalted symbolism, and thus their critique of language and literary theory is certainly political. Because science supplies a pool of information rather than truth, this body of information can be either disseminated throughout society or ignored altogether. Either way, the polity is no longer held hostage by a single knowledge base, simply because science is given special attention.

As a result of the postmodern critique of science, the acquisition of knowledge is still possible. All postmodernists destroy is the metaphysics of knowledge. What this means is that all forms of knowledge, even scientific, are left intact, although they are now socially restricted. Only within a limited framework does a knowledge base have relevance. Yet this maneuver is disastrous for positivism, with its aim the development of a universal mode of understanding. Critical knowledge is made available by postmodernists, but only as an enticement to liberation. No guarantees are offered, as when a revolt is thought to be instigated by natural forces. Likewise, no revolution is final, because symbols do not command this sort of respect. In *Signéponge-Signsponge*, Derrida makes this point when he suggests that signs absorb everything and thus are not clean.[27] Nothing, he says, is excluded from a sign. Like a sponge, words take in everything and sometimes overflow with meaning. Liberation, accordingly, is a result of persons exhibiting determination and rejecting fate. Because words do not possess a destiny, the politico-linguistic domain is not certain. Only discussion is possible.

Within this context, the promise of democracy can come to fruition. The ideal speech situation discussed by Habermas can possibly be realized, but not as a utopia.[28] While somewhat different from the situation he describes, which is replete with elitism, postmodernism fosters full political participation on the part of citizens. As opposed to Habermas' portrayal of non-repressive dialogue, democratization does not occur in a realm divorced from power struggles. For according to postmodernists, discourse is part of a political reconciliation process. Discourse is not simply a matter of persons beginning to speak properly. Non-repressive interaction, in other words, occurs at the same time as the relativity of knowledge is recognized. Hence political enlightenment does not follow from philosophical inspiration or occur as a result of mastering certain strategies.

Habermas and Plato are similar in one respect, for both imply that societal harmony is derived from a philosophical ideal. Plato's cave is Habermas' ideal speech situation. However, postmodernists believe that both conditions are unjustifiable. Instead, the leveling of knowledge that is vital to liberation is related to the linguistic praxis that unites persons. Escapism is not advocated by postmodernists, for the destruction of hierarchies and the development of the rules for non-coercive discourse take place between persons. And in any case, how can persons withdraw from language? An important ingredient of linguistic intersubjectivity is the awareness that domination is illegitimate. Hence, repression must be reinforced by language use. This means that political guidance does not arrive from outside of the polity, and that the role played by various types of knowledge is specified through interaction. All political activity occurs within the realm of the mundane. Therefore, asymmetrical social relations are an aberration that have no linguistic justification. Neither liberation nor repression is sustained by a political ideal.

POLITICS OF EMBODIMENT

Social discourse is central to politics. In addition to acquiring information, persons must be able to influence others. Engaging in productive social discourse, however, is no small task. Persons must view themselves as capable of changing institutions. If this is not the case apathy will result, and persons will flee from the political process. Further, those who wield power must be understood as vulnerable. Only if the polity can be penetrated, will politics inspire enthusiasm on the part of the public. Involvement, however, must not be limited to the periphery of the polity. It is not enough to allow persons to voice their opinions, but, more important, they must be able to define the course of events. Democratization, in other words, relates to far more than participation in a few political rituals. The entire political process, instead, must be democratized. This means that the polity must be accessible, responsive, multidimensional, and malleable. Politics must not be allowed to become an impenetrable labyrinth.

Many writers claim that today fewer persons than ever participate in politics. Marxists, for example, argue that this is by design. Yet critics on both the right and the left agree that persons are prevented from becoming involved in politics by social structures. The political system has become simply too bureaucratic. In short, power is exercised by those who control the party apparatus. But why is this misuse of power tolerated? Lefort supplies some insight into this question. He notes that many people believe ordinary citizens do not possess the skills necessary to operate the political system. Of course, those who strive to protect their privileged positions are the most obvious beneficiaries of this retreatism. If the polity appears to be implacable, traditional political wisdom is encouraged. Jockeying for position within the system becomes the order of the day. Leftists and rightists, however, differ greatly with respect to why politics has become ineffectual.

As might be expected, Marxists contend that the objectification of the political system is a product of the ideology promulgated by the bourgeoisie. Conservatives, on the other hand, believe that government interference stifles political participation. Both sides, however, overlook the social imagery that undermines widespread enthusiasm about politics. The polity is portrayed as autonomous, and presumed to be the primary source of reason. As mentioned earlier, this penchant for realism is ubiquitous to the Western conception of order.

With reason identified with political institutions, mass action is unlikely for a variety of reasons.[29] First, the identity of persons is thought to be derived from these organizations. To challenge the establishment is tantamount to rushing headlong into the wilderness. When persons are this dependent, their raison d'être becomes easily associated with the programs approved by those who have power. And second, activism presupposes that possibilities are opened by policies that formerly were thought to be incredible. This is what Bloch and Moltmann mean when they state that hope is interjected into the world.[30] What they mean is that liberating political proposals are anything but realistic. But how can transcendence of the status quo be inspired by realism? The exhortations of leftist European students during the 1960s to entertain only the impossible exemplify this position. In this sense, one is reminded by Magritte's painting, "This is not a pipe."[31] Although a picture of a pipe is obviously presented, observers are warned not to trust their vision. Magritte's message is clear enough: reality is not necessary. With regard to liberation politics, an appropriate call for change might be, "this is not a state." Similar to Magritte's assessment of painting, political excitement stems from a concern for the impossible and not the obvious. Nonetheless, according to postmodernists, imagination in this case is not synonymous with fiction. Instead, genesis is allowed to occur; spontaneous generation is promoted.

Liberation is not necessarily brought about by institutions. In fact, what is absent in coercive institutions ignites revolutions—hope. The aim of a repressive society is to prevent persons from imagining and thus desiring a different way of life. "Surplus repression," as stated by Marcuse, prevails.[32] Yet into this darkness bursts a spark of hope. Hope is not merely a psychological sense of optimism, but a crack in the facade of oppression. Hope occurs when persons begin to understand that they can successfully defy their oppressors. When desire is released—the ambition to remake reality—progressive action occurs. In other words, hope is present when reality is no longer obtrusive. Magritte's confusion about the identity of a pipe should provide inspiration to would-be revolutionaries.

The "copy theory" of knowledge, rejected by postmodernists, results in hierarchy and asymmetrical political discourse. The usual justifications for political institutions, such as social forces and biological themes related to the "anatomy is destiny" argument, cannot be challenged.[33] Quite simply, if cognition is mimetic, reality is reinforced. Once human action is equated with the recollection of facts and the impossible is superseded by the real, the traditional sources of power go unscathed. The "reality principle," or what Sartre calls the "serious attitude," dominates all discussions.[34] Postmodernists, however, hint that this uninspired ontologizing is a product of human forgetfulness. At this juncture, a Heideggerian theme is manifest. Persons fail to remember that the original purpose of politics was to upgrade the human condition, as a result of enabling them to achieve perfection. Yet is this possible when realism guides politics? Reaching perfection is a challenge, and implies a break with normalcy. Uncertainty is central to proposals that improve society by rectifying untenable conditions.

Political realism, however, is characterized by expediency.[35] Proposals are advanced that are safe, for they must not offend the members of any constituency. Consultants are hired who create slogans that appeal to everyone, but obviously lack substance. Also, messages are packaged so that they can be circulated widely in the media. And as is clearly witnessed nowadays, these ideas cannot be very complex. Television, for example, is not well adapted to handling lengthy or in-depth analyses of candidates or issues, particularly after viewers have been socialized by regular programming. Certainly a political campaign consisting of one-liners, similar to those digested for years by the television audience, cannot be very substantial. Nonetheless, after citizens have been sufficiently cajoled, their views are solicited.

Traditionally, voting is assumed to provide an accurate index of their political philosophies. This belief is dubious, for the candidate who garners the most votes does not necessarily represent a well-known position. This entire process overlooks the ideals that sustain political positions. The one thing political consultants want to avoid is a discussion of philosophy.[36] Such discussions can easily become unmanageable. Therefore, the ability of a particular theory of government to deliver social justice is most often not addressed. Political technique is substituted for debate on moral or ethical principles. A situation is merely manipulated by those who are politically astute. Hence contemporary political campaigns have become contests to assess who is most adroit at controlling public sentiment. Obviously, enlightenment is not likely to result from this process. The aim of technique is precision, and not inspiration.

Postmodernists do not consider politics to be a technique, but rather an answer to the question of social meaning. Rather than being a method of societal maintenance, issues related to the meaning of personal and social existence should be addressed through political activity. In point of fact, postmodernists hold that manipulation implies a disregard for the wishes of those who are governed. Furthermore, due to the linguistic base of knowledge, such arrogance is not justified. In this sense, the polity must be viewed as what Bourdieu calls a "literary field."[37] This is a space where literary styles and intentions clash. Traditional and avant-garde artists compete in this domain for the public's admiration. His point is that when reality is understood to be a literary field, a struggle must take place to determine the words that will be accepted as real. Accordingly, politics represents competition between language games, none of which is inherently more important than any other. The polity is where realities are made, rather than where the techniques of manipulation are instituted.

The polity has no importance, claim postmodernists, except as a facilitator of the commonweal that is revealed through language. Rather than being rarefied, political knowledge is united inextricably with discourse. Yet the question remains: What judgments should be treated as salient? Lyotard's response to this query is that judgments should be made "without criteria."[38] Speaking like a postmodernist, he contends that dogma should not limit discourse. This does not mean that politics becomes directionless. Simply put, no criteria other than those that emerge from solving the problems of daily life are deemed relevant. The decisions made within the literary field should determine the important criteria for establishing policies.

Echoing the sentiment of Marković, postmodernists eschew lazy metaphysics.[39] Yet postmodernism is not a version of pragmatism, which suggests that whatever works should be used. Significantly more germane, Lyotard is questioning the criteria used to assess the pertinence of political judgments. He is arguing that political standards are not functional imperatives, as is claimed by functionalists, systems theorists, and other realists. Politics, to paraphrase Lyotard, is not the power to judge or review but to invent criteria.[40] There is no political ideal, because politics is not didactic. The basis of the polity, accordingly, is the creativity that spawns social ideals. As opposed to voting, discourse is essential to the formation of a government. Rationality is not necessarily exhibited by persons casting a ballot for their favorite candidate, but it is when they demand that the polity embody their desires. Rather than being a trait associated with the state, reason relates to existential concern—*Sorge*, as Heidegger called it. According to postmodernists, the polity is the expression of the all-pervasive praxis that goes unnoticed by realists. Government, claims Lyotard, is "worked out in . . . theoretical discourse."[41] Through the confluence of viewpoints a polity is established. As should be noted, this style of theory is not *theoria*, the product of abstraction. Instead, this theory is linked directly to discursive practice. Unrelated to pure speculation, theory can be liberating. Every polity is theoretical, or created, rather than necessary.

Because of his statement that political discourse does not culminate in "consensus," Lyotard has been misrepresented as an advocate of anarchy. This view is inaccurate on two counts.[42] First, Lyotard is not a proponent of egotism. As he notes regularly, the protection of differences is the keystone of a postmodern polity. Postmodern society is based on the toleration of difference. Intersubjectivity is thus presupposed. And second, most anarchists suggest that natural laws would guarantee a just order, if only formal government were eliminated. Due to the linguistic nature of all ontologies, natural laws and any other reality *sui generis* are impossible to sustain. And deprived of an ultimate identity, a postmodern society is comprised of nothing but differences. These differences, accordingly, co-exist. Further, because these points of difference are related, an inherent state of disorganization cannot be said to exist. In Hasidic fashion, Buber adequately portrays this view of the polity when he writes that a community is "the being no longer side by side but *with* another or a multitude of persons."[43] Recognizing and integrating otherness is the hallmark of the community in the postmodern world. Clearly, the promotion of anarchy is not the hidden agenda of postmodernism.

With realism undermined, the polity is quite fragile, although government is not impossible to maintain. Like other *moralistes* in the French tradition, Lyotard's concern for order is not ancillary to his epistemology.[44] Of utmost concern for him and other postmodernists is the establishment of a just society. Natural or divine laws, however, are not relied upon for this purpose. Rather, postmodernists contend that nothing can justify politics but political acts. In more concrete terms, the polity is identified to consist of only discursive practices. Therefore, the state is certainly vulnerable, while persons have no other choice but to be political. As Sartre might say, persons are condemned to be political, for even repressed human action reaches to the core of reality. For a reality that does not touch the flesh would be truly ominous.

DIALOGICAL REALITY

Postmodernists are not left to wallow in darkness subsequent to their subversion of "phallocracy"—a state sustained by principles that represent a *causa sui*.[45] Order does not dissolve simply because the state is no longer envisioned as an untamed phallus. Because the Cartesian ego is undermined, persons are able to come into contact with one another. Solipsism, in other words, is avoided. Yet, as previously noted, the discourse that occurs should not be construed as similar to the mode prescribed by Habermas. Dialogue is not organized with respect to theoretical or practical a prioris, contrary to what is suggested by his ideal speech situation. In this regard, Lyotard writes that "one gives oneself one's own laws."[46] The dialogue that occurs, accordingly, is marred in many ways by desire, uncertainty, and situational exigencies. There is no pristine dialogue, despite the claims made by Habermas, but merely the possibility of preserving the concoction of interpretations and misinterpretations that constitute reality. Persons are able to establish social relationships among themselves, yet without the benefit of complete knowledge. Reality might be called a mélange of (mis)understanding, a "collective utterance" rather than a prison.[47] Paul Nougé, a Belgian surrealist, is acting as a postmodernist when he states that reality is "the metaphor that lasts."

For a variety of reasons, dialogue should not be referred to as simply intersubjective. According to Lyotard, discourse is sustained by "intersubjective pragmatics"; he thereby modifies the standard rendition of intersubjectivity.[48] First, as already noted, the subject no longer exists, but is an ephemeral manifestation of reading, writing, and other forms of action. Second, dialogue does not result from separate entities somehow coming together, for they are never completely together or apart. The traditional version of intersubjectivity seems to suggest that interaction is optional. And third, discourse is never finalized or formalized, in that any style of social meaning must be constantly reaffirmed. The polity does not consist of subjects that are joined, but of discursive formations that are invented and accepted. Politics consists of collective imagination. Accordingly, from within a web of practice (praxis), identities, laws, and realities emerge.

This denial of intersubjectivity does not represent a fatal contradiction in postmodernism. Social reality still exists between persons. Postmodernists are merely reluctant to be associated closely with phenomenology, because of the charges of solipsism that dogged Husserl. Nonetheless, as should be noted throughout this text, many phenomenological themes are found in postmodernism. The point postmodernists are making is that interaction is not somehow derived from subjectivity. According to writers such as Luhmann, phenomenology suggests that interaction occurs only after the certainty of the subject is ascertained.[49] While this interpretation of phenomenology is outdated, for quite some time Husserl's work was understood in this way. In fact, structuralism arose as a response to the perceived inability of phenomenologists to address political or social issues. Postmodernists did not want to be linked with a tradition that has a checkered past in Europe.

Postmodernists are hostile to both statism and liberalism. They contend that the focus of each of these systems of government is social control. For example, many Marxist societies are currently regulated by a bureaucratic élite, who do little more than reinforce the hierarchy from which their perks are derived. On the other hand, many advanced liberal societies are also governed by a select corps of specialists, referred to by C. Wright Mills as the "power élite."[50] These experts labor to secure government stability, even if an alternative course of action would be in the best interest of the citizenry. In each case, a governmental framework is assumed to exist and is maintained, with little regard for popular opinion. This approach to government is understandable, for both systems are sustained by a belief in natural order. Appeals to natural law can be discovered in the work of Locke and Marx. Yet when order is assumed to reflect natural tendencies, these abstractions become the focus of attention. Consequently, the survival of government becomes the purpose of the polity. The essential structures of society must be protected at all costs.

In terms of political organization, postmodernists make no distinction between the center and periphery of the polity. The absence of dualism prevents this distinction from being made. Again reminiscent of the rebelliousness of the 1960s, many leftist students have declared that the periphery is everywhere. With no one occupying a privileged position, the idea of flat political organizations suddenly gains credibility. In actual practice, this means that decision making should be localized, in the form of worker or citizen councils. Yet persons must be socialized into their new roles as political activists. Because they are not simply recipients of political dictums, citizens must be provided with the knowledge and technical skills necessary for them to create and implement policies. The information that was formerly restricted to managers and government officials must be more widely disseminated. Hence political dependency is no longer fostered. This is not to say that political leadership may not emerge, but, contrary to Michels's "iron law of oligarchy," these persons are not automatically given a license to dominate discussions and all other facets of policy formation.[51] The presence of leaders, in other words, does not necessarily signal the decline of democracy. For according to postmodernists, authority is not derived from divine right or genetic properties, for example, but from social assignment. Lefort makes an interesting observation that is important at this juncture: competence and power are not identical.[52]

Because a person has expertise in a particular area, he or she is not necessarily guaranteed a seignorial position in society. This belief in privilege is fostered, however, when skills are thought to be a divine or natural gift, and when particular jobs are cited, a priori, to be vital to the survival of society. With this abstract ontology undermined, talents are understood to be situationally relevant. Contra Chomsky, for example, competence is revealed in performance, and not defined according to inherent standards.[53] Every ability has certain socially established value, with none able to be identified as unquestionably important. In short, all jobs have dignity. However, even when a particular ability is elevated in importance due to social need, this designation does not have a supernatural origin. Therefore, these select persons should remember their obligation to the collective, the origin of their worth, and not inflate their importance or demands. On the other hand, those who bestowed this status should not forget that their role in this process must be socially confirmed. Accordingly, if both groups appreciate their social relationship, Michels' law can be easily tempered. Mannheim refers to this leveling activity as "democratization," whereby every hierarchy of values is undermined.[54]

Yet democratic theory seems to be in a state of crisis.[55] The post–World War II optimism about liberal democracy has faded. For instance, pluralism must now be treated as somewhat naive, because the market mechanism has not optimized political participation. Many groups have not received the resources required for them to obtain all of the benefits they deserve from the political system. Further, those who reside at the bottom of the social pyramid are systematically excluded altogether from politics, due to structural and ideological barriers. The so-called marketplace of ideas, in short, has been influenced disproportionately by specific segments of the population. Accordingly, postmodernists attempt to debunk the claim that ideas circulate randomly, as well as the falsehood that power accrues to those who proffer the best political proposals. Traditional democratic theory ignores the asymmetry of social relations, which stifles open discourse and the proliferation of novel ideas. Through their criticism of Western epistemology and social ontology, postmodernists strive to expand political discourse. They try to show that power is based on other than material factors.

DEBUNKING IDEAS, DISCOURSE, AND THE POLITY

Clearly Jameson's objection that "Alliance Politics" is prevented by postmodernists is ill-founded. Contrary to this charge, postmodernists offer novel social imagery, which allows persons to encounter one another freely, to exchange points of view, and to suggest alternatives to the reigning political reality. Postmodernists disallow, however, the claim that the victory of a political party is preordained by natural law or any other metaphysical force. Moreover, the formation of oppositional views is not only permitted but encouraged. Actually, the demythologization of reality undertaken by postmodernists is designed for this purpose. An absolutely autonomous political reality is shown to be unjustified, thereby suggesting that politics occurs between persons. This being the case, structural or ideological imperatives cannot limit action. With traditional ontology destroyed, persons are advised to be suspicious of all purveyors of truth. Specifically noteworthy, the totalitarian idea of the "People-as-One" is denied credence by postmodernists.[56] In a manner of speaking, the desired result of postmodernism is true pluralism. This denouement is quite radical, for according to traditional realism, any unplanned or spontaneous division within society is unproductive.

Liberal critics, however, charge that this advocacy of pluralism inadvertently absolves repressive governments of their heinous deeds. Likewise, Marxists fear that capitalism is endorsed indirectly by postmodernists. Yet these worries are completely unfounded. Any system that arrogates to itself the autonomy required to oppress persons will not receive solace from postmodernists. In point of fact, postmodernists consider this kind of absolutism to be illegitimate, and a harbinger of terrorism. Anyone who is permitted to act without regard for the "other," is well on the way to becoming a demigod. For once the opinions of a particular group are imagined to be unaffected by situational contingencies, these views are placed beyond reproach. As should be noted, postmodernism is anathema to this "bad infinity," or metaphysics.[57] Obviously dictators will be unlikely to find anything in postmodernism to justify their rule, yet capitalists too will not be ecstatic about this philosophy. Specifically, the advantages that accrue to the owners of capital are also called into question. As Marx commented, the dead weight of capital, oppressive symbolism, is lifted from the backs of workers. As a consequence of postmodernism, discourse among all parties is rendered symmetrical. This is because different viewpoints are merged at the level of language use, and thus are reversible.

A government established at the level of experience cannot be oppressive. The reason for this is simple: how can persons repress themselves? Repression implies that a heteronomous referent has the power to condition experience.

Yet this possibility is clearly discredited by postmodernism. To quote Lefort, postmodernism restores the "substance of the body politic."[58] His point is that only after the body has been mutilated, or made into an object, is the flesh unkind. When the flesh is not reified, the body does not block but provides access to the world. A government that is not immortalized, likewise, will not inhibit expression. Linked to the flesh, the polity can never be more than the "social imaginary"—a reality that embodies a promise.[59] The thrust of a postmodern polity is reflected in the surrealist theme that only unfinished things are acceptable.

The flesh is not reified by postmodernism because dualism is abandoned. Action, language, and the body are united. This unity allows postmodernists to extend beyond contract theory and liberalism, in order to make these theories socially responsible. Even Marcuse recognized that liberalism has the potential to be a radical theory, yet this possibility has been blunted by dualism.[60] Control has become more important than freedom. Yet what could be more radical than understanding order to originate from the vox populi? Government, stresses Lyotard, is nothing more than names and signs. Attributing the legitimacy of government to the people's voice is obviously consistent with the aims of postmodernism. However, postmodernists differ from liberals in a crucial respect. As opposed to Locke, for example, the maintenance of a social contract does not require that citizens relinquish their power to a higher authority, such as the state. Readers should recognize by this time that according to postmodernists such an exalted position cannot be sustained, for outside of a linguistic contract, nothing survives.

In view of postmodernism, the concept of the vox populi assumes renewed meaning. The voice is reality, while the social contract is the basis of norms. The state does not protect interlocutors, but embodies dialogue. Mutual respect among persons, rather than a Leviathan, insures discourse. Locke needed a state to secure order, because his theory was flawed in an important respect: he made persons appear incapable of regulating themselves, for he treated the preservation of the common good as secondary to the pursuit of personal happiness. Therefore, collective action is not likely. But because postmodernists undermine this dualism, the state is not necessary to secure order. Language is not deficient in this regard: speech is capable of self-review and self-preservation.

CONCLUSION

Postmodernists dismantle the traditional political ontology. As suggested earlier, order without control is the outcome desired by postmodern political theorists. With the usual structural means of social control abandoned, they claim, self-management is the only acceptable form of government. Stated simply, when they are proposing new laws, persons have no other alternative but to rely on the precedents that have been established, which can always be challenged. Yet this courage seems to be lacking in today's society. Citizens are mostly sycophantic and look to their leaders for guidance. Furthermore, government officials look to God, science, or some other metaphysical scource to infuse them with wisdom. As recognized by Husserl in his critique of the lassitude inundating Europe during the 1930s, leaders and citizens want security that cannot be provided by scientists, technocrats, or prophets without sacrificing human freedom.[61] Surely order is not worth such a high cost.

Most proposals for self-management are not well-received. Indeed, these ideas are thought to be impractical and naive. Yet this unflattering appraisal is understandable for several reasons. First and foremost, order is not viewed traditionally to be a product of human praxis. And second, self-control is assumed to be a trait that is conditioned by institutions. Subjectivity is thus too dangerous to support order. To invoke Hobbes' imagery, nothing less than an ominous force can control passion. Therefore, persons appear to have no other recourse but to seek out authorities for political counsel.

No wonder most citizens balk at the prospect of self-management. Images of despair are conjured up, with frenzied persons running amok. Accordingly, workers admit openly that they are incapable of managing the production process. Managers, on the other hand, are often led to believe that because they are scientific, they are a key defense against impending chaos. Leaders thus become dogmatic, while the remainder of society becomes overly submissive. Such a combination of factors will most likely result in political disaster. As described by Erich Fromm, the stage is set for authoritarianism to be embraced as a rational approach to politics.[62]

What is forgotten, however, is that this scenario is fostered by specific social imagery. It must be remembered that the absence of an absolute reality does not inevitably produce barbarism. This is the case only when persons are crippled to the extent that they distrust their ability to govern themselves through discourse. Moreover, competence is equated with power when role placement is based on supernatural considerations. The idea that a division of labor can be created, with citizens assigning themselves tasks, should not necessarily scandalize anyone. After all, democratic theory has been available for quite some time. Cartesianism, nonetheless, comes into conflict with democracy. Specifically, a dualistic mode of social control is required that stifles the personal autonomy essential to democratic behavior. Democracy is thus perverted and becomes synonymous with rituals that have little to do with self-government.

Postmodernism is consistent with what might be called radical democracy. With the periphery suddenly everywhere, a decentralized polity is not an anomaly.[63] Likewise, self-control as a political imperative is no longer a fantasy. Following the elimination of realism, collective initiatives are encouraged, and new forms of political representation are possible. With the omnipotence of authority placed in question, decisions can finally be made that embrace public sentiment. Self-government is mandatory, for no other source of order can be summoned. Repression, therefore, is revealed to be an obscene style of self-control. Most important, postmodernism encourages socially responsible government. Regardless of the institutions that may emerge, human action supplies them with legitimacy. The body politic is thus instituted. This is the thrust of what Lyotard calls "libidinal politics"—desire becomes real. And desire is not self-effacing. Following the appearance of postmodernism, desire does not need to be infused with reason in order for society to survive; creativity is a sufficient political motive.

NOTES

1. Eagleton, *Walter Benjamin*, pp. 131–142.

2. Terry Eagleton, *The Rape of Clarissa* (Oxford: Basil Blackwell, 1982), pp. 64–67.

3. Edward W. Said, "The Problem of Textuality: Two Exemplary Positions," *Critical Inquiry* 4.4 (1978), pp. 673–714.

4. Jameson, *The Political Unconscious*, p. 54.

5. Eagleton, *Walter Benjamin*, p. 134.

6. John M. Ellis, "What Does Deconstruction Contribute to Theory of Criticism," *New Literary History* 19.2 (1988), pp. 259–279.

7. Mark Edmundson, "A Will to Cultural Power," *Harper's* (July 1988), pp. 67–71; James Atlas, "The Case of Paul de Man," *New York Times Magazine*, 28 August 1988; Jon Weiner, "Deconstructing de Man," *The Nation*, 9 January 1988, pp. 22–24; Geoffrey Hartman, "Blindness and Insight," *The New Republic*, 7 March 1988, pp. 26–31; Jacques Derrida, "Like the Sound of the Sea Deep within a Shell: Paul de Man's War," *Critical Inquiry* 14.3 (1988), pp. 590–652.

8. Thompson, *Studies in the Theory of Ideology*, p. 42.

9. Frantz Fanon, *The Wretched of the Earth* (Middlesex, England: Penguin, 1967); see also Albert Memmi, *Dominated Man* (New York: Orion Press, 1968); Albert Memmi, *The Colonizer and the Colonized* (Boston: Press, 1967).

10. Gunnar Myrdal, *The American Dilemma* (New York: Harper and Brothers, 1944).

11. Edward W. Said, *Orientalism* (New York: Pantheon, 1978), p. 3.

12. Jean-Paul Sartre, *Anti-Semite and Jew* (New York: Schocken, 1948), esp. pp. 17–31.

13. Friedrich Nietzsche, *The Genealogy of Morals*, vol. 13 (New York: Russell and Russell, 1964), pp. 34ff.

14. Roland Barthes, "Inaugural Lecture, Collège de France," in *A Barthes Reader*, ed. Susan Sontag (New York: Hill and Wang, 1982), pp. 457–478; see also Jonathan Culler, *Roland Barthes* (New York: Oxford University Press, 1983), p. 13.

15. Jacques Derrida, *Limited Inc.* (Baltimore: Johns Hopkins University Press, 1977), pp. 75–79.

16. Joseph Pilotta, John W. Murphy, Elizabeth Wilson, and Trica Jones, "The Contemporary Rhetoric of the Social Theories of Law," *Central States Speech Journal* 34.4 (1983), pp. 211–220.

17. Foucault, *Discipline and Punish*, pp. 184–194.

18. Ryan, *Marxism and Deconstruction*; Jonathan Arac, ed., *Postmodernism and Politics* (Minneapolis: University of Minnesota Press, 1986).

19. Hayden White, "Historical Pluralism," *Critical Inquiry* 12.3 (1986), pp. 480–493.

20. Lewis Mumford, *Techniques and Civilization* (New York: Harcourt, Brace, and World, 1963), pp. 31ff.

21. Jacques Ellul, *The Technological Society* (New York: Vintage, 1964), p. 84.

22. Herbert Marcuse, *One Dimensional Man* (Boston: Beacon Press, 1966).

23. Jürgen Habermas, *Theory and Practice* (Boston: Beacon Press, 1974), pp. 268–276.

24. Karl Mannheim, *Ideology and Utopia* (New York: Harcourt, Brace, and World, 1936), pp. 155ff.

25. Lyotard, *The Postmodern Condition*, pp. 53–60.

26. Paul A Bové, "The Ineluctability of Difference: Scientific Pluralism and the Critical Intelligence," in *Postmodernism and Politics*, ed. Jonathan Arac, pp. 3–25.

27. Jacques Derrida, *Signéponge-Signsponge* (New York: Columbia University Press, 1984), pp. 54, 64–70.

28. Jürgen Habermas, "Toward a Theory of Communicative Competence," in *Recent Sociology*, vol. 2, ed. Hans Peter Dreitzel (New York: Macmillan, 1970), pp. 115–148.

29. Lefort, *The Political Forms*, pp. 272–291.

30. Moltmann, *Theology of Hope*; Ernst Bloch, *The Principle of Hope*, vol. 1 (Cambridge, Mass.: MIT Press, 1986), pp. 195–205.

31. Foucault, *This is not a Pipe*.

32. Herbert Marcuse, *Eros and Civilization* (New York: Vintage Books, 1962), pp. 34ff.

33. Lynda Birke, *Women, Feminism, and Biology* (New York: Methuen, 1986), pp. 13–35. See also Lynda Miller and Jean Baker, *Toward a New Psychology of Women* (Boston: Beacon Press, 1976).

34. Jean-Paul Sartre, *Being and Nothingness* (New York: Philosophical Library, 1956), pp. 39–40.

35. Joseph F. Freeman, "Politics and Technology," in *The Underside of High-tech*, pp. 109–120.

36. Larry Sabato, *The Rise of Political Consultants* (New York: Basic Books, 1981), pp. 143–153.

37. Pierre Bourdieu, "Flaubert's Point of View," *Critical Inquiry* 14.3 (1988), pp. 539–562.

38. Lyotard and Thébaud, *Just Gaming*, p. 16.

39. Mihailo Marković, *From Affluence to Praxis* (Ann Arbor: University of Michigan Press, 1974), p. xiii.

40. Lyotard and Thébaud, *Just Gaming*, p. 17.

41. Ibid., p. 21.

42. Ibid., p. 27; see also Lyotard, *The Postmodern Condition*, pp. 61, 65–66.

43. Buber, *Between Man and Man*.

44. Karlis Racevskis, "The Modernity of *moralistes* and the (a)morality of postmodernists," *Antioch Review* 45.3 (1987), pp. 275–279.

45. Guattari, *Molecular Revolution*, p. 233.

46. Lyotard and Thébaud, *Just Gaming*, p. 31.

47. Guattari, *Molecular Revolution*, p. 43.

48. Lyotard and Thébaud, *Just Gaming*, p. 77.

49. Luhmann, *Trust and Power*, p. 7.

50. C. Wright Mills, *The Power Elite* (New York: Oxford University Press, 1956).

51. Robert Michels, *Political Parties* (New York: The Free Press, 1966), pp. 342–356.

52. Lefort, *The Political Forms*, pp. 268–272.

53. Noam Chomsky, *Aspects of the Theory of Syntax* (Cambridge, Mass.: MIT Press, 1965), pp. 3–18.

54. Karl Mannheim, "The Democratization of Culture," in *From Karl Mannheim* (New York: Oxford University Press, 1971), pp. 271–346.

55. Gary Thom, *Bringing the Left Back Home* (New Haven: Yale University Press, 1979), pp. 13–51; Fred F. Dallmayr, *Polis and Praxis* (Cambridge, Mass.: MIT Press, 1984), pp. 15–46.

56. Lefort, *The Political Forms*, pp. 292–306.

57. John W. Murphy, "Deconstruction and the Subversion of 'Affirmative Culture,' " *New Orleans Review* 13.2 (1986), pp. 90–97.

58. Lefort, *The Political Forms*, p. 306.

59. Ibid., pp. 195–204.

60. Herbert Marcuse, "Repressive Tolerance," in Robert Paul Wolff, Barrington Moore, Jr., and Herbert Marcuse, *A Critique of Pure Tolerance* (Boston: Beacon Press, 1968), pp. 81–117.

61. Husserl, *The Crisis in European Science*, pp. 269–299.

62. Erich Fromm, *Man for Himself* (New York: Holt, Rinehart, and Winston, 1964), pp. 8–14, 144–158.

63. Lefort, *The Political Forms*, pp. 262–270.

8

Conclusion—Social Rehabilitation

Not only Marxists, but a variety of critics argue that modern society must be on the brink of collapse, for social priorities are clearly misguided. The questions asked by philosophers, for example, have come to be viewed as trite, even disruptive. Nowadays those who devote themselves to raising ethical and moral issues are considered either fanatics, or hustlers who are no better than con artists. Every aspect of society seems to be driven by a single motive: efficiency that leads to the accumulation of material goods. In fact, considerations related to human welfare are thought to interfere unnecessarily with the acquisition of wealth and the pursuit of pleasure.

As suggested throughout this book, modernism has not gone unchallenged. Jacques Ellul claims that modernity should be characterized as a "technological civilization."[1] This theme can be found throughout the history of modern thought.[2] Ferdinard Tönnies wrote that society was changing from a *Gemeinschaft* to a *Gesellschaft*. A similar trend was noted by Durkheim, which he conceptualized as the movement from mechanical to organic solidarity. And Weber, simply put, believed that the world is becoming increasingly rationalized. What these authors shared is the view that social life is shifting inexorably in a negative direction. Namely, consistent with the leitmotif of efficiency, both nature and society are being systematically deanimated.[3] Through the use of quantification, technology, and cybernetics, the human side of existence is becoming unduly regulated. Some commentators go so far as to charge that modern society is nothing more than a lifeless shell. The world has become disenchanted, they claim, as persons feel trapped within a system of their own devise.

In contrast to Tönnies, Durkheim, and Weber, Marxists argue that this trend is neither natural nor evolutionary. Instead, this formalization of existence is politically inspired and quite diabolical. Even Charles Babbage and Adam Smith, who were hardly leftists, recognized the deleterious political consequences of rationalizing social life.[4] They believed that technology dulls the mind. Nonetheless, Marxists like to claim credit for discovering that technical or instrumental reasoning may actually reduce productivity, contrary to most expectations. When workers are imagined to be appendages of machines, the quality of both working and social life deteriorates. For instance, mental acuity and a worker's overall level of skill atrophy.[5] Marxists claim the apathy that results benefits the owners of production, because workers become pliable. Increased formalization, therefore, is not a natural tendency, but a surreptitious means of social control. As work is standardized and workers are deskilled, the worth of labor power declines. Also, the division of labor that is enforced begins to reduce the viability of critical thought.

In terms of either the Marxists or the liberal account of history, the alienation persons are experiencing is increasing. This has assumed a variety of forms. First, persons are treated merely as a source of the energy necessary to keep the social system operating. In point of fact, this is how humans are described in cybernetic theory. The energy that persons exhibit is simply channeled as efficiently as possible into the prevailing division of labor. This is referred to by the innocuous title "systems design." The labor force must be made manageable. As portrayed by Frederick Taylor, a worker must become merely "one of a train of gear wheels."[6] If a cheaper source of energy becomes available, humans may be removed altogether from the production process. Machines that are self-directed, through automation, may make workers obsolete. After all, what could possibly be more efficient than a machine that does not need to be directed by an outside source?

Second, examined from a broader perspective, this dehumanization of the individual results in society being described as a mass. In fact, referring to social existence as a mass society is currently commonplace. This imagery, accordingly, is very suggestive. If humans are an important resource, similar to coal or wood, then the citizenry logically constitutes an energy mass. While workers are "retooled" or "retreaded" in order to be marketable, society must be preserved and cultivated. Similar to an inert but valuable object, the populace must be protected and readied for use. To reach this end, a sort of social ecology now prevails, whereby human capital is preserved. Obviously, citizens who defy authority, for example, would be unacceptable as laborers. Capital must not be recalcitrant, but rather must be "liquid" and ready to be invested at any time.

As suggested earlier, politics and most other social activities have become a game of manipulation. A mass of persons must be enticed into acting, but only within well-defined parameters. For example, at the workplace, cost-efficiency has become the chief means for boosting productivity. Workers are instructed in how to make uncomplicated movements, in order to streamline a job. Most disturbing, however, schools have become the key means for creating a docile work force. John Scudder notes correctly that schools have become "factories," with students their "most important products."[7] In point of fact, many high schools offer little more than vocational training, while even liberal arts colleges have increased their business programs. And with the introduction of computers into the classroom as early as possible, students do not have much choice but to equate formal logic with reasoning. Yet as Heidegger remarks, critical analysis cannot be forthcoming from this form of education. "Calculative thinking never stops, collects itself," and thus is not thinking that "contemplates the meaning which reigns in everything that is."[8] Hence education is unreflexive. In general, the purpose of institutions in the modern world, like schools, is to remove passion from humans. The rationale for this goal is actually straightforward—nothing is more unpredictable and inefficient than passion.

In the *Winds of Doctrine*, Santayana suggests that modernism is destructive. Particularly important is his point that utilitarian values come to dominate the social scene.[9] Hence, everything is rationalized. But because human action is negative, a sort of absence, selflessness is accepted as normal until a certain amount of goods is acquired. Hope, enthusiasm, and desire, because they are difficult to analyze and control, are dismissed as irrational. Yet without inspiration, the self can only reflect objects in the world. Mimicry is all that is possible. Intelligence is thus identified as the ability to memorize and discuss various themes pertaining to reality. And testing is the main means used to evaluate scholastic ability or a willingness to work. Subsumption within reality is the aim of learning and practically every other endeavor. Reflection on the question of meaning is surely impossible. Like Narcissus, the modern identity is only a secondary quality, derived from a reflection of reality. No wonder writers such as Christopher Lasch refer to modernity as a "culture of Narcissism," wherein an ephemeral self must be obsessively reaffirmed. The new narcissist "doubts even the reality of his own existence."[10] How can such persons question their source of their existence?

How does alienation result from the modern preoccupation with the control of spontaneity? With the focus on efficiency, utilitarian values are paramount. Any improvement in the division of labor, especially with regard to logistical rigor, is applauded. However, notwithstanding the views of realists, what is less utilitarian than language? Indeed, language is excessive, always defying codification. According to postmodernists, the programs instigated by structuralists and members of the Vienna Circle to transform language into a stable system were doomed to fail. Language, simply put, cannot be made into an inanimate object. Accordingly, with language capable of destroying order, persons must repress themselves if society is to be efficiently ordered. For example, instructions are concocted that are not assumed to require interpretation, so that jobs are completed and policies implemented without the complications that result from critical reflection. Hence language is formalized, even mathematized, as outlined by Bertrand Russell and Rudolf Carnap.[11] At all cost, language must be prevented from infecting a task, for a decrease in efficiency will likely be the result of this imprudent action.

This denial of language is practically a textbook example of alienation. Human praxis is repressed, while sources outside of the individual determine the boundaries of reality. Through self-alienation, persons turn control of their lives over to alien forces. If political power is part of this scheme, this desire to mimic reality is disastrous. Those in authority, that is, must be emulated if ordinary folks are to acquire a proper identity. Authority figures thus begin to serve unquestioningly as role models for everyone. This process can take many forms. For example, through advertising persons are informed about how they can acquire everything from success in a career to sex appeal. Even the stock market is thought to fluctuate according to how fashion designers alter women's skirts. And the fact that *Playboy* dictates the ideal appearance of women makes feminists livid. As one writer stated recently, advertisers have become the "captains of consciousness."[12] Most important is not that television and magazines influence public opinion, but the way in which they do so. Those who control these media are able to create the impression that they have insight others cannot possess. Consequently, these moguls are treated as visionaries.

Knowledge is placed in a context that gives it objectivity, and thus power. Mechanically reproduced information, writes Benjamin, loses its "aura," or existential value.[13] As a brute force, this knowledge can overwhelm everyday consciousness. For example, persons almost begin to swoon in the presence of famous television personalities. Consequently, these stars are employed to endorse almost every political viewpoint and product. In Adorno's study, "The Stars Down to Earth," astrology is treated as superstition, whereby persons deny their social condition in order to discover their fate. Hence Adorno concluded that astrology is an "ideology of dependence."[14] Certainly his claim could be extended nowadays to many other areas of social life. Moreover, postmodernists suggest that this externalization of destiny leads to centralized administration.

As TV stars, scientists, and technical experts increase in stature, the rest of existence decreases in importance. When persons are convinced that their ability to make judgments is a weakness, their repression is complete. Once judgments are viewed as an expression of uncertainty, persons become their own worst enemy. Portrayed as lacking reason or sensibility, they feel meaningless and devote a minimal amount of effort to controlling their environment. Powerlessness, in short, accompanies the censorship of the self. Obviously, denying the world is unproductive. With passion discredited, persons are consigned to an endless cycle of monitoring. For society must be kept safe from sudden, unplanned excitement. Students in the 1960s, following John Cage, called these spontaneous uprisings "happenings." Unregulated occurrences are anathema to modernity, because they are difficult to incorporate into budgets and other methods of planning. Although social control is certainly sometimes violent, those who are efficient want to avoid this sort of display.

Obviously, culture does not dissolve merely because persons are alienated. A strange type of society has to be invented, nonetheless, in order for alienation to be considered normative. Such a system must inevitably be fragmented, for persons are unable to relate to themselves or others. Because the self is basically hollow until a sufficient number of authority symbols are purchased, a large part of a persons's life is spent seeking recognition from those who bestow identities. Of course, those who fail to be recognized need help to adjust to this unsavory condition. Rehabilitation has to be provided to persons who are unsuccessful at propitiating authority, in addition to the unwise few who may become rebels. Normalcy, in short, is defined in terms of selfless individuals who are mesmerized by their possessions, yet at the same time believe they have no social responsibility. All the while, these persons wonder whether they are ever adequate. Furthermore, anyone who rejects these feelings of inadequacy is labelled as an ingrate, as overaggressive, or, in the case of those who are religious, as impious or blasphemous. In fact, turning oneself over to God appears to be fashionable today. Some time ago, Erich Fromm called this trend an "escape from freedom."[15] The flight into fantasy made possible by language is prevented, as persons clamp on to reality to get rid of the burden or insecurity associated with freedom. Persons abandon freedom as part of a quest to discover proof for their existence.

The downside of postmodernism, writes Jameson, is that it is all too compatible with the anomie and serialization endemic to today's consumer culture.[16] Probably more so than any other social philosophy, capitalism verges on nihilism. For example, tradition must be sacrificed, because increasing levels of consumption are necessary in order for the capitalist economy to grow. Anything that is old must be abandoned, so that new products can be purchased.[17] Accordingly, in addition to being dominated by their goods, persons adopt whatever moral principles happen to be fashionable. This unseemly activity is referred to euphemistically as the ability to "adjust," or to "play the game." Of course, fickleness is a natural by-product of utilitarianism. Also, personal gain is a measure of this system's worth. Egoism is encouraged, while the social cost of any action is, at most, an afterthought. Even the most intimate relationship is referred to as a contract, thereby suggesting that no one can be trusted. Someone who violates another's rights is not filled with remorse, but merely hires a skillful lawyer. The only consideration that prevents persons from attacking their fellow citizens outright is the fear of incarceration. Stated simply, capitalism is organized around inhumane acts. And as a reward, those who survive this barbarism are granted social mobility.

Stated another way by Fromm, capitalism is sustained by the "pathology of normalcy."[18] Due to the market orientation, persons come to view themselves as things to be purchased, instead of active agents. They believe that their worth is determined by their socioeconomic role. In short, the self is nothing but a commodity. In the *Sane Society*, Fromm writes: "man does not experience himself as an active bearer of his own powers and richness, but as an impoverished 'thing,' dependent on powers outside of himself, unto whom he has projected his living substance."[19] Fromm refers to this enslavement to objects as "idolatry." Earlier, in his book *The Acquisitive Society*, R.H. Tawney foretold the domination of persons by their possessions.[20] As with Ibsen's Peer Gynt, after peeling off layer after layer of pretense, humans in the modern world are left with nothing. In modernity, persons are merely the bearers of structural imperatives. In the face of social change, persons ask, "where would we be without a 'system'?" The social system becomes the surrogate for an identity. Humanity as a whole must be protected, as is the claim of fascist governments.

Why is postmodernism thought to lend support to capitalism? According to Jameson, postmodernists restore respect to subjectivity. The individual, or Cartesian point, is resurrected. Because reality is an outgrowth of subjectivity, anything is possible: relativity reigns supreme. Therefore, unlimited personal consumption is supposedly sanctioned. Is there a difference between relativity and the capriciousness spawned by utilitarianism? Critics of postmodernism claim that there is no noticeable difference. Moreover, if morality is private, almost any kind of behavior can be justified. What constitutes an immoral act in the modern world—questioning someone else's right to maximize profit or to rape the environment? Certainly not, because no one should presume to have the knowledge necessary to tell another person how to behave. Hayek, who provides the key theoretical support for supply-side economics, chastises advocates of a planned economy for claiming that they are able to integrate various sources of information into a comprehensive economic program.[21] Due to the indefinite nature of truth, persons are assumed to be helpless to control themselves and advise others. Only an extremely presumptuous person would try to base social policy on *doxa*.

Within this environment, those who appeal for moral restraint appear to be zealots. After all, morality cannot be achieved without overcoming the limits imposed by subjectivity. Usually this means that moral guidance can be dispensed only by a supernatural being. And accordingly, direct contact with God must take place before this insight can be obtained. Yet anyone who makes such a claim is viewed with suspicion, especially in a world based on utilitarianism. In a capitalist society, morality is finite, and thus is altered with respect to changing circumstances. And only someone who is irrational would choose to be unrealistic. Therefore, sometimes outlandish announcements are made by religious leaders, in the hope of capturing people's attention. Considering the obsession in a consumer society with material success, no wonder hyperbole is required to distract persons from their headlong pursuit of pleasure. Religion becomes extravagant; yet this exaggeration tends to make citizens even more leery of those who talk about ethics. References made to the sublime are dismissed as fantastic. Bourgeois morality, in other words, is measured and pragmatic, and thus devoid of enthusiasm.

Postmodernism is associated with bourgeois morality for a simple, but erroneous reason: Postmodernists are believed to work within the strictures imposed by Cartesianism. Again, Lyotard is at fault for providing an obvious opportunity for postmodernism to be misconstrued in this way. He states that postmodernism is not the most recent period in the history of literature, but a movement within modernism.[22] In other words, postmodernism lies dormant within modernism. Clearly this account could mean that postmodernism is merely an extension of modernism, an attempt at refinement. However, this is not Lyotard's intention. His point, instead, is that at the basis of modernism, and every style of art, is an element that has come to be obscured. Perhaps more to the point, this factor was actively repressed, for example, by many earlier modes of artistic expression. To use Merleau-Ponty's distinction, postmodernists allow the "invisible" to penetrate the "visible."[23]

What is the invisible? The invisible is the thrust that propels a brush stroke forward. Moreover, this factor prevents impressionistic paintings from dissolving into patches of color. And without the invisible, the pain and loneliness displayed in Van Gogh's picture of a peasant's shoes would be missing, as Heidegger shows.[24] In postmodernism what was formerly unrepresented is presented—the background is made manifest. The human presence, in short, is revealed to pervade every attempt at artistic expression, even those designed to deny any association between reality and imagination. According to postmodernists, art is an event, regardless of the aesthetic theory it espouses. Postmodernist art exists "*à découvert*, or "without the cover" supplied by a codified system. The art engendered by postmodernists does not remain in the shadow of reality.[25]

This human background is replete with the "silences" alluded to by postmodernists. These unmentionables constitute assumptions persons make about reality, or the *Hinterfragen* explored by Nietzsche. In this regard, postmodernists imagine a world where knowledge is not severed from expression and where the self is not a threat to reality. Postmodernist art, in other words, allows what Susan Sontag calls the "erotics of art" to become manifest.[26] The assumptions that make reality are not concealed, but permitted to flourish.

A postmodern artistic event, accordingly, is not placid, but full of surprises. Suggested by this description is that artworks gather together, rather than portray reality. In the last sentence of *Nadja*, Breton clearly conveys this idea when he writes that "Beauty will be convulsive or it will not be at all."[27] According to Breton and postmodernists, the desire for order pervades a painting. Additionally, bereft of this organizational capacity, artworks, along with social life, could not exist at all. Without the "excitement" Breton acknowledges to pervade beauty, art would have no purpose.

While impressionists, for example, claim to capture the essence of light, postmodernists argue that this is impossible. Light is never pure. The light by which a novel is read in a drafty, spartan room, is different from the warm glow that is experienced when examining one of Van Gogh's spring or summer landscapes. Light, therefore, has meaning only in terms of where the human element is situated. Postmodernists recognize that the human spirit resides in the midst of an artwork, as the backdrop of all that is visible. This is the assumption that, if questioned, would render reality ineffable, due to the implied uncertainty of perception. As a *hypokeimenon*, or fundamental being around which existence gathers, the human presence cannot be dispatched. Kristeva calls this primordial base the "semiotic zone." "The *semiotic*," she writes, "assumes the role of a linguistic signifier signifying an *object* for an *ego*, and thus constituting them both as thetic."[28] Art is thus literally with the world.

The problem with the critics who understand postmodernism to be a product of modernism is that they are unable to overcome dualism. Their Cartesian anguish propels them to place postmodernism in the traditional mold. Individualism, therefore, becomes egoism, while a lack of objectivity is thought to lead to moral decay. But as noted throughout this text, postmodernists are not intimidated by dualism. They break through the veil erected by Descartes, in order to cavort with reality. Postmodernists immerse themselves in reality, because they are not afraid of adulterated truth. Like Dali, they approach truth as if it is "edible."[29] The future of humankind is not despoiled, contend postmodernists, simply because interpretation has crept into society's supply of knowledge. Because a flower is not treated as a sum of molecules, this does not mean that reality is defiled. Instead, the flower of experience is given credence by postmodernists.

In order to subvert the dualism that is central to metanarratives, postmodern society is sustained by so-called minor literature.[30] This sort of literature is affected with the drama of existence, and thus is thoroughly political.[31] Postmodern art is dramatic because its expression is not bound by reality. Minor literature is not representation, but the embodiment of speech. Specifically, postmodernists argue that the stories handed down from one generation to another should be seriously studied, for these tales are the heart and soul of history. Verbal history, the language that not merely recalls but creates the past, present, and the future, circumscribes a specific reality. The world of magic is not something to be explained and dismissed by science, but a realm that is very real to its inhabitants. Every linguistic world has interesting secrets. And because language extends to the horizon and beyond, it provides a path for travelers. However, Benjamin contends that the storyteller has become an anachronism in modern society.[32] In other words, why does knowledge have to be disseminated to persons? Talking about a reality that is obvious undoubtedly would be redundant.

Nonetheless, all forms of artistic expression are meaningful, precisely because they defy reality. As Marcuse demonstrates, the appearances conveyed by art are sufficient to challenge political realities as menacing as the Third Reich.[33] In point of fact, Hitler, like most authoritarians, was suspicious of imagination. Literature or painting, therefore, is not moribund, because the character of its reality is not obvious. Minor literature is written by ordinary persons, not "great men," with powerful language. Hence everyone is a potential revolutionary, for reality is contaminated further with every additional statement, and persons cannot escape from their responsibility to language.

As discussed throughout this book, when dualism is overcome in this way, every aspect of society must be conceptualized anew. The absence of an ultimate reality does not precipitate the demise of truth, and, likewise, individual spontaneity does not necessarily conflict with the commonweal. These distinctions are irretrievably outmoded. Actually, instead of destroying culture, postmodernists radically democratize society. Max Scheler refers to this as a "democracy of emotions," while Mannheim uses the phrase "democratization of culture" to describe this metamorphosis.[34] As a result of infecting reality with language, culture is opened or expanded, not abolished. As expressed by Macherey, culture becomes "determinate reverie." Because culture is not their adversary, persons are able to "freely associate." Stated more explicitly, political will is not thwarted by structural barriers. "Language," like politics, "stops being representative in order to now move toward its extremities or its limits."[35]

To suggest that the cultivation of democracy is a cultural affair is important. In this regard, Mannheim's use of the term *Geist* is particularly significant, when he is discussing culture. This term implies the interpenetration of culture, mind, and human action. Democracy, accordingly, does not result from instituting a few practices, such as parliamentary procedures and universal suffrage. Modern society provides enough testimony to justify this conclusion. Political participation in most democracies has reached new lows. The reason for this decline may be that the cultural imagery essential for supporting widespread political involvement has not been spawned. Citizens, stated differently, have not been infused with the spirit of democracy. And until this occurs, democracy will continue to consist of nothing more than a limited number of hollow activities. For a democratic mode of existence must be inaugurated before a democratic polity is possible. What this book seeks to suggest is that postmodernism encourages the inculcation of democratic principles—an ethos of democracy, so to speak.

Mannheim identifies four reasons why he believes the promise of democracy has not been fulfilled.[36] First, the cliques of power brokers have not been dismantled. What this means is that the knowledge, skills, and other resources necessary to form, advocate, and implement policies are highly concentrated. Therefore, pluralism remains a platitude. To paraphrase modern feminists, a democracy is fatherless, for no one ought to have privileged access to the information required to produce a government. Nothing should be authorized in the "name of the Father."[37]

Second, Mannheim argues that persons have understood democracy to be merely another approach to rationalizing the status quo. This view, he states, is both unfortunate and wrong. Stated simply, democracy is not just the most efficient method for securing social order. Many other styles of government are more efficient, because discussion can lead in an almost unlimited number of directions. Nonetheless, to suggest that democracy rationlizes order implies that this form of government is simply a means of social control. Just the opposite is true. In a democratic society, the government embodies rather than constrains desire. There should be nothing necessary about order in a democracy; the only restrictions that should be operative are imaginary ones.

Third, personal autonomy has not been encouraged. According to Fromm, "pseudo-autonomy" has prevailed, because undue importance has been attributed, for example, to common sense, science, public opinion, normalcy, and public health.[38] Hence a type of "herd conformity" prevails, similar to that discussed by Heidegger with respect to the influence of *das Man*—the anonymous person who strives to be acceptable. Instead of these concerns, as Tillich might say, the "courage to be" should be the guiding principle of a democracy.[39] Individuals must have the confidence to develop and assert their opinions, despite opposition. If this element is lacking, dogmatism can all too easily begin to stifle discussion and planning. To counteract their adversaries, persons must be able to state their case. Blind faith, accordingly, has no place in a democratic society.

And fourth, the interpersonal character of reality has been de-emphasized in modern society. Individualism has been stressed to the extent that social concerns are almost deemed irrelevant. If particular persons are not affected by a policy, they will probably not protest the adverse treatment of others. But in a democracy everyone must be vigilant, so that injustice does not spread throughout a society. For if persons are only willing to challenge their own mistreatment, a society may collapse before corrective action can be taken. In a democracy, persons must understand that they are not insulated from one another, and thus one negative precedent can proliferate. What is to prevent repression from spreading, besides prayers to an unknown God? As noted by Sartre, everyone's freedom is based on the freedom of each person—freedom does not exist in the abstract.[40] If persons do not protect one another, no one else will guarantee their security. Individualism, therefore, must not obscure social responsibility.

Postmodernists strive to rectify these shortcomings. Truth is decentered, or disassociated from any specific social constellation. Neither a particular social class nor empirical referent can serve as an unquestioned source of knowledge. Furthermore, with the undecidable element of interpretation vital to knowledge acquisition, every conceivable system is derationalized. The basis of the "pathology of normalcy" is thus inadvertently questioned. The claim cannot be sustained, in other words, that systems are shrinking. Implosion such as this would mean that languages are naturally efficient, and this is simply not the case. Rather, persons must constantly redouble their effort to stabilize an interpretation of reality. What postmodernists show is that left unattended, language will proliferate instead of wither. Surely normalcy is anything but obvious.

With reality condemned to reside within language, nothing sustains norms other than choice. Interpretation implies that truth and error are merely momentarily separated with respect to a judgment. Only tenacity keeps truth from vanishing. This means that interpretive hegemony is the result of personal effort, and nothing else. Therefore, the ability to exhibit autonomy in the face of uncertainty is required for knowledge to survive. These choices, however, are not made in a vacuum, but presuppose the availability of possibilities. Simply put, every choice has impact on the remaining options. Modalities of interpretation are thus not self-contained—the "I" co-exists with the "other." Through choice, the interpersonal character of knowledge is revealed. Solipsism, accordingly, is dismissed by postmodernists. Democracy is thus immanent, something closely associated with human action.

To use a postmodern conception introduced by Jean Gebser and Karl Jaspers, the origin of a democratic society is the "present."[41] This means that the genesis of government is not anathema to human intoxication. Gebser writes: "we can speak of *origin's development toward the self-realization of man.*"[42] The conscious acts, or linguistic fulminations, that shape the future are the origin of self, knowledge, and order. In a democracy this is crucial, because the locus of social control must be self-imposed. Accordingly, democracy is achieved when persons acquire a sense of "mature autonomy," or when they are able to constrain themselves, understand when a particular form of constraint is outmoded, discuss new modes of interaction, and forge an appropriate course of action.[43] The origin of democracy, in short, is the democratic process.

If there is a metaphysic associated with postmodernism, it is similar to the one suggested by Jaspers and Gebser. That is, the fundamental characteristic of existence can best be described as "world-openness." With the breakdown of dualism, Gebser contends that the world is now witnessing the "concretion of the spiritual."[44] This phrase might better be rendered the "*con-crescere*" of the cultural.[45] Stated differently, culture is the coalescence of consciousness or praxis; postmodernists might say the condensation of desire. In any case, the point is that persons are not imprisoned within space, time, or history, but upsurge with these dimensions. Escape is possible from what Macherey calls the "tomb of structures."[46] As the eye turns, so does the earth. What does this mean for politics? Simply this: social existence is rehabilitated. Society is not cured of an illness, but, more important, in line with the original intent of *therapeia*, the social is returned to the place where "I" and "Thou" meet. Postmodernists provide an educational program that allows persons to return to themselves. Society is restored to its original state, before the crisis that ensued following the acceptance of dualism. Persons can live their lives without accepting or rejecting reality.

Postmodernists allow culture to be lived. Because nothing exceeds direct experience, every facet of social life is a manifestation of the human spirit. Reality is simply irrelevant for the creation of order. As a result of this realization, postmodernists avert the tragedy Georg Simmel argues is endemic to modernism.[47] Specifically, he contends that cultural products tend to turn against their creators, unless action is taken to prevent this from happening. With passion and reality existing in concert, this debacle cannot be justified. Objects offer no solace, other than to suggest that their inventors are creative, wise, and able to tame, at least temporarily, their passions. Persons have no choice but to make and remake reality, and are provided with the skills required for this ominous task. Postmodernists never let persons forget their role in history: to make a home in a world that has no justification.

Certainly postmodernists could be more overt about their radicalism. Indeed, this could be said about any writer, even Marx. Supplying prescriptions, however, would defeat their purpose: their aim is not to enslave persons to another authority. Nonetheless, they do not retreat from the world. Postmodernism is not anti-art or anti-philosophy. On the contrary, the world of experience that subtends reality is the focus of their attention. And what could be more radical than setting the stage for persons to create reality, if they can summon the courage to meet this challenge. Accordingly, postmodernists ask persons to assume responsibility for their lives. Revolutions cannot be orchestrated or order imposed by experts without repression. Postmodernists want order to survive because ideologies have been penetrated and persons have chosen to regulate themselves in a particular way. This is rational order—order without control. Postmodernists want to avoid the image of hell described by Camus, where streets are "filled with stop signs and no way of explaining oneself. One is classified once and for all."[48]

NOTES

1. Jacques Ellul, *The Technological Society*, pp. 61–147.

2. Anthony Giddens, *Capitalism and Modern Social Theory* (Cambridge: Cambridge University Press, 1971).

3. Don Ihde, *Technics and Praxis* (Dordrecht, Netherlands: D. Reidel, 1979), pp. 3–39.

4. Robert Brown, *The Nature of Social Laws* (Cambridge: Cambridge University Press, 1984), pp. 70–95.

5. Harry Braverman, *Labor and Monopoly Capital* (New York: Monthly Review Press, 1974), pp. 139–152.

6. Frederick W. Taylor, "Why Manufacturers Dislike College Students," cited in Samuel Haber, *Efficiency and Uplift: Scientific Management in the Progressive Era, 1890–1920* (Chicago: University of Chicago Press, 1964), p. 24.

7. John R. Scudder, "Excellence in Education: Production or Productivity," in *Technology and Human Productivity*, ed. John W. Murphy and John T. Pardeck (Westport, Conn.: Quorum Books, 1986), pp. 39–49.

8. Martin Heidegger, *Discourse on Thinking* (New York: Harper and Row, 1966), pp. 45–57.

9. George Santayana, *Winds of Doctrine* (New York: Scribner's, 1913), pp. 25–57.

10. Christopher Lasch, *The Culture of Narcissism* (New York: Norton, 1978), p. xvi.

11. Bryant, *Positivism in Social Theory and Research*, pp. 109–116.

12. Stuart Ewen, *Captains of Consciousness: Advertising and the Social Roots of Consumer Culture* (New York: McGraw-Hill, 1979).

13. Benjamin, "The Work of Art in the Age of Mechanical Reproduction," *Illuminations*, pp. 217-251.

14. Jay, *The Dialectical Imagination*, pp. 196-197.

15. Erich Fromm, *Escape from Freedom* (New York: Farrar & Rinehart, 1941).

16. Fredric Jameson, "Postmodernism and Consumer Society," in Hal Foster, ed., *The Anti-Aesthetic* (Port Townsend, Wash.: Bay Press, 1983), pp. 111-125.

17. Charles Newman, *The Postmodern Aura* (Evanston, Ill.: Northwestern University Press, 1985), p. 51.

18. Erich Fromm, *The Sane Society* (New York: Rinehart & Company, 1955), p. 6.

19. Ibid., p. 124.

20. R.H. Tawney, *The Acquisitive Society* (New York: Harcourt Brace and Company, 1920), pp. 183-184.

21. John W. Murphy, "An Examination of Hayek's Theory of Social Order," *Journal of Interdisciplinary Economics* 1.1 (1985), pp. 5-17.

22. Lyotard, *The Postmodern Condition*, p. 79.

23. Maurice Merleau-Ponty, *The Visible and the Invisible* (Evanston, Ill.: Northwestern University Press, 1968).

24. Martin Heidegger, *Poetry, Language, and Thought* (New York: Harper and Row, 1971), pp. 32ff.

25. Lyotard, *The Postmodern Condition*, p. 81.

26. Susan Sontag, *Against Interpretation* (New York: Farrar, Straus and Giroux, 1966), p. 14.

27. André Breton, *Nadja* (New York: Grove Press, 1960), p. 160.

28. Kristeva, *Revolution in Poetic Language*, p. 67.

29. Salvador Dali, *On Modern Art* (New York: The Dial Press, 1957), p. 45.

30. Deleuze and Guattari, *Kafka: Toward a Minor Literature*, pp. 16-27.

31. Ibid., p. 16.

32. Benjamin, "The Storyteller: Reflections on the Works of Nikolai Leskov," *Illuminations*, pp. 83-109.

33. Herbert Marcuse, *The Aesthetic Dimension* (Boston: Beacon Press, 1978).

34. Karl Mannheim, *Man and Society* (New York: Harcourt, Brace and Company, 1951), pp. 44-49; see also Karl Mannheim, "The Democratization of Culture," in *From Karl Mannheim*, ed. Kurt H. Wolff (New York: Oxford University Press, 1971), pp. 271-346.

35. Deleuze and Guattari, *Kafka*, p. 23.

36. Mannheim, "The Democratization of Culture."

37. Nelly Furman, "The Politics of Language: Beyond the Gender Principle," in Gayle Green and Coppélia Kahn, eds., *Making a Difference: Feminist Literary Criticism* (London: Methuen, 1985), pp. 59-79.

38. Fromm, *The Sane Society*, pp. 152-164.

39. Paul Tillich, *The Courage to Be* (New Haven: Yale University Press, 1952).

40. Jean-Paul Sartre, *Existentialism* (New York: Philosophical Library, 1947), pp. 44-45, 54.

41. Gebser, *The Ever-Present Origin*, pp. 280-281.

42. Ibid., p. 41.

43. Habermas, *Theory and Praxis*, p. 17.

44. Gebser, *The Ever-Present Origin*, p. 541.

45. Ibid., p. 542.

46. Pierre Macherey, *A Theory of Literary Production* (London: Routledge and Kegan Paul, 1978), pp. 136–156.

47. Georg Simmel, *The Conflict in Modern Culture and Other Essays* (New York: Teachers College Press, 1968), pp. 27–46.

48. Albert Camus, *The Fall* (New York: Knopf, 1961), p. 47.

Selected Bibliography

Arac, Jonathan; Godzich, Wlad; and Wallace, Martin. *The Yale Critics: Decon-struction in America*. Minneapolis: University of Minnesota Press, 1983.

Atkins, G. Douglas. *Reading Deconstruction; Deconstructive Reading*. Lexington: University of Kentucky Press, 1983.

Barthes, Roland. *Writing Degree Zero*. New York: Hill and Wang, 1968.

_____ . *The Pleasure of the Text*. New York: Hill and Wang, 1975.

_____ . *Image-Music-Text*. New York: Hill and Wang, 1977.

_____ . *The Rustle of Language*. New York: Hill and Wang, 1986.

_____ . *Criticism and Truth*. Minneapolis: University of Minnesota Press, 1987.

Baudrillard, Jean. *In the Shadow of the Silent Majorities*. New York: Semiotext(e), 1983.

Carroll, David. *Paraesthetics*. London: Routledge Chapman and Hall, 1987.

Cixous, Hélène and Clément, Catherine. *Newly Born Woman*. Minneapolis: University of Minnesota Press, 1986.

Culler, Jonathan. *The Pursuit of Signs*. Ithaca, N.Y.: Cornell University Press, 1981.

_____ . *On Deconstruction*. Ithaca, N.Y.: Cornell University Press, 1983.

_____ . *Roland Barthes*. New York: Oxford University Press, 1983.

Deleuze, Gilles. *Proust and Signs*. New York: George Braziller, 1972.

_____ . *Cinema 1: The Movement-Image*. Minneapolis: University of Minnesota Press, 1986.

Deleuze, Gilles and Guattari, Félix. *Anti-Oedipus*. New York: Viking Press, 1977.

_____ . *On the Line*. New York: Semiotext(e), 1983.

_____ . *Kafka: Toward a Minor Literature*. Minneapolis: University of Minnesota Press, 1986.

de Man, Paul. *Allegories of Reading*. New Haven: Yale University Press, 1979.

_____ . *Blindness and Insight*. Minneapolis: University of Minnesota Press, 1983.

_____ . *The Resistance to Theory*. Minneapolis: University of Minnesota Press, 1986.

Derrida, Jacques. *Speech and Phenomena*. Evanston, Ill.: Northwestern University Press, 1973.

_____ . *Of Grammatology*. Baltimore: Johns Hopkins University Press, 1976.

_____ . *Writing and Difference*. Chicago: University of Chicago, 1979.

_____ . *Dissemination*. Chicago: University of Chicago Press, 1981.

_____ . *Positions*. Chicago: University of Chicago Press, 1981.

Descombs, Vincent. *Modern French Philosophy*. Cambridge: Cambridge University Press, 1980.

Eagleton, Terry. *Walter Benjamin or Towards a Revolutionary Criticism*. London: NLB, 1981.

Felman, Shoshana. *The Literary Speech Act*. Ithaca, N.Y.: Cornell University Press, 1983.

_____ . *Writing and Madness*. Ithaca, N.Y.: Cornell University Press, 1985.

Felperin, Howard. *Beyond Deconstruction*. Oxford: Clarendon Press, 1985.

Fischer, Michael. *Does Deconstruction Make any Difference*. Bloomington: Indiana University Press, 1985.

Foster, Hal, ed. *The Anti-Aesthetic*. Port Townsend, Wash.: Bay Press, 1983.

Foucault, Michel. *Madness and Civilization*. New York: Random House, 1965.

_____ . *The Archaeology of Knowledge*. New York: Harper and Row, 1972.

_____ . *The Birth of the Clinic*. New York: Vintage, 1975.

_____ . *Discipline and Punish*. New York: Pantheon, 1979.

_____ . *Power/Knowledge*. New York: Pantheon, 1980.

_____ . *This is not a Pipe*. Berkeley: University of California Press, 1982.

Gebser, Jean. *The Ever-Present Origin*. Athens: Ohio University Press, 1985.

Guattari, Félix. *Molecular Revolution*. New York: Penguin Books, 1984.

Hartman, Geoffrey H. *Saving the Text*. Baltimore: Johns Hopkins University Press, 1981.

Johnson, Barbara. *The Critical Difference*. Baltimore: Johns Hopkins University Press, 1980.

Kristeva, Julia. *Desire in Language*. New York: Columbia University Press, 1980.

_____ . *Revolution in Poetic Language*. New York: Columbia University Press, 1984.

Lacan, Jacques. *Ecrits*. New York: Norton, 1977.

_____ . *Feminine Sexuality*. New York: Norton, 1982.

Lefort, Claude. *The Political Forms of Modern Society*. Cambridge, Mass.: MIT, 1986.

Lentricchia, Frank. *After the New Criticism*. Chicago: University of Chicago Press, 1980.

Lingis, Alphonso. *Libido*. Bloomington: Indiana University Press, 1986.

Lyotard, Jean-François. *The Postmodern Condition: A Report on Knowledge*. Minneapolis: University of Minnesota Press, 1984.

_____ . *Driftworks*. New York: Semiotext(e), 1984.

_____ . *The Differend*. Minneapolis: University of Minnesota Press, 1988.

Lyotard, Jean-François and Thébaud, Jean-Loup. *Just Gaming*. Minneapolis: University of Minnesota Press, 1985.

MacCannel, Juliet Flower. *Figuring Lacan*. Lincoln: University of Nebraska Press, 1986.

Melville, Stephen W. *Philosophy Beside Itself*. Minneapolis: University of Minnesota Press, 1986.

Mitchell, Juliet and Rose, Jacqueline. *Feminine Sexuality: Jacques Lacan and the Ecole Freudienne*. New York: Norton, 1985.

Moi, Toril. *Sexual-Textual Politics*. London: Routledge Chapman and Hall, 1985.

Norris, Christopher. *Deconstruction: Theory and Practice*. London: Methuen, 1982.

_____ . *The Deconstructive Turn*. London: Methuen, 1983.

_____ . *The Contest of Faculties: Philosophy and Theory after Deconstruction*. London: Methuen, 1985.

Ryan, Michael. *Marxism and Deconstruction*. Baltimore: Johns Hopkins University Press, 1982.

Said, Edward W. *Orientalism*. New York: Pantheon, 1978.

_____ . *The World, the Text, and the Critic*. Cambridge, Mass.: Harvard University Press, 1983.

Scholes, Robert. *Textual Power*. New Haven: Yale University Press, 1985.

Showalter, Elaine, ed. *The New Feminist Criticism*. New York: Pantheon, 1985.

Index

ABOUT THE AUTHOR

JOHN W. MURPHY is Associate Professor of Sociology at the University of Miami, Coral Gables, Florida. He received his Ph.D. from Ohio State University. His present interests include social philosophy and sociological theory.